MW01716442

'Sheila Zamar's *Filipino: An Essential Grammar* responds to frequently asked questions about Filipino grammar through clear and thorough explanations, illustrative examples, and illuminating clarifications, making it a must-read for language learners. Moreover, it brings the language to the present by recognizing that Filipino, the national language of the Philippines, although primarily based on Tagalog, has evolved. This book stands out as an essential contemporary resource in both teaching and learning.'

Joi Barrios, *Filipino Language Lecturer, University of California, Berkeley, USA*

'This is an exciting and long-awaited grammar, produced by a highly talented linguist and language instructor with over 20 years of experience teaching Filipino. This grammar will greatly facilitate Filipino language learning and at the same time serve as a critical and user-friendly reference for understanding the grammatical intricacies of the national language of the more than a hundred million Filipinos and their rapidly growing global diaspora.'

Michael Cullinane, *Director, Southeast Asian Studies Summer Institute, University of Wisconsin–Madison, USA*

'Filipino language is one of the most difficult languages to acquire, not because of a different writing system, but because of its unique internal working with its use of cases, markers, different verb families, and other unique features that fascinate linguists. Zamar's *Filipino: An Essential Grammar* provides an easy-to-understand and clear grammar explanation for both teachers and students who have no formal linguistics background.'

Nenita Pambid Domingo, *Filipino Language Lecturer, University of California, Los Angeles, USA*

'Filipino grammar is complex and unique – fascinating for linguists but often difficult for students. Zamar's approach combines the precision of a linguist with the accessibility of an experienced language teacher. The result is an invaluable resource for learners of Filipino at any level. If you want to finally "get" Filipino grammar, look no further than this book.'

Noah Theriault, *Assistant Professor of Anthropology, Carnegie Mellon University, USA*

'Sheila Zamar's Filipino language instruction has helped so many learners work towards language competency. Zamar simplifies challenging grammar concepts and helps learners develop a strong foundation for language learning and usage. This book distills invaluable classroom lessons that have greatly benefitted countless students, including myself. Aspiring students of Filipino will undoubtedly benefit from this invaluable resource.'

Mark John Sanchez, *Assistant Professor in Asian American Studies, Vanderbilt University, USA*

'Sheila Zamar has written an indispensable book on Filipino grammar. Clearly organized with lucid, reader-friendly content, this reference guide is a vital resource for teachers and students of all levels.'

Emmanuel David, *Associate Professor in Women and Gender Studies, University of Colorado Boulder, USA*

'*Filipino: An Essential Grammar* is a smart book that provides linguistic fundamentals to enhance the language-learning and pedagogical experience. In addition to being a valuable resource for language acquisition and instruction, this is an exquisite text for researchers and a must-have for fieldwork. Zamar deploys her expertise in linguistics to make the text indispensable to those engaged in lexicographical studies, literary analysis, ethnography, and other humanistic and social scientific research that relies on Filipino. Even more meaningfully, this book is absorbing for those eager to learn the nuances of the language and the linguistic elements that make it profound.'

Kathleen Gutierrez, *Assistant Professor of History, University of California, Santa Cruz, USA*

Filipino

Filipino: An Essential Grammar is a comprehensive and practical reference guide introducing the key grammatical forms and structures in the Filipino language.

This book offers a detailed exploration of key phonological, morphological, and syntactic features of Filipino that are essential to achieving high levels of proficiency in the language. Across 14 chapters are concise explanations of important grammatical categories and linguistic features relevant in the description of Philippine languages, complemented by examples relevant for everyday conversations and easy-to-understand rules for navigating Filipino grammar.

Taking into consideration the most salient grammatical aspects that need to be presented by teachers and mastered by learners of Filipino, this is the ideal reference grammar for researchers, teachers, and learners of the Filipino language. This book is designed for both independent and class-based studies by learners of Filipino at all levels.

Sheila Zamar is Assistant Professor of ESL and Tagalog Language Instruction in the Defense Critical Language and Culture Program at the Mansfield Center, University of Montana, Missoula, MT, USA.

Routledge Essential Grammars

Essential Grammars describe clearly and succinctly the core rules of each language and are up-to-date and practical reference guides to the most important aspects of languages used by contemporary native speakers. They are designed for elementary to intermediate learners and present an accessible description of the language, focusing on the real patterns of use today.

Essential Grammars are a reference source for the learner and user of the language, irrespective of level, setting out the complexities of the language in short, readable sections that are clear and free from jargon.

Essential Grammars are ideal either for independent study or for students in schools, colleges, universities and adult classes of all types.

Essential Grammars are available for the following languages:

Bosnian, Croatian, Montenegrin and Serbian
Catalan
Chinese
Czech
Danish
Dutch
English
Filipino
Finnish
German
Greek
Hindi
Hungarian
Icelandic
Korean
Latvian
Modern Hebrew
North Sámi
Norwegian
Polish
Portuguese
Romanian
Serbian
Spanish
Swedish
Thai
Turkish
Urdu
Vietnamese
West Greenlandic

For more information about this series, please visit: www.routledge.com/Routledge-Essential-Grammars/book-series/SE0549

Filipino

An Essential Grammar

Sheila Zamar

Routledge
Taylor & Francis Group
LONDON AND NEW YORK

First published in 2023
by Routledge
4 Park Square, Milton Park, Abingdon, Oxon OX14 4RN

and by Routledge
605 Third Avenue, New York, NY 10158

Routledge is an imprint of the Taylor & Francis Group, an informa business

British Library Cataloguing-in-Publication Data
A catalogue record for this book is available from the British Library

Library of Congress Cataloging-in-Publication Data
Names: Zamar, Sheila, author.
Title: Filipino : an essential grammar / Sheila Zamar.
Description: New York : Routledge, 2023. | Includes bibliographical references and index.
Identifiers: LCCN 2022014413 (print) | LCCN 2022014414 (ebook) | ISBN 9781138826274 (hardback) | ISBN 9781138826281 (paperback) | ISBN 9781315739427 (ebook)
Subjects: LCSH: Tagalog language—Grammar. | Tagalog language—Phonology. | Tagalog language—Morphology. | Tagalog language—Syntax.
Classification: LCC PL6053 .Z28 2023 (print) | LCC PL6053 (ebook) | DDC 499/.211—dc23/eng/20220712
LC record available at https://lccn.loc.gov/2022014413
LC ebook record available at https://lccn.loc.gov/2022014414

ISBN: 978-1-138-82627-4 (hbk)
ISBN: 978-1-138-82628-1 (pbk)
ISBN: 978-1-315-73942-7 (ebk)

DOI: 10.4324/9781315739427

Typeset in Sabon
by Apex CoVantage, LLC

For Dolores, Nacer, Rudy, and Jun.

Maraming salamat po.

Contents

Contents

Introduction

Filipino, the Tagalog-based national language of the Philippines, belongs to the Western Malayo-Polynesian branch of the Austronesian language family. Spoken natively by about 30 million speakers at the time of this writing, it is also used and understood by about 90 percent of the Philippine population, currently around 100 million. It serves as the lingua franca or common language of multilingual Filipino communities and is one of two official languages of the country, along with English. There are significantly large Filipino-speaking communities in most urban centers of the developed world, particularly in the United States and Canada.

Linguistically, Filipino is a variety – and is mutually intelligible with all dialects – of Tagalog. Its standardized form is taught in schools and used by the mass media. This variety, however, is used by more non-native speakers and in more domains than any other Tagalog dialect due to its wide use in popular culture and in education. As a result, Filipino tends to be more open to loanwords from other languages, more recently from English, and to have some features that are not considered to be part of Tagalog, for instance, the sounds /f, v, j, z/.

Due to the archipelago's history and geographic location in maritime Southeast Asia, Philippine languages, especially Tagalog and its varieties, including Filipino, have incorporated many loanwords from several languages, some of them belonging to other language families, such as Spanish, Hokkien Chinese, English, Malay, Sanskrit, and Arabic. Undoubtedly, the primary source language of borrowings in Filipino is Spanish, owing to the country's 330 years under Spain's colonial rule from the 16th century until the last decade of the 19th century. English introduced many loanwords to Filipino during the nearly 50 years of American occupation in the first half of the 20th century. It continues to influence Filipino today due to the country's close political and economic ties with the United States and the global impact of American

DOI: 10.4324/9781315739427-1

popular culture. Borrowings from Chinese, Malay, Arabic, and Sanskrit mostly came into the language prior to European contact, as Manila and other major coastal areas were vital trading hubs in maritime Southeast Asia in the 14th and earlier centuries. Merchants and workers passing through these ports brought their own languages with them, influencing local communities with whom they came into contact.

This book is a reference grammar for learners, researchers, and teachers of the Filipino language. It takes into consideration the most salient grammatical aspects that need to be presented by teachers and mastered by learners of Filipino. The book covers in detail key phonological, morphological, and syntactic features of Filipino that are essential to achieving high levels of proficiency in the language. It also provides concise explanations of important grammatical categories and linguistic features relevant in the description of Philippine languages.

Chapter 1

Phonology and spelling

1.1 Consonants

Filipino has the following consonant sounds, shown in the table by their orthographic symbols. The sounds indicated by bold, italicized symbols are not considered to be part of the Tagalog sound system.

Manner and point of articulation	*Bilabial*	*Labio-dental*	*Dento-alveolar*	*Palatal*	*Velar*	*Glottal*
stop, voiceless	p		t		k	'
stop, voiced	b		d		g	
affricate, voiceless				***ty/ch***		
affricate, voiced				***dy/j***		
fricative, voiceless		***f***	s	***sy/sh***		h
fricative, voiced		***v***	***z***			
lateral			l			
Flap			r			
Nasal	m		n	ñ	ng	
Glide	w			y		

1.1.1 Stops /p, t, k, ', b, d, g/ in Filipino are unaspirated and unreleased in final position. The only time a glottal stop /'/ is orthographically represented is by using a hyphen when it occurs word medially between a consonant and a vowel, as in the words /pag-ibig/ *love* and /mag-alay/ *to offer*. It occurs but is not orthographically represented in the following positions: word initial, word final, and predictably between two vowels, as in the examples /'awit/ *song*, /bata'/ *child*, and /'i'ukit/ *to carve*.

DOI: 10.4324/9781315739427-2

1.1.2 The **fricatives** /f, v, z, sh/ and the **affricates** /ch, j/ are relatively recent additions to the sound inventory of Filipino and are usually found in English loanwords. Often, these sounds are replaced by Tagalog sounds closest to their point of articulation. Thus, the sounds /f/ and /v/ are replaced by /p/ and /b/, respectively; /z/ and /sh/ are replaced by /s/ and /sy/, respectively; and /ch/ and /j/ are replaced by /ts/ and /dy/, respectively. These orthographic symbols are retained for writing proper names, as in the names /Zuñiga/, and /Joshua/. Common nouns with these sounds often have competing ways of spelling, as in the following examples: /vidyo/ or /bidyo/ *video*, /sabjek/ or /sabdyek/ *subject*, and /syampu/ or /shampoo/ *shampoo*. The **palatal nasal** /ñ/ is limited in its use to proper names, as in the names /Peñafrancia/ and /Añonuevo/.

1.1.3 The **velar nasal** /ng/ occurs in word-initial, medial, and final positions. Here are some examples: /ngayon/ *today/now*, /hangin/ *air/wind*, and /bawang/ *garlic*.

1.2 Consonant morphophonemics

1.2.1 The **glottal fricative** /h/ is not written when occurring in word-final position. It appears, however, when the suffix *-in* or *-an* is attached to a root ending in a vowel (non-glottal stop). The following are some examples, contrasted with words that end in a consonant, (-) glottal stop being one of them.

Root	Root with suffix *-in* or *-an*
gupit *cut*	gupitin *to cut*
gulo *confusion*	gulu**h**in *to confuse*
punta *go*	punta**h**an *to go to*
tago(-) *hide*	taguan *hide and seek*

1.2.2 The **consonants** /d/ and /r/ often appear in native words as variants of the same underlying consonant. The consonant /d/ may become /r/ in between vowels. Here are some examples.

Root	Root with affix/es
dating *to arrive*	da**r**ating *will arrive*
pahid *wipe*	pahi**r**an *to wipe*
unlad *development*	paunla**r**in *to develop*

1.2.3 **Palatalization**. The dento-alveolar sounds /t/, /d/, and /s/ palatalize to /ty/, /dy/, and /sy/, respectively, when they come before an unstressed vowel /i/ followed by the glide /y/. Here are some examples.

Word	Palatalized pronunciation
tiyan *stomach*	**ty**an *stomach*
diyan *there*	**dy**an *there*
siyam *nine*	**sy**am *nine*

1.2.4 Nasal assimilation. The velar nasal /ng/ in the prefixes *kasing-/magkasing-*, *mang-*, *nang-*, and *pang-* assimilates to the point of articulation of the first consonant of the root to which they attach. This prone to assimilation /ng/ is represented by the symbol /N/ here. Before the labial stops /p, b/ the nasal /ng/ becomes /m/, and before the dental consonants /t, d, l, r, s/ the nasal /ng/ becomes /n/. In all other environments, the velar nasal /ng/ remains. Here are some examples.

kasiN- + bait	→	kasi**m**bait	*as kind as*
magkasiN- + laki	→	magkasi**n**laki	*of the same size*
paN- + palo	→	pa**m**palo/pa**m**alo	*(instrument) for hitting*
paN- + sulat	→	pa**n**sulat/pa**n**ulat	*(instrument) for writing*
maN- + loko	→	ma**n**loko	*to deceive*

1.2.5 Metathesis or reordering of sounds. The infix *-in-* metathesizes to *ni-* when attached to the lateral /l/, the flap /r/, and the fricative /h/. Here are some examples.

– *in-* + luto	= linuto	→	**ni**luto	*Cooked*
– *in-* + labhan	= linabhan	→	**ni**labhan	*did the laundry*
– *in-* + iregalo	= irinegalo	→	**ini**regalo	*gave as a present*
– *in-* + irespeto	= irinespeto	→	**ini**respeto	*respected*
– *in-* + ihalo	= ihinalo	→	**ini**halo	*mixed in*
– *in-* + ihanap	= ihinanap	→	**ini**hanap	*find something for . . .*

1.3 Vowels

Filipino has five vowels, often described to be phonetically most similar to the vowels of Spanish or Italian: /a/ a low central vowel, /e/ a mid-front vowel, /i/ a high front vowel, /o/ a mid back vowel, and /u/ a high back vowel.

Tongue position	Front	Central	Back
High	i		u
Mid	e		o
Low		a	

Before the introduction of Spanish loanwords, Tagalog was essentially a three-vowel language, with [i] and [e] in free variation, and [o] and [u] were also alternate pronunciations of the same sound. The high variants /i/ and /u/ occurred everywhere except in syllable-final position, where they are lowered to /e/ and /o/, respectively. This explains the observed change in form and spelling of roots with final syllable /o/ when a suffix is attached, as shown by the following examples:

pulot + *-in*	→	Pulutan	*to pick up*
bilog + *-an*	→	Bilugan	*to encircle*
kape + *-han*	→	Kapihan	*coffee shop*

This also accounts for the variation in pronunciation of certain words with a final /i/ sound, as in the following examples:

Lalaki	~	lalake	*male* or *man*
Katabi	~	katabe	*next to*
Kasi	~	kase	*Because*

Each adjacent vowel comprises a syllable. A glottal stop between the vowels separates the syllables, especially noticeable in careful speech. It should also be noted that there are no vowel-initial syllables in the language. Here are some examples.

/ta'o/	Tao	*person*
/'a'alis/	aalis	*will leave*
/mano'od/	manood	*to watch*

1.4 Stress

Stress, which is syllable prominence, symbolized here with a colon /:/, is contrastive in Filipino. When stress falls on a particular syllable, its vowel is usually the longest and the loudest relative to other vowels in the word. Here are some examples showing contrast.

/ga:bi/	*Taro*	/gabi:/	*night*
/bu:kas/	*Tomorrow*	/buka:s/	*open*
/li:kas/	*Evacuate*	/lika:s/	*natural*
/ba:lat/	*birthmark*	/bala:t/	*skin*
/bu:not/	*Pull*	/buno:t/	*coconut husk*
/pu:no'/	*Tree*	/puno:'/	*full*

Older Tagalog texts marked stress with the symbol /'/ above the stressed vowel. However, in modern Filipino orthography, stress is no longer represented in writing. Readers are expected to know the appropriate meaning of the word from context. This poses a challenge to language learners, but if you have to guess, stress generally falls on the penultimate or second to the last syllable.

1.4.1 Stress shifting happens due to grammatical factors or with the addition of a suffix, like *-an* or *-in*. It involves movement of stress one syllable to the right, as shown by the following examples:

lu:to' + -in	→	lutu:in	*to cook*
pata:y + -in	→	patayi:n	*to kill*
pu:nas + -an	→	puna:san	*to wipe*
laka:s + -an	→	lakasa:n	*to make louder*

1.5 Syllabification

Filipino has a relatively simple way of syllabification. For most words, especially indigenous words, the basic syllable shape is CV(C). A syllable is comprised minimally of a consonant followed by a vowel. No two vowels can share a syllable. A glottal stop /'/ in word-initial position is not written or orthographically represented. Thus, any word spelled with a vowel-initial syllable is pronounced with a glottal stop (') at the onset. Consonant clusters in word medial position are broken between syllables, but keep in mind that velar nasal /ng/ is considered to be a consonant that cannot be broken. Here are some illustrative examples. The semicolon is used to symbolize secondary stress, while the period /./ marks syllable boundary.

Pakikibaka	[pa.ki;.ki.ba:.ka]	*Struggle*
Makipagsuntukan	[ma.ki.pa;g.sun.tu:.kan]	*to be in a fistfight*
pag-aaralan	[pag.a;.a.ra:.lan]	*will study*

1.6 Reduplication

Reduplication or repetition of a word or a part of a word is common in Filipino morphology. Full reduplication, repetition of the entire root word, and partial reduplication, repetition of a segment, are both used in the language. Some examples of full reduplication are /araw-araw/ *everyday* and /magandang-maganda/ *very beautiful*. Words with partial reduplication often only repeat the first consonant–vowel segment of the stem. Some examples are /takbo + rep1stCV = tatakbo/ *will run* and /alis + rep1st(C)V = aalis/ *will leave*. Sometimes, the first two syllables are also reduplicated, as in the following examples: /tahimik + rep1st2CV = tahi-tahimik/ *somewhat quiet* and /minuto + rep1st2CV = minu-minuto/ *every minute*.

1.7 Spelling

Before the arrival of the Spanish colonizers, Tagalog used an Indic syllabary consisting of three vowels and 15 consonants. In this system, final consonants were not written. In keeping with the phonology of the pre-Hispanic Tagalog language, the consonants /d/ and /r/ were represented by one symbol, as well as the vowels /e/ and /i/, and /o/ and /u/. Diacritics were used to distinguish vowels that accompanied the consonant (e.g., [ba, be/bi, bo/bu]). The ancient syllabary was later replaced with the Romanized alphabet based on Spanish orthography.

Present-day Filipino uses a spelling system based on Tagalog phonology, consisting primarily of 15 consonants (B, K, D, G, H, L, M, N, NG, P, R, S, T, W, Y) and five vowels (A, E, I, O, U). Loanwords are respelled using these letters. In addition, the letters C, F, J, Ñ, Q, V, X, Z have been incorporated into the language, bringing the total number of consonants to 23. However, these additional consonants are mainly used to spell proper names. For common nouns, loanwords with the sounds /f/ and /v/ are often replaced with /p/ and /b/, respectively. Loanwords with the sounds /ch/ and /j/ are spelled with the digraphs /ks/ and /dy/, respectively. Loanwords with the letter Z as well as those that contain the letter C pronounced as /s/ are respelled with an /s/. The letters Ñ, Q, and X are replaced by the symbols /ny/, /k/, and /ks/, respectively.

Chapter 2

Nouns and pronouns

2.1 Nouns in Filipino may be simple bare root words or morphologically complex derived forms composed of a root word + affix/es. Here are some examples where the affix/es are in bold.

Root word	***Root + one affix***	***Root + two or more affixes***
araw *sun* or *day*	aklat**an** *library*	**ka**buti**han** *goodness* or *kindness*
buhay *life*	**taga**linis *janitor*	**ka**balintuna**an** *irony*
gubat *forest*	**ka**klase *classmate*	**pagpapa**tupad *enforcement*
kulay *color*	**ka**trabaho *coworker*	**pagsasa**ulo *memorization*
nayon *village*	sayaw**an** *ball*	**pakikipag**-ugnay**an** *interaction*
puno *tree*	kain**an** *feast*	**sangka**tau**han** *humanity*
yaman *wealth*	**pag**-ibig *love*	**tala**salita**an** *vocabulary list*
wakas *end*	**pag**-asa *hope*	**ka**isip**an** *idea*

2.1.1 There are a number of derivational affixes used to derive new nouns from existing words. The most common ones are outlined here.

2.1.1.1 The suffix -(*h*)*an* may be used to indicate source or location.

Root word	Word + -(*h*)*an*
tinda *merchandise*	tindahan *store*
hukom *judge*	hukuman *courtroom*
daan *path*	daanan *passageway*
tulog *sleep*	tulugan *sleeping quarters*
mangga *mango*	manggahan *mango orchard*

2.1.1.2 The prefixes *taga-*, *mag-*, and *mang-* (*maN-*) with CV reduplication, repetition of the first consonant + first vowel, indicate occupation

DOI: 10.4324/9781315739427-3

or the person responsible for performing the action expressed by the root.

Root word	Word + *taga-*
hugas *wash*	tagahugas *dishwasher*
linis *clean*	tagalinis *janitor* or *person assigned to clean up*
sulat *write*	tagasulat *person assigned to take notes*

Root word	Word + *mag*CV-
saka *farm*	magsasaka *farmer*
lako *sell*	maglalako *street vendor*
taho *sweet tofu*	magtataho *sweet tofu vendor*

Root word	Word + *mang*CV-
gawa *do* or *make*	manggagawa *laborer*
habi *weave*	manghahabi *weaver*
gamot *heal*	manggagamot *healer* or *doctor*

2.1.1.3 The **prefix *mag-* without CV reduplication** is also used to express a reciprocal relationship.

Root word	Word + *mag-*
asawa *spouse*	mag-asawa *husband and wife*
kapatid *sibling*	magkapatid *brother and sister* or *siblings*
ama *father*	mag-ama *father and child*
kaklase *classmate*	magkaklase *classmates*

2.1.1.4 The **affix combination *ka – an*** is used to derive abstract nouns from adjective roots and collective nouns from other nouns.

Root word	Word + *ka – an*
tamad *lazy*	katamaran *laziness*
baliw *crazy*	kabaliwan *craziness*
sipag *hard work*	kasipagan *diligence*
babae *female*	kababaihan *womenhood*
bata *young* or *child*	kabataan *youth* or *young people*
bundok *mountain*	kabundukan *mountain region*

2.1.1.5 The **prefix *tag-*** is used to indicate a season or period of time.

Root word	Word + *ka – an*
ulan *rain*	tag-ulan *rainy season*
init *hot*	tag-init *warm season* or *summer*
gutom *hungry*	taggutom *famine*
ani *harvest*	tag-ani *harvest time*

2.1.1.6 The <u>prefix *pa-*</u> is used to form causative nouns or nouns of utility.

<u>Root word</u>	<u>Word + *pa-*</u>
kain *eat*	pakain *dinner treat*
hatid *deliver*	pahatid *notice* or *message*
gawa *do* or *make*	pagawa *work order*
luto *cook*	paluto *catering request or order*

2.1.1.7 The <u>infix *-in-*</u> (indicating completed action) forms nouns made by the process. Some of the most commonly used words of this category refer to food prepared using specific cooking techniques.

<u>Root word</u>	<u>Word + *-in-*</u>
tapa *to smoke*	tinapa *smoked fish or meat*
ihaw *to grill*	inihaw *something grilled*
sigang *to stew-sour*	sinigang *something stewed in sour broth*
gisa *to sauté*	ginisa *something sautéed*

2.1.1.8 The **<u>prefix *saN-/sangka-* or affix combination *saN-/sangka – an*</u>**, from the cardinal number *isá* 'one' and the linker *-ng*, forms nouns that express oneness, wholeness, or completeness.

<u>Root word</u>	<u>Word + *saN-* (*-an*)</u>
daigdig *world*	sandaigdigan *whole universe*
langit *heaven*	sangkalangitan *entire heaven*
pulo *island*	sangkapuluan *whole archipelago*
tao *people*	sangkatauhan *entire humanity*

2.1.1.9 The <u>affix combination *pala – an*</u> is used to indicate the method, art, rules, or basis of what is denoted by the root.

<u>Root word</u>	<u>Word + *pala – an*</u>
isip *think*	palaisipan *puzzle* or *riddle*
tanda *mark*	palatandaan *identifying mark* or *sign*
tunton *follow*	palatuntunan *program* (*of event*)
baybay *spell*	palabaybayan *spelling rules*

2.1.1.10 The <u>affix combination *tala – an*</u> comes from *tala* 'note, record, or list' and is used to indicate lists.

<u>Root word</u>	<u>Word + *tala – an*</u>
araw *day*	talaarawan *diary*
salita *word*	talasalitaan *word list*
awit *song*	talaawitan *song book*
hulog *equivalent*	talahulugan *dictionary*

2.1.1.11 Actor-focus (AF) verbs may be nominalized (i.e., turned into nouns by adding specific affixes) through a process called **nominalization**.

AF verb form	*Nominalizing affix*	*Example: verb→noun*	
- *um*- verb	*pag*- + root word	tumakbo > *to run* >	**pag**takbo *act of running*
mag- verb	*pag*C_1V_1- + root word	magluto > *to cook* >	**paglu**luto *the act of cooking*
ma- verb	*pagkaka*- + root word	matulog > *to sleep* >	**pagkaka**tulog *the act of sleeping*
maN- verb	*paN*C_1V_1- + root word	manggamit > *to use (people)* >	**pangga**gamit *act of using (people)*
maki- verb	*pakiki*- + root word	makikain > *to eat with others* >	**pakiki**kain *act of eating with others*
makipag- verb	*pakikipag*- + root	makipag-usap > *to converse with* >	**pakikipag**-usap *act of conversing*
magpa- verb	*pagpapa*- + root	magpagupit > *to get a haircut*>	**pagpapa**gupit *act of getting a haircut*
mag – an verb	*pag*C_1V_1- + root + -*an*	magtulungan > *to help one another*>	**pagtu**tulung**an** *act of helping one another*

***Note**: C_1 = initial consonant of the root word; V_1 = first vowel of the root word

2.1.2 Although there are a few animate nouns that express inherent gender, Filipino nouns do not generally carry **gender**. However, there are a few Spanish loanwords in which masculine forms end in a consonant or /o/ and feminine forms end in /a/. Some examples are shown here.

Nouns that do not carry gender or have inherent gender		*Nouns that express gender*			
		Feminine		*Masculine*	
asawa	*husband* or *wife*	tiya	*aunt*	tiyo	*uncle*
kapatid	*brother* or *sister*	abogada	*lawyer*	abogado	*lawyer*
tagaluto	*chef* or *cook*	doktora	*doctor*	doktor	*doctor*
magsasaka	*farmer*	musikera	*musician*	musikero	*musician*
		tindera	*salesclerk*	tindero	*salesclerk*
kuya	*older brother*	kahera	*cashier*	kahero	*cashier*
ate	*older sister*	gobernadora	*governor*	gobernador	*governor*

2.1.3 Pluralization is indicated by the particle */manga:/* (spelled as mga) placed immediately before the noun. When other indicators of plurality are used, such as numbers, the particle */mga/* is deemed redundant, and hence, its use in this context is avoided.

Singular	Plural
bahay *house*	mga bahay *houses*
anak *child*	mga anak *children*
kotse *car*	tatlong kotse *three cars*
bisita *guest*	maraming bisita *many guests*

2.2 Pronouns

Personal and demonstrative pronoun paradigms in Filipino align neatly with the noun marker sets in that they also indicate case. These sets of pronouns are here thus labeled **subject set or *ang* pronouns, genitive set or *ng* pronouns**, and **oblique set or *sa* pronouns**, substituting for *ang* phrases, *ng* phrases, and *sa* phrases, respectively.

2.2.1 Personal pronouns in Filipino encode person and number but do not encode gender. There are two pronoun forms for first-person plural, distinguishing between the 'inclusive we' that includes the addressee and the 'exclusive we' that excludes the addressee. The full sets are shown here.

Person number	***Ang pronouns (subject set)***	***Ng pronouns (genitive set)***	***Sa pronouns (oblique set)***
I (first-person singular)	ako	ko	sa akin
you (second-person singular)	ikaw/ka	mo	sa iyo
he/she (third-person singular)	siya	niya	sa kanila
we; exclusive (first-person plural)	kami	namin	sa amin
we; inclusive (first-person plural)	tayo	natin	sa atin
you (second-person plural)	kayo	ninyo	sa inyo
they (third-person plural)	sila	nila	sa kanila

2.2.1.1 *Ang* pronouns behave like enclitics, usually occurring in the second position within their clause, except when occurring with adverbial enclitics or in an inverted order (i.e., ay sentence or identificational sentences;

see chapter on adverbs and sentences). The second-person singular /ikaw/ can occur at the beginning of a clause, while /ka/ cannot. Politeness in the second-person singular can be expressed with three degrees of respect: /ka/ for informal, intimate, or familiar; /kayo/ for formal; and /sila/ for very formal context. The subject set is used to replace subjects or *ang* phrases (i.e., noun phrases with the marker *ang*, *si*, or *sina*).

Sentences with *ka* and *ikaw*	English equivalent
Kumain **ka** sa kusina.	***You*** *eat in the kitchen.*
Ikaw ay kumain sa kusina.	***You*** *eat in the kitchen.* (ay sentence)
Ikaw ang kumain sa kusina.	***You*** *be the one to eat in the kitchen.*

Politeness in second-person plural	English equivalent
Kumusta **ka**?	*How are* ***you****?*
Kumusta po **kayo**?	*How are* ***you****?* (plural or singular; formal)
Kumusta po **sila**?	*How are* ***they****?* (singular; very formal)

Sentences with *kami* and *tayo*	English equivalent
Manonood **kami** ng sine.	***We*** *will watch a movie.* (I and other/s)
Manood **tayo** ng sine.	*Let* ***us*** *watch a movie.* (I and you [and maybe others/s])

2.2.1.2 ***Ng*** **pronouns** are used to replace *ng* phrases that express either the possessor of a noun or the actor of a non-AF verb (see chapter on verbs). *Ng* pronouns come first when they occur with *ang* pronouns in the same clause. The portmanteau pronoun *kita* is used when the first-person singular /ko/ is followed by the second-person singular /ka/ instead of *ko* + *ka*, which is ungrammatical.

Ng pronoun as possessor	English equivalent
Libro niya ito.	*This is* ***his/her book*** .
Kinuha ko ang **mga papel nila**.	*I took* ***their papers*** .
May bagong kotse ang **kuya ko**.	***My older brother*** *has a new car.*

Ng pronoun as actor of OF verb	English equivalent
Binasa **niya** ang diyaryo.	***He/she*** *read the newspaper.*
Ipinagluto **nila** kami ng hapunan.	***They*** *cooked dinner for us.*
Itapon **ninyo** ang basura.	***You*** *throw away the trash.*

Ng pronoun with *ang* pronoun	English equivalent
Ibinili **ko** siya ng sapatos.	***I*** *bought shoes for him/her.*
Binigyan **nila** kami ng pera.	***They*** *gave us money.*
Tatawagan **kita** bukas.	*I will call* ***you*** *tomorrow.*

2.2.1.3 *Sa* **pronouns** are used to replace oblique or *sa* phrases, which express nouns that are not verbal arguments (i.e., neither actor nor [direct] object), often translated in English by prepositional phrases. They can often be moved around without changing the meaning of the sentence. They may also be used as an alternative way of expressing possession. Its structure is different from that which uses *ng* pronouns. It comes before the noun and has a linker in between possessor + noun and the /sa/ is often dropped (see chapter on linkers).

Sa pronoun	English equivalent
Tumulong si Ben **sa kanila**.	*Ben gave assistance* ***to them****.*
Ibinigay niya **sa akin** ang lapis.	*He/she gave* ***me*** *the pencil.*
Magluluto siya para **sa inyo**.	*He/she will cook for* ***you****.*

Sa pronoun as possessor	English equivalent
(Sa) Kanyang libro ito.	*This is* ***his/her book****.*
Kinuha ko ang **kanilang mga papel**.	*I took* ***their papers****.*
May bagong kotse ang **aking kuya**.	***My older brother*** *has a new car.*

2.2.2 **Demonstrative pronouns**. Filipino divides space into three domains: the proximate, close to the speaker; the medial, close to the addressee or not too far from either; and the distal, far from the speech event. There is a distinction between the singular and plural forms.

2.2.2.1 Like personal pronouns, demonstratives also inflect for case corresponding to the noun marker sets. These pronouns substitute for phrases expressing inanimate noun referents. However, in spoken Filipino, some speakers also use the third-person personal pronouns (*siya* and *sila*) for this.

Proximity	***Ang pronouns (subject set)***	***Ng pronouns (genitive set)***	***Sa pronouns (oblique set)***
proximal; singular	ito	nito	dito
proximal; plural	ang mga ito	ng mga ito	sa mga ito
medial; singular	iyan	niyan	diyan
medial; plural	ang mga iyan	ng mga iyan	sa mga iyan
distal; singular	iyon	niyon/noon	doon
distal; plural	ang mga iyon	ng mga iyon	sa mga iyon

Ang demonstratives	English equivalent
Mahal **ang mga ito**.	***These*** *are expensive.*
Binili ko **iyan** sa internet.	*I bought* ***that*** *online.*
Nakikita mo ba **iyon**?	*Do you see* ***that*** *over there?*

Ng demonstratives	English equivalent
Saan ka kumuha **ng mga ito**?	*Where did you get **these**?*
Gumawa rin sila **niyan**.	*They also made **that**.*
Naghahanap kami **niyon**.	*We are looking for **that** (distal/absent).*

Sa demonstratives	English equivalent
Nag-aplay sila ng trabaho **dito**.	*They applied to work **here**.*
Dahil **sa mga iyan**, nagbago na siya.	*Because of **those** (reasons), he/she changed.*
Bukod **doon**, relihiyoso rin siya.	*Aside from **that**, he/she is also religious.*

The subject-set demonstrative pronouns may be used with noun markers to point out or emphasize their referent nouns. It is not limited to animate nouns. In this construction, the demonstrative comes after the noun, and there is a linker between the noun and the demonstrative pronoun. Here are a few examples.

With *ang* marker	English equivalent
Mabuti **ang kaisipang ito**.	***This idea** is good.*
Binili niya **ang mga bagay na iyan**.	*He/she bought **those things**.*
Binisita ko **ang mga lugar na iyon**.	*I visited **those places over there**.*

With *ng* marker	English equivalent
Dinala **ng batang ito** ang bulaklak.	***This child** brought the flower.*
Kinuha **ng taong iyan** ang pera.	***That person** took the money.*
Mabait ang guro **ng klaseng iyon**.	*The teacher **of that class** is kind.*

With *sa* marker	English equivalent
Nakatira sila **sa lugar na ito**.	*They live **in this place**.*
Tumulong sila **sa mga taong iyan**.	*They helped **those people**.*
Tumutol kami **sa mga patakarang iyon**.	*We objected **to those policies**.*

In spoken Filipino, many speakers use /iyong/ (*iyon* + linker /*-g*/) as a substitute for the marker *ang*, especially when the noun referent is not physically present or remote in time/space. Sometimes, it is pronounced and written as /'yung/. Here are some examples.

'Yung substituting for *ang*	English equivalent
Napanood mo na ba **'yung sine**?	*Have you watched **the movie**?*
Iniwan ko **'yung kompyuter ko**.	*I left **my computer**.*
Lumabas **'yung estudyante**.	***The student** went outside.*

2.2.2.2 Aside from the preceding three basic demonstrative pronoun sets, there are **other pronoun sets** in Filipino that carry the same proximity of referents logic. The most common ones are mentioned here, followed by some illustrative sentences.

Proximity	*Location/ existence* ***(is here; is there)***	*Deictic* ***(here it is; there it is)***	*Direction* ***(this direction; that direction)***	*Manner* ***(in this manner; in that manner)***
proximate	nandito/narito	heto	parito	(pa)ganito
medial	nandiyan/nariyan	hayan	pariyan	(pa)ganiyan
distal	nandoon/naroon	hayun	paroon	(pa)ganoon

Examples	English equivalent
Nandito ako sa labas.	*I am here outside.*
Hayun ang bahay ni Mario.	*There is Mario's house.*
Lumiko pariyan ang bus.	*The bus turned toward that direction.*
Tumakbo siya nang ganito.	*He/she ran in this manner.*

Chapter 3

Markers and prepositions

3.1 Markers

Filipino has a closed lexical class called *noun markers*. This may be thought of as equivalent to the word *class* referred to as articles or determiners in other languages. Noun markers immediately precede the nouns they qualify. There are three sets of noun markers in Filipino: the subject set (*ang* markers), genitive set (*ng* markers), and oblique set (*sa* markers). In verbal sentences, they assign case to the nouns they qualify: *ang* phrases are marked for subjective (or nominative) case; *ng* phrases are marked for genitive (or ergative) case; and *sa* phrases are marked for oblique case, which, depending on the meaning and form of the verb, may encode dative case (which answers the question 'for whom?'), locative case (which answers the question 'where or to/from whom?'), and instrumental case (which answers the question 'with/by/through what?').

***Ang* markers** precede the subject of a sentence. ***Ang* phrases** are generally interpreted as definite. However, there are instances when *ang* phrases with the common noun marker may be indefinite: one, when the word /isang/ *one* follows it and precedes the rest of the noun phrase; two, in some cases, when it occurs with verbs that are not actor focus (AF) (see chapter on verbs).

***Ng* markers** have three functions: (1) they mark or precede a possessor noun, (2) they mark or precede the object of an AF verbal sentence, and (3) they mark or precede the actor of a non-actor focus (non-AF) verbal sentence (e.g., OF, LF/DF, and BF; see chapter on verbs). The genitive marker is pronounced [nang]. *Ng* phrases with personal noun markers are always definite and specific. However, *ng* phrases with common noun markers may be interpreted as either definite or indefinite depending on the context in which they occur.

***Sa* markers** mark everything else, functioning like prepositions in English. Oblique markers may combine with prepositions to make

DOI: 10.4324/9781315739427-4

the referent location or direction more specific. *Sa* phrases are always definite.

Noun markers are further categorized into common or personal. **Common noun markers** precede inanimate nouns or generic animate nouns. **Personal markers** precede names, terms of address, and sometimes kinship terms. There are distinct personal markers for singular and plural referents. Generally, a singular personal marker precedes a single name and a plural marker precedes two or more names. However, a plural marker may also precede a single name. In this context, the referent is interpreted as plural (i.e., the named person and others with him/her).

Noun markers	***Ang set (subject)***	***Ng set (genitive)***	***Sa set (oblique)***
common	ang	ng [nang]	Sa
personal; singular	si	ni	Kay
personal; plural	sina	nina	kina

The following sentences show the functions of noun markers. The relevant illustrative phrases are in bold.

Sentences with *ang* phrases	English equivalent
Malaki **ang bahay nila**.	***Their house*** *is big.*
Umalis **ang guro**.	***The teacher*** *left.*
Nasa kusina **si Ben**.	***Ben*** *is in the kitchen.*
Nag-aaral **sina Beth at Elsa**.	***Beth and Elsa*** *are studying.*

Sentences with *ng* phrases	English equivalent
Bago ang kotse **ni Karen**.	***Karen's*** *car is new.*
Dumating ang tatay **ng bata**.	***The child's*** *father arrived.*
Bumili **ng mga bulaklak** si Jun.	*Jun bought* ***flowers***.
Kinain **nina Lito at Juan** ang pansit.	***Lito and Juan*** *ate the noodles.*

Sentences with *sa* phrases	English equivalent
Naglalaro ang bata **sa kuwarto**.	*The child is playing* ***in the bedroom***.
Ibinigay ko ang pera **kay Mila**.	*I gave the money* ***to Mila***.
Tumawag siya **sa mga magulang niya**.	*She made a call* ***to her parents***.
Lumapit ako **kina Jon at Meg**.	*I approached* ***Jon and Meg***.

As already mentioned, markers assign case to the nouns that they qualify in verbal sentences: *ang* phrases are marked for subjective or nominative case, *ng* phrases are marked for genitive case, and *sa* phrases are marked for oblique case.

3.1.1 The **noun phrase with subjective case marker /ang/** is the focus or topic of the sentences. This is also sometimes referred to as nominative or absolutive in some Tagalog grammar descriptions. The focus marking in the verb indicated by a focus affix must agree with the subjective case marking on the focused noun phrase. In this sense, Filipino is similar to English in having a subject–verb agreement rule. The focus affix on the verb triggers the subjective marking on the noun phrase matching its case. In some grammar books, the non-AF sentences are analyzed as different forms of passive sentence constructions. However, in practical terms, the type of focusing in English that approximates grammatical focus in Filipino is the fronting of a noun phrase for emphasis. The following examples demonstrate this rule:

AF sentence

Bumili ng mga bulaklak sa tindahan **ang bata** para sa kanyang nanay.
The child bought *flowers at the store for his/her mother.*

Object-focus (OF) sentence

Binili ng bata sa tindahan para sa kanyang nanay **ang mga bulaklak**.
The flowers, *the child* ***bought*** *at the store for his/her mother.*

Locative-focus (LF) sentence

Binilhan ng bata ng mga bulaklak para sa kanyang nanay **ang tindahan sa tabi ng simbahan**.
At the store next to the church, *the child* ***bought*** *flowers for his/her mother.*

Benefactive-focus (BF) sentence

Ibinili ng bata ng mga bulaklak sa tindahan **ang kanyang nanay**.
For his/her mother, *the child* ***bought*** *flowers at the store.*

Experiencer-focus (EF) sentence

Natakot ang mga turista dahil sa pagsabog ng bulkan.
The tourists got scared *because of the volcanic eruption.*

Reason-focus (RF) sentence

Ikinatatakot ng mga turista **ang pagsabog ng bulkan**.
Because of the volcanic eruption, *the tourists* ***got scared***.

Instrumental-focus (IF) sentence

Ipinanghiwa niya ng mga mangga **ang maliit na kutsilyo**.
With a small knife, he/she sliced *the mangoes.*

3.1.2 The **genitive case marker /ng/**, as mentioned earlier, can mark a noun phrase that is either the direct object in an AF sentence or the actor in a non-AF sentence. Some Tagalog grammar descriptions refer to this case as accusative or ergative. Using the same sentences in the preceding section, the genitive case-marked noun phrases (NPs) are highlighted as follows to illustrate the use of this case marking.

AF sentence

Bumili **ng mga bulaklak** sa tindahan ang bata para sa kanyang nanay.
*The child bought **flowers** at the store for his/her mother.*

OF sentence

Binili **ng bata** sa tindahan para sa kanyang nanay ang mga bulaklak.
*The flowers, **the child** bought at the store for his/her mother.*

LF sentence

Binilhan **ng bata ng mga bulaklak** para sa kanyang nanay ang tindahan.
*At the store, **the child** bought **flowers** for his/her mother.*

BF sentence

Ibinili **ng bata ng mga bulaklak** sa tindahan ang kanyang nanay.
*For his/her mother, **the child** bought **flowers** at the store.*

In the immediately preceding examples, the first sentence has a *ng* phrase, which is the direct object of an AF sentence. The second example has a *ng* phrase, which is the actor of an OF sentence. In the last two examples, both the actor and direct object are *ng* phrases because these are not the grammatical focus or subject of the locative and benefactive sentences. When both actor and direct object are *ng* phrases, the actor noun phrase usually occupies the position next to the verb.

3.1.3 The **oblique case marker /sa/** marks any NP that is not the grammatical focus of a verbal sentence other than the actor or direct object. By itself or in combination with different conjunctions, this marker can encode a number of grammatical functions. It can mark the locative or directional phrase that is not the grammatical focus of the verb. Co-occurring with certain conjunctions, it can also mark the case role of other NPs in a sentence. These functions are discussed in detail in the following section.

3.1.3.1 The **marker /sa/** specifies the location or direction of an action, event, or noun, concrete or abstract. Combined with adverbs and prepositions, it can also indicate specific time and position. In the following examples, these functions are illustrated:

The marker /sa/ specifying the location of an event/action

Kumain sina Amy at Lina **sa Barrio Fiesta**.
Amy and Lina ate at Barrio Fiesta (restaurant).

Bumaha **sa aming probinsya** noong isang linggo.
*There was flooding **in our province** last week.*

Binili ko ang mga prutas na ito **sa palengke**.
*I bought these fruits **at the market**.*

The marker /sa/ specifying the direction of an event/action

Pumunta ang mga bata **sa parke** para maglaro.
*The kids went **to the park** to play.*

Itinapon nila ang basura **sa ilog**.
*They threw trash **into the river**.*

Tumulong sila **sa mga biktima ng bagyo**.
*They gave assistance **to the hurricane victims**.*

The marker /sa/ indicating time

Manonood kami ng sine **sa Sabado**.
*We will watch a movie **on Saturday**.*

Nag-eehersisyo si Ben **sa hapon**.
*Ben exercises **in the afternoon**.*

Aalis na ang mga bisita **sa makalawa**.
*The guests are leaving **on the day after tomorrow**.*

The marker /sa/ indicating position

Maraming puno **sa paligid ng lawa**.
*There are lots of trees **around the lake**.*

Inilagay ni Mario ang susi **sa ibabaw ng libro**.
*Mario put the key **on top of the book**.*

Isasabit ko ang parol **sa harap ng bahay**.
*I will hang the Christmas lantern **in front of the house**.*

3.1.3.2 The **marker /para sa/** marks the benefactive noun phrase in a non-BF verbal sentence. The benefactive phrase is roughly equivalent to the grammatical case in other languages called dative, which is the beneficiary noun for whom the action expressed by the verb is performed. Here are some examples.

Nagluto si Jun ng hapunan **para sa kanyang mga kapatid**.
*Jun cooked dinner **for his siblings**.*

Ginawa nila ang mga kakanin **para sa mga bisita**.
*They made rice cakes **for the guests**.*

Pinitas ng bata ang mga bulaklak **para sa kanyang lola**.
*The child picked flowers **for his/her grandmother**.*

3.1.3.3 The **marker /dahil sa/** marks the reason noun phrase in a non-RF verbal sentence. The reason phrase expresses the reason for the event or action expressed by the verb. Here are some examples.

Nalungkot siya **dahil sa balitang nabasa niya sa diyaryo**.
*He/she felt sad **because of the news that he/she read in the newspaper**.*

Gumaling ang aking lolo **dahil sa gamot na ibinigay ng doktor**.
*My grandfather got better **because of the medicine that the doctor gave him**.*

Naiinis si Pablo **dahil sa masamang lagay ng trapiko sa daan**.
*Pedro is annoyed **because of the bad traffic conditions on the road**.*

3.1.3.4 The marker **/sa pamamagitan ng/** marks the instrumental noun phrase in a non-IF verbal sentence. The instrumental phrase expresses the instrument used in performing the action expressed by the verb. Here are some examples.

Pinutol ni Mila ang lubid **sa pamamagitan ng kutsilyo**.
*Mila cut the rope **with a knife**.*

Nililinis nila ang balkonahe **sa pamamagitan ng walis**.
*They are cleaning the balcony **(by) using a broom**.*

Nagbubungkal ng lupa ang aking tiyo **sa pamamagitan ng traktora**.
*My uncle tills the land **using a tractor**.*

3.2 Prepositions

A preposition connects a noun or pronoun to a verb or adjective in a sentence. In Filipino, these can be classified into two general categories based on their specific function, either to indicate location/direction or to indicate relation. They all combine with the oblique marker /sa/ and usually followed by the genitive marker /ng/ to complete the form.

3.2.1 Location prepositions. Location in Filipino is expressed by the word **/nasa/**, for common nouns (i.e., non-personal nouns), **/na kay/** for singular personal nouns, and **/na kina/** for plural personal nouns. These are shortened forms of the full phrase **/naroon sa, naroon kay, naroon kina/**, respectively.

Sentences with *nasa* preposition	English equivalent
Nasa Davao si Mario.	*Mario is **in Davao**.*
Na kay Gina ang telepono ko.	*My phone is **with Gina**.*
Na kina Jim at Luis ang gamit namin.	*Our things are **with Jim and Luis**.*

The marker /sa/ functions as a preposition indicating location preceding common nouns in non-verbal sentences. However, its equivalent personal markers almost always indicate ownership or possession when used in similar constructions.

Sentences with *sa* preposition	English equivalent
Sa bahay ni Sara ang pagdiriwang.	*The party is **at Sara's house** .*
Sa Batangas ang piyesta.	*The festival is **in Batangas**.*
Kay Tina ang kompyuter na ito.	*This computer **belongs to Tina**.*
Kina Jon at Rita ang pagkain.	*The food **belongs to Jon and Rita**.*

More specific locations are often expressed by combining /nasa/ or /sa/ with other location indicators. The most commonly used ones are listed here.

Location indicator	***English equivalent***	***Example***
tabi	*beside, next to, or by*	**Nasa tabi ng ilaw** ang silya. *The chair is **beside the lamp**.*
		Nakatayo siya **sa tabi ng pintuan**. *He/she is standing by the doorway.*
kaliwa	*left*	May halaman **sa kaliwa ng sopa**. *There is a plant **to the left of the couch**.*
		Nasa kaliwa ng simbahan ang aming paaralan. *Our school is **on the left of the church**.*
kanan	*right*	Malaki ang bintana **sa kanan ng kama**. *The window **to the right of the bed** is big.*
		Binili ko ang halamang **nasa kanan ng telebisyon**. *I bought the plant that is **on the right side of the television**.*

harap	*front*	**Nasa harap ng klase** ang bisita. *The guest is **in front of the class**.* May maliit na hardin **sa harap ng aming bahay**. *There is a small garden **in front of our house**.*
likod	*at the back* or *behind*	May malaking puno **sa likod ng bahay namin**. *There is a big tree **at the back of our house**.* **Nasa likod ng sopa** ang pusa. *The cat is **behind the sofa**.*
ibabaw	*on top of* or *on*	**Nasa ibabaw ng kabinet** ang pitaka ko. *My wallet is **on top of the cabinet**.* **Sa ibabaw ng kama** mo ilagay ang mga damit. *Put the clothes **on the bed**.*
ilalim	*under* or *beneath*	**Nasa ilalim ng mesa** ang aso. *The dog is **under the table**.* Marami ang regalo **sa ilalim ng krismas tri**. *There are lots of gifts **underneath the Christmas tree**.*
taas	*above* or *up*	**Nasa taas ng telebisyon** ang relo. *The clock is **above the television**.* Umakyat ang pusa **sa taas ng puno**. *The cat climbed **up the tree**.*
baba	*below* or *down*	May bangko **sa baba ng hagdan**. *There is a bench **below the stairs**.* **Nasa baba ng gusali ang tindahan ng prutas**. *The fruit stand is **down the building**.*
sulok	(*inner*) *corner*	**Nasa sulok ng kuwarto** ang pusa. *The cat is **in the corner of the room**.* Pumunta rin ang aso **sa sulok ng silid**. *The dog also went **to the corner of the room**.*
kanto	(*outer*) *corner*	**Nasa kanto** ang tindahan ni Nena. *Nena's store is **on the street corner**.* Tumama ang aking tuhod **sa kanto ng mesa**. *I accidentally hit my knee **on the corner of the table**.*

tapat	*directly in front*	**Nasa tapat ng gusali** si Pedro. *Pedro is **directly in front of the building**.* Pumunta siya sa klinika **sa tapat ng aming opisina**. *He/she went to the clinic **directly in front of our office**.*
kabila	*other side*	May parke **sa kabila ng kalye**. *There is a park **across the street**.* **Nasa kabila ng lawa** ang bayan ng aking lolo. *My grandfather's town is **on the other side of the lake**.*
loob	*inside*	**Nasa loob ng simbahan** ang mga pari. *The priests are **inside the church**.* Nagdiwang sila **sa loob ng kuweba**. *They celebrated **inside the cave**.*
labas	*outside*	**Nasa labas** ang mga musikero. *The musicians are **outside**.* Tumakbo ang mga bata **sa labas ng paaralan**. *The children ran **outside the school**.*
dulo	*edge* or *end*	**Nasa dulo ng kalye** ang kaninan. *The eatery is **at the end of the street**.* Nakarating kami **sa dulo ng tulay**. *We reached **the end of the bridge** .*
gitna	*middle* or *center*	May mataas na monumento **sa gitna ng lunsod**. *There is a tall monument **in the middle of the city**.* **Nasa gitna ng mesa** ang pagkaing niluto ko. *The food that I prepared is **at the center of the table**.*

3.2.2 **Relation prepositions**. Aside from location prepositions, Filipino has a class of words used for relating the function of a noun to the rest of a sentence. Many of these combine with the oblique noun marker /sa, kay, kina/; some combine with the genitive noun marker /ng/, and some can stand alone. The most commonly used ones are listed with examples here.

Relational preposition	*English equivalent*	*Example*
para sa	*for*	Bumili siya ng regalo **para sa kapatid niya**. *He/she bought a gift* ***for his/her sibling***.
tungkol sa	*about*	Nagkuwento siya **tungkol kina Maria at Ana**. *He/she talked* ***about Maria and Ana***.
mula sa	*from*	Sumakay siya ng bus **mula sa Bikol**. *He/she rode a bus* ***from Bikol***.
hanggang sa	*until*	Tumakbo ang mga estudyante **hanggang sa parke**. *The students ran* ***up to the park***.
bukod sa	*aside from*	**Bukod sa Baguio**, pinuntahan din niya ang Iloilo. ***Aside from Baguio***, *he/she also visited Iloilo.*
maliban sa	*except for*	Dumating ang lahat **maliban kay Benito**. *Everyone came* ***except for Benito***.
laban sa	*against*	Nagprotesta sila **laban sa pagtatayo ng dam**. *They protested* ***against the building of a dam***.
(sang-) ayon sa	*according to*	**Ayon kay Mara**, marami ang biktima ng sunog. ***According to Mara***, *there were many fire victims.*
batay sa	*based on*	**Batay sa mga datos na ito** ang desisyon ng alkalde. *The mayor's decision was* ***based on these data***.
dahil sa	*because of*	Inilikas ang mga tao **dahil sa malakas na bagyo**. *The people were evacuated* ***because of the strong typhoon***.
alinsunod sa	*in accordance with*	Magkakaroon ng mga pagbabago sa mga gawain ng kompanya **alinsunod sa mga bagong patakaran**. *There will be changes in company practices* ***in accordance with new policies***.

depende sa	*depends on*	**Depende sa bilis ng tren** kung anong oras ang dating natin sa probinsya. *It **depends on the speed of the train** what time our arrival will be in the province.*
alang-alang sa	*in consideration of*	Tumigil na ako sa pag-inom at paninigarilyo **alang-alang sa aking lola**. *I quit drinking and smoking **in consideration of my grandmother**.*
hinggil sa	*regarding* or *concerning*	Nagbigay ng pahayag ang opisyal ng pamahalaan **hinggil sa mga bagong patakaran sa paglalakbay sa labas ng bansa**. *The government official gave a statement **regarding the new policies for travel outside the country**.*
kaugnay ng	*in connection with* or *in relation to*	Ilang tao sa aming baranggay ang iniimbestigahan ngayon ng pulisya **kaugnay ng pagnanakaw na naganap noong isang linggo**. *Several people on our block are being investigated by the police **in connection with the robbery that happened last week**.*
pagkatapos ng	*after*	Manonood sila ng pelikula **pagkatapos ng hapunan**. *They will watch a movie **after dinner**.*
katumbas ng	*equivalent to*	Ang pistang bayan sa Pilipinas ay **katumbas ng pagdiriwang ng Araw ng Pasasalamat sa USA**. *A town festival in the Philippines is **equivalent to Thanksgiving Day celebrations in the USA**.*
bilang	*as*	Nagtatrabaho si Pedro **bilang** mekaniko. *Pedro works **as** a mechanic.*
lingid sa	*unbeknownst to*	**Lingid sa kaalaman ng aking tatay**, bumili ng bagong kotse ang aking nanay. ***Unbeknownst to my father**, my mother bought a new car.*

taliwas sa	*contrary to*	**Taliwas sa inaasahan ng marami**, nanalo siya sa paligsahan. ***Contrary to people's expectations**, he/she won the contest.*
sa pamamagitan ng	*by using* or *through the use of*	Pinutol niya ang punungkahoy **sa pamamagitan ng lagaring de-baterya**. *He/she cut down the tree **by using a battery-operated saw**.*
sa kabila ng	*in spite of* or *despite*	**Sa kabila ng pagtutol ng publiko**, pinayagan ng pamahalaan ang pagtaas ng pamasahe sa LRT. ***Despite public protests**, the government approved the LRT fare increase.*
kasama ng	together with	Lumabas ako noong Biyernes **kasama ng** aking mga kaibigan. *I went out **with** my friends last Friday.*

Chapter 4

Adjectives and linker

4.1 The vast majority of adjectives in Filipino are either **simple adjectives** or ***ma* adjectives**. Simple adjectives are bare roots or single morpheme words (i.e., there is no affix attached to it). *Ma* adjectives are formed by attaching the prefix /ma-/ to a root word that expresses a quality. The bulk of adjectives in Filipino are *ma* adjectives.

Simple adjectives		***Ma adjectives***	
mura	*cheap*	malayo	*far*
mahal	*expensive*	malinis	*clean*
payat	*thin*	matalino	*intelligent*
bobo	*stupid*	masipag	*hardworking*
bago	*new*	masaya	*happy* or *fun*
luma	*old*	mahaba	*long*
gutom	*hungry*	maulan	*rainy*
sira	*broken*	mainit	*hot*

4.1.1 Filipino adjectives inflect for degree to express **moderate and intensified quality**. Both forms involve reduplication but applied differently. Moderate quality using *ma* adjectives is expressed through reduplication (i.e., repetition) of the first two syllables of the root. A hyphen is used to mark the reduplicated part of the root. To express moderate quality using simple adjectives, the word *medyo* is used immediately preceding the adjective, although reduplication of the first two syllables of the root may also yield the same meaning for some roots. For example, /mura-mura/, /bago-bago/, and /gutom-gutom/ are acceptable synonyms of /medyo mura/, /medyo bago/, and /medyo gutom/, respectively. However, when reduplication is applied to other simple forms, a completely different meaning is expressed. For example, the word /sira-sira/ does not mean *slightly broken*, but it rather means *completely*

DOI: 10.4324/9781315739427-5

broken or *irreparably damaged*. Because of this unpredictability and inconsistency, it is advisable to use the qualifier /medyo/ with all simple adjectives to express moderate quality.

Moderate quality (somewhat, kind of, a bit having the quality expressed by the root word)			
Simple adjectives		***Ma- adjectives***	
medyo mura	*somewhat cheap*	malayo-layo	*somewhat far*
medyo mahal	*somewhat expensive*	malinis-linis	*somewhat clean*
medyo payat	*somewhat thin*	matali-talino	*somewhat intelligent*
medyo bobo	*somewhat stupid*	masipag-sipag	*somewhat hardworking*
medyo bago	*somewhat new*	masaya-saya	*somewhat happy or fun*
medyo luma	*somewhat old*	mahaba-haba	*somewhat long*
medyo gutom	*somewhat hungry*	maulan-ulan	*somewhat rainy*
medyo sira	*somewhat broken*	mainit-init	*somewhat hot*

Intense quality is expressed through reduplication of the full adjective form. A linker is used to connect the reduplicated forms. This reduplication rule applies to both simple adjectives and *ma* adjectives.

Intensified quality (having intense quality expressed by the root word)			
Simple adjectives		***Ma- adjectives***	
murang mura	*very cheap*	malayong malayo	*very far*
mahal na mahal	*very expensive*	malinis na malinis	*very clean*
payat na payat	*very thin*	matalinong matalino	*very intelligent*
bobong bobo	*very stupid*	masipag na masipag	*very hardworking*
bagong bago	*very new*	masayang masaya	*very happy or fun*
lumang luma	*very old*	mahabang mahaba	*very long*
gutom na gutom	*very hungry*	maulang maulan	*very rainy*
sirang sira	*very broken*	mainit na mainit	*very hot*

There are other ways of expressing intensified quality in Filipino. One is through the use of adverbial phrases immediately preceding the adjective, for instance, the phrases /ubod ng . . ./ *the core of*, /saksakan ng . . ./ *injected with*, and /puno ng . . ./ *full of*. Another way is through the use of the prefix /napaka-/. And yet another way is to use the marker /ang/ before the root, with or without reduplication of the first two syllables. The last two methods affect the sentence structure in which the adjectives occur (see chapter on non-*ang* sentences).

Intensified quality (having intense quality expressed by the root word)			
Simple adjectives		***Ma- adjectives***	
saksakan ng mura	*very cheap*	saksakan ng layo	*very far*
ubod ng mahal	*very expensive*	ubod ng linis	*very clean*
napakapayat	*very thin*	napakatalino	*very intelligent*
napakabobo	*very stupid*	napakasipag	*very hardworking*
ang luma	*very old*	ang saya	*very happy* or *fun*
ang bago-bago	*very new*	ang haba-haba	*very long*

4.1.2 Adjectives in Filipino also inflect for degree to express **comparative and superlative qualities**. Unequal comparison is expressed by placing the word /mas/ immediately before the adjective. There are two ways to express equal comparison. One is with the use of the affix /mag-kasinN-/ and another is through the use of the affix /kasiN-/. Although these are alternate ways of equal comparison, their sentence structures differ. The superlative is expressed by the affix /pinaka-/.

Adjective	***Equal comparison***		***Unequal comparison***	***Superlative***
	kasinN ***(as . . . as)***	*magkasiN* ***(. . . are equally . . .)***	***mas (more . . .)***	*pinaka-* ***(most . . .)***
payat *thin*	kasimpayat	magkasimpayat	mas payat	pinakapayat
bago *new*	kasimbago	magkasimbago	mas bago	pinakabago
mura *cheap*	kasingmura	magkasingmura	mas mura	pinakamura
tahimik *quiet*	kasintahimik	magkasintahimik	mas tahimik	pinakatahimik
maliit *small*	kasinliit	magkasinliit	mas maliit	pinakamaliit
maganda *pretty*	kasingganda	magkasingganda	mas maganda	pinakamaganda
mabait *kind*	kasimbait	magkasimbait	mas mabait	pinakamabait
malapit *near*	kasinlapit	magkasinlapit	mas malapit	pinakamalapit

4.1.3 There are other derivational affixes in Filipino, although these are less productive than the *ma* affix. The most commonly used ones are discussed in this section.

4.1.3.1 ***Nakaka-*** **adjectives** express the meaning 'feeling/emotion-inducing,' whatever the feeling or emotion is expressed by the root. When the root indicates quality, the meaning of the adjective could be 'quality-causing' or 'quality-producing.' Here are a few examples.

Root	*Nakaka-* adjective English equivalent
inis *irritated*	nakakainis *annoying* or *irritating*
tawa *laughter*	nakakatawa *funny*
lungkot *sadness*	nakakalungkot *saddening*
gulat *shock*	nakakagulat *shocking*
inip *bored*	nakakainip *boring*
lito *confused*	nakakalito *confusing*
taba *fat*	nakakataba *fattening*
payat *thin*	nakakapayat *slimming*
ganda *beauty*	nakakaganda *beautifying*

4.1.3.2 ***Maka-*** **adjectives** may be used to indicate support or affinity for the referent expressed by the root. This is a relatively small set of adjectives.

Root	*Maka-* adjective English equivalent
bayan *country*	makabayan *patriotic*
diyos *god*	makadiyos *godly*
luma *old*	makaluma *conservative*
bago *new*	makabago *modern*
tao *people*	makatao *humanitarian*
kaliwa *left*	makakaliwa *left-leaning*
Amerikano *American*	maka-Amerikano *pro-American*
pigil-hininga *stop-breath*	makapigil-hininga *breath-taking*

4.1.3.3 ***Ma – in***, ***mapag-***, and ***pala-*** **adjectives** express the meaning frequent or habitual nature. This is also not a very large set.

Root	Adjective English equivalent
awa *pity* or *mercy*	maawain *merciful*
tulong *help*	matulungin *helpful*
mahal *love*	mapagmahal *loving*
husga *judge*	mapaghusga *judgmental*
away *quarrel*	palaaway *quarrelsome*
kain *eat*	palakain *frequent eater*
simba *go to church*	palasimba *frequent churchgoer*

4.1.3.4 ***Mala-*** **adjectives** indicate the meaning of having similar qualities as the referent of the root.

Root	*Mala-* adjective English equivalent
kristal *crystal*	malakristal *crystal-like*
anghel *angel*	malaanghel *angelic*
diyosa *goddess*	maladiyosa *goddess-like*
hayop *animal*	malahayop *beast-like* or *beastly*
sutla *silk*	malasutla *silken* or *silky smooth*

4.1.3.5 ***Pang-*** **adjectives** denote instrument, use, or intention. Some of these forms may be used as nouns.

Root	*Pang-* adjective English equivalent
Pasko *Christmas*	pamasko *for Christmas*
bahay *house*	pambahay *for use in the house*
punas *wipe*	pampunas *for wiping*
tulog *sleep*	pantulog *for sleeping*
bayad *payment*	pambayad *for use in paying*
luto *cook*	panluto *for cooking*
gabi *night*	panggabi *for nighttime*
opisina *office*	pang-opisina *for use in the office*

4.1.3.6 ***Taga-*** **adjectives** indicate origin. This is generally only used to describe people.

Root	*Taga-* adjective English equivalent
Leyte *Leyte*	taga-Leyte *from Leyte*
Canada *Canada*	taga-Canada *from Canada*
bundok *mountain*	tagabundok *from the mountain*
baryo *village*	tagabaryo *from the village*
bukid *farm*	tagabukid *from the farm*
ilog *river*	tagailog *from the river*

4.1.3.7 There are some Spanish loanwords with the suffix ***-ado*** that are also used as **adjectives** in Filipino.

Root	*-ado* adjective English equivalent
sara *close*	sarado *closed*
kalma *calm*	kalmado *calm*
deklara *declare*	deklarado *declared*
pirma *signature*	pirmado *signed*
amin *admit*	aminado *admitted*
kumpirma *confirm*	kumpirmado *confirmed*

4.1.3.8 Optional plurality encoding number agreement between a modifier and the noun it modifies may be expressed through reduplication of the first syllable (C_1V_1) of the root. This rule generally applies only to *ma-* adjectives, but in limited contexts it may also apply to bare or unaffixed adjective root words, colors, and shapes. The pluralizer /mga/ is deemed redundant when the noun modifier indicates plurality and hence usually dropped, although it is not ungrammatical when the pluralizer /mga/ is overtly expressed. The following examples demonstrate the structure of the modifier–noun number agreement, where the indicator of plurality is in bold.

Modifier + noun plural	Modifier plural + noun plural	English equivalent
magandang **mga** bestida	ma**ga**gandang bestida	*beautiful dresses*
maliit na **mga** bata	ma**li**liit na bata	*small children*
malayong **mga** bayan	ma**la**layong bayan	*remote towns*

Ang payat ng **mga** manok.
Ang **pa**payat ng mga manok. *The chickens are very thin.*

Ang bilog ng **mga** mangga.
Ang **bi**bilog ng mangga. *The mangoes are very round.*

Ang pula ng **mga** bulaklak.
Ang **pu**pula ng bulaklak. *The flowers are so red.*

4.1.3.9 Other adjective-forming affixes

4.1.3.9.1 Denominal affix *ga-* meaning 'comparable/similar to . . .'

Examples:

ga- + noun having the characteristic/quality similar to noun
ga- + bundok *mountain* gabundok *towering like a mountain*
ga- + langgam *ant* galanggam *small like an ant*

4.1.3.9.2 Denominal affix *hugis-* meaning 'having the shape of . . .'

Examples:

hugis- + puso *heart* hugis-puso *heart-shaped*
hugis- + bahay *house* hugis-bahay *house-shaped*
hugis- + kabayo *horse* hugis-kabayo *horse-shaped*

4.1.3.9.3 Denominal affix *kulay-* meaning 'having the color of . . .'

Examples:

kulay- + kape *coffee* kulay-kape *coffee-colored* or *brown*
kulay- + abo *ash* kulay-abo *ashen* or *gray*
kulay- + kahel *orange fruit* kulay-kahel *orange-colored*

4.1.3.9.4 Denominal affix *buhay-* meaning 'having a life similar to that of . . .'

Examples:

buhay- + alamang *baby shrimp* buhay-alamang *living like a shrimp* or *difficult life*
buhay- + baboy *pig* buhay-baboy *living like a pig* or *lazy*

buhay- + mayaman *wealthy* or *rich*	buhay-mayaman *living like a wealthy person*

4.1.3.9.5 Denominal affix *tunog-* meaning 'sounds like a . . .'

Examples:

tunog- + aso *dog*	tunog-aso *sounds like a dog*
tunog- + ambulansya *ambulance*	tunog-ambulansya *sounds like an ambulance*

4.1.3.9.6 Denominal affix *boses-* meaning 'having a voice that sounds like a . . .'

Examples:

boses- + bata *child*	boses-bata *having a child-like voice*
boses- + multo *ghost*	boses-multo *having a ghost-like voice*

4.1.3.9.7 Denominal affix *de-* meaning 'encased in or operated by/with . . .'

Examples:

de- + lata *can*	de-lata *canned* or *in can*
de- + kahon *box*	de-kahon *boxed*
de- + kuryente *electricity*	de-kuryente *electric*
de- + baterya *battery*	de-baterya *battery operated*
de- + hila *pull*	de-hila *operated by pulling*
de- + tulak *push*	de-tulak *operated by pushing*
de- + susi *key*	de-susi *operated with a key*

4.1.3.9.8 Reduplication + *-an* suffix meaning 'pretending to be . . .'

Examples:

bulag *blind* + reduplication + *-an*	bulag-bulagan *pretending to be blind*
bingi *deaf* + reduplication + *-an*	bingi-bingihan *pretending to be deaf*
kasal *wedding* + reduplication + *-an*	kasal-kasalan *pretend wedding*
baril *gun* + reduplication + *-an*	baril-barilan *pretend gun* or *gunfight*
doktor *doctor* + reduplication + *-an*	doktor-doktoran *pretend doctor*
pulis *policeman* + reduplication + *-an*	pulis-pulisan *pretend policeman*

4.1.3.9.9 Compounding

4.1.3.9.9.1 Noun–noun

buhay *life* + alamang *shrimp*	buhay-alamang *shrimp-like life* = *poor*
biyahe *trip* + probinsya *province*	biyaheng-probinsya *province-bound trip*

4.1.3.9.9.2 Verb–noun

luto *cook* + bahay *house*	lutong-bahay *home-cooked*
lakad *walk* + pagong *tortoise*	lakad-pagong *slow-paced walk*
laki *grow* + siyudad *city*	laking-siyudad *raised in the city*
bukas *open* + palad *palm*	bukas-palad *generous* or *helpful*
langoy *swim* + aso *dog*	langoy-aso *dog-like swimming*
pasa *pass* + awa *pity*	pasang-awa *barely passing grade*
tubo *profit* or *earn* + lugaw *rice porridge*	tubong-lugaw *high-earning*

4.1.3.9.9.3 Verb–verb

bantay *watch* + salakay *attack*	bantay-salakay *untrustworthy* or *disloyal*
bukas *open* + sara *close*	bukas-sara *open and close motion*
ligaw *woo* + tingin *glance*	ligaw-tingin *very shy suitor*
labas *exit* + pasok *enter*	labas-pasok *going in and out anxiously*
akyat *climb* + baba *go down*	akyat-baba *going up and down anxiously*
taas *raise* + baba *lower*	taas-baba *raise and lower anxiously*
atras *backward* + abante *forward*	atras-abante *foward and backward*
patay *kill* or *turn off* + sindi *light up*	patay-sindi *flickering*

4.1.3.9.9.4 Adjective–noun

ganda *beauty* + diwata *fairy*	gandang-diwata *fairy-like beauty*
busog *satisfaction* + kalusugan *health*	busog-lusog *healthfully satisfied*

4.1.3.9.9.5 Adverb–adverb

paroon *that direction* + parito *this direction*	paroo't-parito *to and fro*
pababa *going down* + pataas *going up*	pataas-pababa *going up and down*

4.2 Linker

Like other Philippine languages, Filipino has a linker that has several functions in the syntax of the language. It has two phonologically conditioned variants, **/na/** after consonants and **/-ng/** after vowels, [*n*], or a final glottal stop [']. When the linker /-ng/ is attached to a word that ends in /n/, only the letter /g/ is added. The major uses of the linker are outlined here with accompanying examples.

4.2.1 The linker is used to connect single-word modifiers to their noun referents. When multiple adjectives are used to modify the same noun, only the adjective immediately preceding the noun is followed by a linker. When multiple modifiers belonging to different categories (e.g., number, shape, color, and adjective) are used to modify a noun, each modifier must be followed by a linker. Although it is not considered ungrammatical for adjectives, shapes, or colors to come after the nouns they modify, there is a preference for them to precede the noun.

adjective + noun noun + adjective	malaki**ng** bahay/bahay **na** malaki *big house*
	matamis **na** mangga/mangga**ng** matamis *sweet mango*
	mahangin**g** panahon/panaho**ng** mahangin *windy weather*
color + noun noun + color	pula**ng** sapatos/sapatos **na** pula *red shoes*
shape + noun noun + shape	rektanggulo**ng** mesa/mesa**ng** rektanggulo *rectangular table*
numeral + noun	lima**ng** aso *five dogs*
multiple adjectives + noun	mabait, matalino, at masipag **na** bata *kind, intelligent, and hardworking kid*
multiple modifiers + noun	dalawa**ng** malaki**ng** bilog **na** pula**ng** mesa *two big, round, red tables*

4.2.2 The linker is used to connect a relative clause, a phrasal modifier, to its noun referent. The relative clause almost always follows the noun it modifies. In the following examples, the noun referent is underlined and the linker + relative clause are in bold.

Maganda <u>ang awit</u> **na kinanta ng mga bata**.
<u>The song</u> ***that the children sang*** *is beautiful.*

Nakilala ko <u>ang guro</u>**ng nagtuturo ng klaseng Matematika**.
I met <u>the teacher</u> **who teaches Mathematics class**.

Nakuha niya <u>ang parangal</u> **na ibinibigay sa pinakamahusay na estudyante**.
He/she got <u>the award</u> ***that is given to the best student***.

4.3 The linker is used to introduce an embedded clause (i.e., a complement clause in the declarative form). Many Filipino speakers use only the form /na/ consistently for this structure. In the following examples, the linker + complement clause is in bold.

Narinig ko**ng darating si Pedro sa Sabado**.
*I heard **that Pedro is arriving on Saturday**.*

Sinabi ng tagaulat **na tataas ang presyo ng gasolina**.
*The reporter said **that oil prices will increase**.*

Gusto ko**ng lumipat sa probinsya**.
*I want **to move to the province**.*

Marunong siya**ng gumawa ng bibingka**.
*He/she knows (**how**)**to make rice cake**.*

Chapter 5

Verbal aspect

Filipino verbs inflect for aspect, focus, and mood. In this book, each of these verbal inflections is treated in a separate section. However, one must keep in mind that these inflections interact with one another to form grammatical sentences. It must also be noted that there are a variety of ways in which these inflectional categories are analyzed by linguists. The particular analysis presented here is a pedagogical one (i.e., it is useful for teaching and learning the language). It is informed by both syntactic analyses from linguistics and practical pedagogical consideration for teaching Filipino as a foreign or second language.

5.1 **Verbal aspect** is a marking in the verb, through affixation or reduplication, that indicates whether the action has started, been completed, or yet to start. It interacts with both verbal focus and mood for verbs to fully express their intended meaning. Each focus form has four aspectual forms: infinitive, completed, incompleted, and contemplated. Here is a table showing examples of indicative actor-focus (AF) verbs and object-focus (OF) verbs.

AF verb root	***Infinitive***	***Completed***	***Incompleted***	***Contemplated***
Takbo	tumakbo	tumakbo	tumatakbo	tatakbo
Luto	magluto	nagluto	nagluluto	magluluto
Tulog	matulog	natulog	natutulog	matutulog
OF verb root	***Infinitive***	***Completed***	***Incompleted***	***Contemplated***
Kain	kainin	kinain	kinakain	kakainin
Bigay	ibigay	ibinigay	ibinibigay	ibibigay
hugas	hugasan	hinugasan	hinuhugasan	huhugasan

DOI: 10.4324/9781315739427-6

5.1.1 The **infinitive form** comprises verb root + focus affix (+ additional mood affix). It has three major functions: (1) it is used to express imperative or command; (2) it is used when the verb occurs with pseudo-verbs in the same clause; and (3) it is obligatorily used with certain conjunctions, such as /para/, /upang/, /at nang/, /bago/, and /pagkatapos/. Here are some examples.

Examples of imperatives

Kumain ka.
Eat–you
(subj.) You eat.

Hugasan mo ang mga plato sa kusina.
Wash–gen.you–subjmark.dishes–oblmark.kitchen
You wash the dishes in the kitchen.

Examples of sentences with pseudo-verbs

Puwede akong magluto ng manok mamaya.
Can–subj.I.lnk–cook–genmark.chicken–later
I can cook chicken later.

Dapat kong ibigay ang pera sa kapatid ko.
Must–gen.I–give–subjmark.money–oblmark.sibling.genmark
I must give the money to my brother/sister.

Examples of obligatory co-occurrence with certain conjunctions

Tumawag siya para magtanong tungkol sa takdang-aralin.
He/she called to ask about the homework.

Kumakanta sila ng pambansang awit bago sila magsimula ng klase.
They sing the national anthem before they start class.

5.1.2 The **completed aspect** form indicates that the action expressed by the verb has been completed or has terminated.

Examples of completed-aspect AF forms

Kumain kami sa kapeterya kanina.
Ate–subj.we–oblmark.cafeteria–earlier
We ate at the cafeteria earlier.

Natulog ang bata sa sopa.
Slept–subjmark.child–oblmark.sofa
The child slept on the sofa.

Examples of sentences with completed-aspect OF verbs

Ibinigay niya ang pera sa simbahan.
Gave-gen.he/she–subjmark.money–oblmark.church
He/she gave the money to the church.

Hinugasan ng lalaki ang mga plato.
Washed–genmark.man–subjmark.dishes
The man washed the dishes.

5.1.3 The **incompleted aspect** form indicates that the action expressed by the verb has started but has not been completed or has not terminated. It always involves affixation + reduplication of the first consonant–vowel (CV sequence) of the root or stem. This form has two functions: (1) to express ongoing action or activity in progress (expressed in English by the progressive aspect /-ing/ form) and (2) to indicate recurring or habitual action or event (expressed in English by the simple present form).

Examples of ongoing action

Kumakain si Mando ngayon.
Eating–subjmark.Mando–presently
Mando is cooking at the moment.

Nagluluto si Nanay ng hapunan nang dumating ako.
Cooking–subjmark.mother–genmark.dinner–when–arrived–I
Mother was cooking dinner when I arrived.

Examples of recurring or habitual action

Natutulog siya sa sopa tuwing hapon.
Sleeps–subj.he/she–oblmark.sofa–every afternoon
He/she sleeps on the sofa every afternoon.

Naglilinis ako ng banyo tuwing Sabado.
Clean–subj.I–genmark.bathroom.every Saturday
I clean the bathroom every Saturday.

5.1.4 The **contemplated aspect** form indicates that the action expressed by the verb has not yet started. It always involves reduplication of the first CV (CV sequence) of the root or stem.

Examples of contemplated-aspect AF forms

Pupunta kami sa palengke bukas.
Will go–subj.we–oblmark.market–tomorrow
We will go to the market tomorrow.

Manonood sila ng sine mamaya.
Will watch–subj.they–genmark.movie–later
They will watch a movie later.

Examples of sentences with contemplated-aspect OF verbs

Ibibigay namin ang mga regalo sa mga bata.
Will give–gen.we–subjmark.gifts–oblmark.the children
We will give the gifts to the children.

Lalabhan ko ang mga kumot mamaya.
Will wash–gen.I–subjmark.sheets–later
I will wash the sheets later.

5.2 Filipino verbal aspect compared to English tense–aspect forms

Filipino verbs encode aspect but not tense, but many speakers and learners often conflate these two concepts resulting in a tendency to equate English tense form variations with Filipino aspectual forms. In this section, verbal tense forms in English are compared with and mapped onto Filipino verbal aspect forms to clarify the overlaps and differences between these forms.

5.2.1 Past tense verb forms in English are used to indicate that something happened in the past, that is, any time before the moment of speaking. There are four variations of past tense in English: simple past, past continuous/past progressive, past perfect/pluperfect, and past perfect continuous. Simple past and past perfect forms are expressed in Filipino as completed/perfective aspect verbs. Past continuous and past perfect continuous are expressed as incompleted/progressive aspect in Filipino. Here are some examples.

Simple past describes events that began and ended in the past. It is expressed as a completed aspect form in Filipino, as illustrated by the following examples:

Examples: *walked* lumakad
cooked nagluto
slept natulog

Lumakad kami sa parke kahapon.
*We **walked** in the park yesterday.*

Nagluto si Mario ng hapunan.
*Mario **cooked** dinner.*

Natulog nang walong oras ang mga bata.
*The children **slept** for eight hours.*

Past continuous describes events that began in the past, continued for a length of time, and ended in the past. In Filipino, the incompleted aspect form is used to capture this information, as shown by the following examples:

Examples:	*was walking*	naglalakad
	was cooking	nagluluto
	was sleeping	natutulog

Biglang umulan nang **naglalakad** kami sa parke kaya bumalik kami sa bahay.
*It rained when we **were walking** in the park, so we went back to the house.*

Nagluluto ang lola nang nahilo siya.
*Grandmother **was cooking** when she felt faint.*

Nanood ako ng pelikula sa internet habang **natutulog ka**.
*I watched a movie online while you **were sleeping**.*

Past perfect/pluperfect describes a past event that occurred before another past event. It is best expressed in Filipino by the completed aspect abilitative/potential mood form (expressed by the use of the affix /maka-/), although the indicative mood may also be used. Here are some examples.

Examples:	*had eaten*	kumain; nakakain
	had cleaned	naglinis; nakapaglinis
	had showered	naligo; nakaligo

Nakakain na ako ng hapunan bago ako pumunta sa palabas.
*I **had** already **eaten** supper before going to the show.*

Nakapaglinis na ang mga estudyante nang dumating ang guro.
*The students **had already done the cleaning** when the teacher came.*

Nakaligo na si Lito kaya puwede na tayong umalis.
*Lito **had showered** already so we can go now.*

Past perfect continuous describes an event that began in the past, continued for a length of time, and was in progress when another past event happened. In Filipino, the incompleted aspect form is used to indicate this information, as shown in the following examples:

Examples:	*had been eating*	kumakain
	had been cleaning	naglilinis
	had been sleeping	natutulog

Isang taon na akong **kumakain** sa karinderya nang nagpasiya ang may-ari nito na ilipat ang kanilang kainan sa Antipolo.
*I **had been eating** at the cafe for a year when the owner decided to move their business to Antipolo.*

Dalawang oras nang **naglilinis** ng garahe si Jim nang dumating si Ben.
*Jim **had been cleaning** the garage for two hours when Ben arrived.*

Ilang oras na silang **natutulog** nang kumatok ang mga pulis.
*They **had been sleeping** for a few hours when the police knocked.*

5.2.2 **Present tense** forms in English are generally used to indicate that an event is happening at the moment of speaking or in the present time. Like the past tenses, there are four variations of present tense in English: simple present, present continuous, present perfect, and present perfect continuous. Present perfect is expressed in Filipino as a completed aspect form. All other present tense forms in English are expressed as incompleted or progressive aspect forms in Filipino. The following are illustrative examples.

Simple present describes an event as happening in the present or happens regularly. It is expressed as an incompleted aspect form in Filipino, as in the following examples:

Examples:	*study* or *studies*	nag-aaral
	run or *runs*	tumatakbo
	watch or *watches*	nanonood

Nanonood siya ng balita sa telebisyon gabi-gabi.
*He/she **watches** the news on TV every night.*

Tumatakbo si Ana sa parke tuwing umaga.
*Ana **runs** at the park every morning.*

Nag-aaral ako sa kapihan kasama ng aking kaibigan.
*I **study** at the coffee shop with my friend.*

Present continuous describes an event as being in progress in the present and likely continuing into the future. It is also expressed as an incompleted aspect form in Filipino, as in the following examples:

Examples:	*is* or *are studying*	nag-aaral
	is or *are running*	tumatakbo
	is or *are watching*	nanonood

Nag-aaral sila ngayon sa aklatan.
*They **are** presently **studying** in the library.*

Nanonood si Mila ng palabas sa telebisyon.
*Mila **is watching** a show on TV.*

Tumatakbo ang mga tao sa labas.
*People **are running** outside.*

Present perfect describes an event that occurred in the past but has some connection to the present. In Filipino, the completed aspect form of the abilitative mood is most commonly used to express this meaning. However, in some instances, the indicative mood completed aspect may also be used.

Examples:	*has* or *have written*	sumulat/nakapagsulat/naisulat
	has or *have read*	nagbasa/nakapagbasa/nabasa
	has or *have listened*	nakinig/nakapakinig/napakinggan

Nabasa ko ang artikulong sinulat mo sa diyaryo.
I ***have read*** *the article that you wrote in the newspaper.*

Nakapagsulat si Linda ng tula para sa kanyang ina.
Linda ***has written*** *a poem for her mother.*

Napakinggan ng mga tao ang balita kaninang umaga.
People ***have heard*** *the news this morning.*

Present perfect continuous describes an event that began in the past but still continues to happen in the present. In Filipino, it is expressed by the incompleted aspect form, as illustrated by the following examples:

Examples:	*has* or *have been writing*	sumusulat
	has or *have been reading*	nagbabasa
	has or *have been listening*	nakikinig

Matagal na akong **nakikinig** sa programang ito.
I ***have been listening*** *to this program for some time.*

Ilang taon na akong **nagbabasa** ng diyaryong iyan.
I ***have been reading*** *this newspaper for a few years.*

Tatlong taon na siyang **nagsusulat** para sa publikasyong iyon.
He ***has been writing*** *for that publication for three years now.*

5.2.3 **Future tense** forms are used to indicate that an event will happen sometime in the future. Like past and present tenses, there are four variations of future tense and tense–aspect combinations in English: simple future, future continuous, future perfect, and future perfect continuous. Simple future and future continuous are both expressed by the contemplated aspect form in Filipino. Future perfect is most appropriately expressed by the completed aspect of the abilitative mood verb form in Filipino. Future perfect continuous verb form in English is expressed by the incompleted aspect in Filipino. Here are some examples.

Simple future describes an event that will begin and end in the future. It is expressed as a contemplated aspect form in Filipino, as shown by the following examples:

Examples:	*will cook*	magluluto
	will watch	manonood
	shall make	gagawa

Magluluto ako ng adobo mamayang hapon.
*I **will cook** adobo this afternoon.*

Manonod sina Martin at Tina ng konsiyerto sa Sabado.
Martin and Tina are watching a concert on Saturday.

Mamayang gabi, **gagawa** ako ng bibingka para sa salu-salo.
*Tonight, I **will make** rice cake for the party.*

Future continuous describes an event that will begin in the future and continue for a length of time. It is also expressed by the contemplated aspect verb form in Filipino, as illustrated by the following examples:

Examples:	*will be cooking*	magluluto
	will be watching	manonood
	will be making	gagawa

Magluluto ako para sa mga tiya ko habang nagbabakasyon sila sa amin.
*I **will be cooking** for my aunts while they are on vacation at our place.*

Manonood ang mga bata ng telebisyon habang naghihintay ng hapunan.
*The kids **will be watching** TV while waiting for supper.*

Gagawa kami ng lumpia sa umaga ng piyesta.
*We **will be making** spring rolls in the morning of the festival.*

Future perfect describes a future event that will happen before another future event. It is best expressed by the abilitative/potential mood completed aspect verb form, often occurring with the enclitic adverb /na/, in Filipino. However, in some cases, the indicative mood completed aspect form may also be used. Here are a few examples.

Examples:	*will have cooked*	nagluto; nakapagluto (na)
	will have watched	nanood; nakapanood (na)
	will have made	gumawa; nakagawa (na)

Malamang na **nakapagluto na** ako ng hapunan mamaya pagdating mo.
*It is likely that I **will have cooked** dinner already when you get home later.*

Nakapanood na siguro kami ng pagtatanghal sa plasa bago magsimula ang parada.
*We **will have watched** a show at the town square before the parade starts.*

Nakagawa na si Minda ng takdang-aralin niya bago umuwi mamaya.
*Minda **will have done** her homework before going home later today.*

Future perfect continuous describes a future event that will begin, continue for a length of time, and still be in progress when another future event occurs. It is expressed as an incompleted aspect verb form in Filipino, as shown by the following examples:

Examples: *will have been cooking* nagluluto (na)
will have been watching nanonood (na)
will have been making gumagawa (na)

Maaga kaming magsisimula kaya baka ilang oras na kaming **nagluluto** paggising ninyo bukas ng umaga.
*We will start early so maybe we **will have been cooking** for a few hours when you wake up tomorrow morning.*

Dahil mahuhuli ka, **nanonood** na siguro kami ng palabas pagdating mo.
*Because you are coming late, we **will have been watching** the show when you arrive.*

Gumagawa na kami ng mga paketeng dadalhin sa probinsya pagpasok ninyo mamaya.
*When you come in later today, we **will have been making** packages for your trip to the province.*

The following chart is a summary and quick reference guide of the English verb tense–aspect and Filipino verbal aspect comparison.

Aspect tense	*Simple*	*Continuous/ progressive*	*Perfect*	*Perfect continuous/ perfect progressive*
Past	***Completed***	***Incompleted***	***Completed***	***Incompleted***
	lumakad	lumalakad	lumakad/nakapaglakad	lumalakad
	walked	*was or were walking*	*had walked*	*had been walking*
	nagluto	nagluluto	nagluto/nakapagluto	nagluluto
	cooked	*was or were cooking*	*had cooked*	*had been cooking*
	natulog	natutulog	natulog/nakatulog	natutulog
	slept	*was or were sleeping*	*had slept*	*had been sleeping*
Present	***Incompleted***	***Incompleted***	***Completed***	***Incompleted***
	lumalakad	lumalakad	lumakad/nakapaglakad	lumalakad
	walk/s	*is or are walking*	*has or have walked*	*has or have been walking*
	nagluluto	nagluluto	nagluto/nakapagluto	nagluluto
	cook/s	*is or are cooking*	*has or have cooked*	*has or have been cooking*
	natutulog	natutulog	natulog/nakatulog	natutulog
	sleep/s	*is or are sleeping*	*has or have slept*	*has or have been sleeping*
Future	***Contemplated***	***Contemplated***	***Completed***	***Incompleted***
	lalakad	lalakad	lumakad/nakapaglakad	lumalakad
	will walk	*will be walking*	*will have walked*	*will have been walking*
	magluluto	magluluto	nagluto/nakapagluto	nagluluto
	will cook	*will be cooking*	*will have cooked*	*will have been cooking*
	matutulog	matutulog	natulog/nakatulog	natutulog
	will sleep	*will be sleeping*	*will have slept*	*will have been sleeping*

5.3 Other aspectual forms

In addition to the major aspectual forms discussed previously, Filipino has other affixes that express other stages of an action or activity being started, repeated, or completed.

5.3.1 *Nearly started action:* pa(pa)- + *verb root*

This form is generally used in the main clause of a complex sentence to specify the time frame of the event or action expressed in the following subordinate clause. In a sentence, it is often followed by the enclitic adverb /na/ *already* and is always used as an AF form. The verb is formed by attaching the prefix /pa-/ or /papa-/ to a verb root (i.e., ***pa*** **(*pa*)- + root word**). Here are some examples.

pa(pa)- + alis *leave* = paalis/papaalis *about to leave*
pa(pa)- + tapos *finish* = patapos/papatapos *about to finish*
pa(pa)- + tulog *sleep* = patulog/papatulog *about to sleep*

Paalis na kami nang dumating sila.
*We **were about to leave** when they arrived.*

Patapos na ang klase namin nang tumunog ang kampana.
*Our class **was about to end** when the bell rang.*

Papatulog na ako nang tumawag ka.
*I **was about to sleep** when you called.*

5.3.2 *Intermittent action:* pa- + $C_1V_1C_2V_2$ *verb root reduplication*

This form is used to indicate action that is performed intermittently or non-continuously. Often, it is used to express the idea that the actor performing the action is doing the action intermittently due to his/her being either very relaxed, highly enthusiastic, or overly anxious. The verb is formed by attaching the prefix /pa-/ to a reduplicated verb root (i.e., ***pa-*** **+ reduplication of the root word**). Here are some examples.

pa- + lakad *walk* + reduplication = palakad-lakad *pacing around*
pa- + sayaw *dance* + reduplication = pasayaw-sayaw *dancing around*
pa- + tayo *stand* + reduplication = patayo-tayo *standing around*

Palakad-lakad si Ben sa labas habang naghihintay ng resulta ng eksamen.
*Ben is **pacing around** outside while waiting for test results.*

Pasayaw-sayaw si Kim ngayon dahil sa magandang balitang natanggap niya.

*Kim is **dancing around** right now because of the good news that she received.*

Paupo-upo na lang ang mga tagalinis dahil tapos na ang kanilang trabaho.
*The cleaners are now **sitting around** because they are done with their work.*

5.3.3 *Immediate post-completed action:* pagka- + *verb root*

This form is generally used in the main clause of a complex sentence to specify the time frame of the event or action expressed in the following subordinate clause. This verb form that means *upon completion of action* is a non-AF form that expresses the meaning *immediately after performing the action* expressed by the verb root. When overtly expressed in a sentence, the actor or doer of the action is in the genitive case. That is, it requires a *ng*-marked actor and a *ng*-marked object when specified. The verb is formed by attaching the prefix /pagka-/ to a verb root (i.e., ***pagka-*** **+ root word**). Here are some examples.

pagka- + laba *do laundry* = pagkalaba *after doing laundry*
pagka- + luto *cook* = pagkaluto *after cooking*
pagka- + ligo *shower* = pagkaligo *after taking a shower*

Pagkagradweyt ni Tina sa kolehiyo, nagtrabaho siya sa Maynila.
***After graduating** from college, Tina worked in Manila.*

Pagkakuha ko ng aking suweldo tuwing katapusan ng buwan, lumalabas ako kasama ng aking mga kaibigan.
***After collecting** my salary at the end of each month, I go out with my friends.*

Pagkakain natin ng tanghalian, manonood tayo ng sine.
***After (we eat) lunch**, we will watch a movie.*

A variation of this form that involves a full reduplication of the verb expresses stronger immediacy, a close equivalent of the English expression 'as soon as X is done.' Here are some examples.

Pagkalabas na pagkalabas ng mga bata sa eskuwela, tumakbo silang lahat sa tindahan.
***As soon as** the kids **got out** of school, they all ran to the store.*

Pagkagising na pagkagising ko bukas, magbibiyahe na tayo papuntang Bikol.
***As soon as** I **wake up** tomorrow, we will start our trip to Bicol.*

Pagkarating na pagkarating ni Pedro sa bahay mula sa trabaho, kumakain agad siya ng hapunan.
***As soon as** Pedro **gets home from work**, he would immediately eat dinner.*

5.3.4 *Recently completed action:* ka- + C_1V_1 *verb root reduplication or* kaka- + *verb root*

This aspectual form expresses the idea of recent completion of an action or event indicated by the verb root. There are two forms in free variation: the use of the prefix *ka-* attached to a verb root with partial reduplication of the first consonant and vowel, or the affix *kaka-* attached to the verb root. **Recent perfective verbs** are non-AF forms, which means that the clause containing this verb has the actor or doer of the action marked with the genitive case. The verb is formed by attaching the prefix /ka-/ to a verb root with a reduplicated first (C)V (i.e., ***ka-*** + **reduplication of first** (C)V **of the root + root word**). Alternatively, the preifix may be reduplicated (*ka-* + *kaka-*) instead of the first CV of the root. In a sentence, the verb is often followed by the adverbial enclitic **lang** *just* or *only*, but without it the sentence would still be grammatical. Here are some examples.

kaka- + dating *arrive* = kakarating *just arrived*
kaka- + kain *eat* = kakakain *just ate*
kaka- + gising *wake* = kakagising *just woke up*
kaka- + basa *read* = kakabasa *just read*

Kalalabas lang ng pelikulang 'Darna.'/**Kakalabas lang** ng pelikulang 'Darna.'
The movie 'Darna' ***just came out***.

Kaaalis lang ng aking nanay./**Kakaalis lang** ng aking nanay.
My mother ***just left***.

Kabibili ko ng bagong telepono pero may problema na agad ito./**Kakabili** ko ng bagong telepono pero may problema na agad ito.
I ***just bought*** *a new phone, but it has issues already.*

Chapter 6

Verbal focus

In addition to verbal aspect, Filipino verbs also encode verbal focus, a grammatical marking in the verb via affixation to indicate which noun phrase will take the subject case marker in a sentence.

Verbal focus is a marking on the verb, through affixation and verb root meaning or semantic content, to indicate which noun in the sentence is the subject (i.e., which noun will be marked by the noun marker /ang/), the focus of the clause. It can be thought of as verb–subject agreement, wherein the affix on the verb must agree with the marker of the subject noun. There are at least seven focus forms in Filipino: actor, object, location–direction, beneficiary, instrumental, experiencer, and reason. Each form will be discussed here using the default indicative mood setting of the verb.

6.1 **Actor-focus** (**AF**) **verbs** indicate that the actor or doer of the action expressed by the verb is the subject or focus of the sentence. In the indicative mood, there are three affixes associated with this focus form: the infix /-um-/, the prefix /mag-/, and the prefix /ma-/. There is a tendency for *um-* verbs to be semantically intransitive, while *mag-* verbs tend to be transitive. **Transitivity** here is used to refer to the property of a verb to either take a direct object (transitive) or not take a direct object (intransitive). Some verb roots can take both /-um-/ and /mag-/ affixes interchangeably, but in general, AF verbs are either ***um-*** **verbs**, ***mag-*** **verbs**, or ***ma-*** **verbs**. There is a very small set of AF *ma-* verbs, so language learners are advised to memorize the most commonly used ones. Actor-focus verbs are considered to be the most basic verbal forms because they can be used as the basis for other forms (see verbal mood). Actor-focus verbal sentences are also considered to have the most basic structure because the noun markers in AF sentences unambiguously distinguish the case roles of noun phrases. The following is a table of commonly used AF verbs and some

DOI: 10.4324/9781315739427-7

illustrative sentences. Take note that the sentences contain verbs that are inflected for both focus and aspect. The affix on the verb and the subject of the sentence are in bold.

AF verbs

Um verbs					
English	**Root word**	*Neutral/* ***infinitive***	*Completed/* ***perfective***	*Incompleted/* ***progressive***	***Contemplated/ imperfective***
sit	upo	umupo	umupo	umuupo	Uupo
stand	tayo	tumayo	tumayo	tumatayo	Tatayo
walk	lakad	lumakad	lumakad	lumalakad	lalakad
run	takbo	tumakbo	tumakbo	tumatakbo	tatakbo
jump	talon	tumalon	tumalon	tumatalon	tatalon
sing	kanta	kumanta	kumanta	kumakanta	kakanta
dance	sayaw	sumayaw	sumayaw	sumasayaw	sasayaw
read	basa	bumasa	bumasa	bumabasa	babasa
write	sulat	sumulat	sumulat	sumusulat	susulat
leave or *go*	alis	umalis	umalis	umaalis	Aalis
eat	kain	kumain	kumain	kumakain	kakain
cry	iyak	umiyak	umiyak	umiiyak	Iiyak
laugh	tawa	tumawa	tumawa	tumatawa	tatawa
turn around	ikot	umikot	umikot	umiikot	Iikot
kneel	luhod	lumuhod	lumuhod	lumuluhod	luluhod
shout or *yell*	sigaw	sumigaw	sumigaw	sumisigaw	sisigaw
drink	inom	uminom	uminom	umiinom	Iinom
count	bilang	bumilang	bumilang	bumibilang	bibilang
go in	pasok	pumasok	pumasok	pumapasok	papasok
go out	labas	lumabas	lumabas	lumalabas	lalabas
go (to)	punta	pumunta	pumunta	pumupunta	pupunta
visit	bisita	bumisita	bumisita	bumibisita	bibisita
ride	sakay	sumakay	sumakay	sumasakay	sasakay
look	tingin	tumingin	tumingin	tumitingin	titingin
buy	bili	bumili	bumili	bumibili	Bibili
kill	patay	pumatay	pumatay	pumapatay	papatay

Word formation rules:

Infinitive: add the affix ***-um-* before the first vowel of the root word**.

takbo + -*um*- = **tum**akbo

Completed: add the affix ***-um-* before the first vowel of the root word**.

takbo + -*um*- = **tum**akbo

Incompleted: (1) **repeat the first consonant–vowel** (**CV**) of the root word

takbo + rep1stCV = **ta**takbo

and (2) add the affix ***-um-* before the first vowel**.

tatakbo + -*um*- = **tum**atakbo

Contemplated: repeat the first CV of the root word.

takbo + rep1stCV = **ta**takbo

Note on reduplication of first CV: repeat only the first vowel if the word starts with a vowel.

Mag- verbs

English	***Root word***	*Neutral/* ***infinitive***	*Completed/* ***perfective***	*Incompleted/* ***progressive***	***Contemplated/ imperfective***
cook	luto	magluto	nagluto	nagluluto	Magluluto
do laundry	laba	maglaba	naglaba	naglalaba	Maglalaba
study	aral	mag-aral	nag-aral	nag-aaral	mag-aaral
play (game)	laro	maglaro	naglaro	naglalaro	Maglalaro
eat breakfast	almusal	mag-almusal	nag-almusal	nag-aalmusal	mag-aalmusal
eat lunch	tanghalian	magtanghalian	nagtanghalian	nagtatanghalian	magtatanghalian
eat supper	hapunan	maghapunan	naghapunan	naghahapunan	Maghahapunan
eat snack	meryenda	magmeryenda	nagmeryenda	nagmemeryenda	magmemeryenda
brush teeth	sipilyo	magsipilyo	nagsipilyo	nagsisipilyo	Magsisipilyo
wash face	hilamos	maghilamos	naghilamos	naghihilamos	Maghihilamos
get dressed	bihis	nagbihis	nagbihis	nagbibihis	Magbibihis
shave	ahit	mag-ahit	nag-ahit	nag-aahit	mag-aahit
watch a movie	sine	magsine	nagsine	nagsisine	Magsisine
relax or rest	pahinga	magpahinga	nagpahinga	nagpapahinga	magpapahinga
drive	maneho	magmaneho	nagmaneho	nagmamaneho	magmamaneho
play basketball	basketbol	magbasketbol	nagbasketbol	nagbabasketbol	magbabasketbol
tell (a story)	kuwento	magkuwento	nagkuwento	nagkukuwento	magkukuwento
give	bigay	magbigay	nagbigay	nagbibigay	magbibigay
bring	dala	magdala	nagdala	nagdadala	magdadala
put	lagay	maglagay	naglagay	naglalagay	maglalagay

converse	usap	mag-usap	nag-usap	nag-uusap	mag-uusap
meet each other	kita	magkita	nagkita	nagkikita	Magkikita

Word formation rules:

Infinitive: add the affix ***mag-* at the beginning of the root word**.

luto + *mag-* = **mag**luto

Completed: change the /m/ of the affix to /n/ and add the affix ***nag-* to the root word**.

luto + *nag-* = **nag**luto

Contemplated: (1) **repeat the first CV** of the root

luto + rep1stCV = luluto

and (2) add the affix ***mag-* at the beginning**.

luluto + *mag-* = **mag**luluto

Incompleted: (1) **repeat the first CV** of the root

luto + rep1stCV = luluto

and (2) add the affix ***nag-* at the beginning**.

luluto + *nag-* = **nag**luluto

Note on reduplication of first CV: repeat only the first vowel if the word starts with a vowel. A hyphen is used between the prefix /mag-/ or /nag-/ when it is attached to a word that starts with a vowel.

Additional notes:

(1) Borrowed words usually take the affix /mag-/ when used as AF verbs (e.g., /magbasketbol/ *play basketball*, /magdrayb/ *drive*, /magdrowing/ *draw*, and /magpinta/ *paint*).

(2) Some *mag-* verbs have inherent reciprocal meaning (i.e., two actors are doing the action expressed by the verb to each other). Examples are /magkita/ *meet with each other*, /mag-usap/ *talk* or *converse with each other*, and /mag-away/ *quarrel* or *fight with each other*.

***Ma-* verbs**

English	***Root word***	*Neutral/* ***infinitive***	*Completed/* ***perfective***	*Incompleted/* ***progressive***	***Contemplated/ imperfective***
shower or *bathe*	ligo	maligo	naligo	naliligo	maliligo
sleep	tulog	matulog	natulog	natutulog	matutulog
stroll	masyal	mamasyal	namasyal	namamasyal	mamamasyal
listen	kinig	makinig	nakinig	nakikinig	makikinig
watch	nood	manood	nanood	nanonood	manonood

Word formation rules:

Infinitive: add the affix ***ma-* at the beginning of the root word**.

nood + *ma-* = **ma**nood

Completed: change the /m/ of the affix to /n/, and add the prefix ***na-* to the root word**.

nood + *na-* = **na**nood

Incompleted: (1) **repeat the first CV** of the root

nood + rep1stCV = nonood

and (2) add the affix ***na-* at the beginning**.

nonood + *na-* = **na**nonood

Contemplated: (1) **repeat the first CV** of the root

nood + rep1stCV = nonood

and (2) add the affix ***ma-* at the beginning**.

nonood + *ma-* = manonood

Note on reduplication of first CV: repeat only the first vowel if the word starts with a vowel.

Here is a quick review of the uses and functions of the different aspectual forms.

The infinitive form is used to

(1) express commands.
(2) used with pseudo-verbs like puwede (*can*) and gusto (*like* or *want*).

The completed aspect form is used to

(1) express completed or finished action or event.

The incompleted aspect form is used to

(1) express action or event that has started but not finished (progressive).
(2) express habitual or recurring action or event (simple present).

The contemplated aspect form is used to

(1) express action or event that has not yet started.

Here are some examples to illustrate the use of the AF verbs.

Infinitive form with a pseudo-verb:

Gusto niyang b**um**ili ng bagong telepono.
*Want–gen.he/she.link–**to buy**–genmark.new.phone*
*He/she **wants to buy** a new telephone.*

Infinitive form expressing a command or imperative:

Matulog **ka** sa salas.
*Sleep–**subj.you**–oblmark.living room*
***You** sleep in the living room.*

Completed form indicating completed action:

T**um**akbo **ang bata** sa parke.
*Ran–**subjmark.child**–oblmark.park*
***The child** ran to the park.*

Incompleted form indicating ongoing action/event:

Nagluluto ng manok **si Mario** ngayon.
*Cooking–genmark.chicken–**subjmark.Mario**–right now*
***Mario** is cooking chicken right now.*

Incompleted form indicating habitual or recurring action/event:

Nanonood ng balita **si Ana** gabi-gabi.
*Watches–genmark.news–**subjmark.Ana**–every night*
***Ana** watches the news every night.*

Contemplated form indicating an action/event that has not yet started:

Mag-aaral **kami** sa aklatan mamaya.
*Will study–**subj.we**–in the library–later*
***We** will study in the library later.*

6.2 **Object-focus (OF) verbs** indicate that the (direct) object or the noun upon which the action expressed by the verb is performed by the actor and is the subject or focus of the sentence. **Only transitive verbs** (i.e., verbs that take an object) have OF forms. In the indicative mood, there are three affixes associated with this focus form: the suffix /-in/, the prefix /i-/, and the suffix /-an/. There is a tendency for *in-* verbs to indicate action that involves movement of the object toward the actor (e.g., eat, take, get, and bring), while *i-* verbs tend to indicate action that involves movement of the object away from the actor (e.g., give, throw, put, and toss). Some verb roots can take both /-in/ and /i-/ affixes interchangeably, mostly verbs associated with cooking, but in general OF verbs are either ***in-* verbs**, ***i-* verbs**, or ***an-* verbs**. There is a very small set of OF *an-* verbs, so language learners are advised to memorize the most commonly used ones. However, there are many de-adjectival OF *an-* verbs (i.e., verbs derived from adjectives) that often mean *make something have the quality expressed by the adjective root* (see *an-* verbs table for examples). A number of OF verb forms undergo phonological changes that are reflected in their spelling so that they may appear to be 'irregular' forms. The tables provided here note some of these forms. The following are tables of commonly used OF verbs with their complete aspectual forms.

-In verbs

English	***Verb root***	*Neutral/* ***infinitive***	*Completed/* ***perfective***	*Incompleted/* ***progressive***	***Contemplated/ imperfective***
kill	patay	patayin	Pinatay	pinapatay	papatayin
eat	kain	kainin	Kinain	kinakain	kakainin
count	bilang	bilangin	binilang	binibilang	bibilangin
borrow	hiram	hiramin	hiniram	hinihiram	hihiramin
look for	hanap	hanapin	hinanap	hinahanap	hahanapin
dance	sayaw	sayawin	sinayaw	sinasayaw	sasayawin
use	gamit	gamitin	ginamit	ginagamit	gagamitin
play musical instrument	tugtog	tugtugin	tinugtog	tinutugtog	tutugtugin
pick up	pulot	pulutin	pinulot	pinupulot	pupulutin
answer	sagot	sagutin	sinagot	sinasagot	sasagutin
sing	awit	awitin	inawit	inaawit	aawitin
study	aral	aralin	Inaral	inaaral	aaralin
fix or arrange	ayos	ayusin	inayos	inaayos	aayusin
remove	alis	alisin	Inalis	inaalis	aalisin
drink	inom	inumin	ininom	iniinom	iinumin
clean	linis	linisin	nilinis	nililinis	lilinisin
cook	luto'	lutuin	niluto	niluluto	lulutuin
read	basa	basahin	binasa	binabasa	Babasahin
copy	kopya	kopyahin	kinopya	kinokopya	kokopyahin
kolekta	kolekta	kolektahin	kinolekta	kinokolekta	kokolektahin
erase	bura	burahin	binura	binubura	buburahin
say	sabi	sabihin	sinabi	sinasabi	sasabihin
*buy**	bili	bilhin	binili	binibili	bibilhin

*bring**	dala	dalhin	dinala	dinadala	dadalhin
*get**	kuha	kunin	kinuha	kinukuha	kukunin
make or *do**	gawa	gawin	ginawa	ginagawa	gagawin
*watch**	panood	panoorin	pinanood	pinapanood	papanoorin

Word formation rules:

Infinitive: add the affix ***-in /-hin*** **at the end of the root word.**
kain + ***-in*** = kain**in**/basa **+ *-hin*** = basa**hin**
Completed: add the affix ***-in-*** **before the first vowel of the root word.**
kain + ***-in-*** = k**in**ain
Incompleted: (1) **repeat the first CV** of the root
kain + **rep1stCV** = **ka**kain
and (2) add the affix ***-in-*** **before the first vowel.**
kakain + ***-in-*** = k**in**akain
Contemplated: (1) **repeat the first CV** of the root
kain + **rep1stCV** = **ka**kain
and (2) add the affix ***-in*** **at the end.**
kakain + ***-in*** = kakain**in**

Note on reduplication of first CV: repeat only the first vowel if the word starts with a vowel.

Additional notes:

(1) Root words that end in a vowel sound (i.e., there is no glottal stop following the vowel) use the suffix /-hin/ instead of /-in/.

(2) Root words that start with the sounds /l/, /r/, and /h/ undergo metathesis or reordering of sounds when the infix /-in-/ is attached to it for the completed and incompleted forms.

(3) Some roots have complicated multiple sound changes so that their forms look like they do not follow the regular pattern of affixation so that they are sometimes referred to as 'irregular' forms. These verbs are marked by an asterisk (*) in the preceding table.

I- verbs

English	***Verb root***	*Neutral/* ***infinitive***	*Completed/* ***perfective***	*Incompleted/* ***progressive***	***Contemplated/ imperfective***
give	Bigay	ibigay	ibinigay	ibinibigay	ibibigay
throw away	Tapon	itapon	itinapon	itinatapon	itatapon
write	Sulat	isulat	isinulat	isinusulat	isusulat
tie	Tali	itali	itinali	itinatali	itatali
add	dagdag	idagdag	idinagdag	idinadagdag	idadagdag

pour	buhos	ibuhos	ibinuhos	ibinubuhos	ibubuhos
hang	sabit	isabit	isinabit	isinasabit	isasabit
point to or *teach*	Turo	ituro	itinuro	itinuturo	ituturo
bring in	pasok	ipasok	ipinasok	ipinapasok	ipapasok
raise	taas	itaas	itinaas	itinataas	itataas
lower	baba	ibaba	ibinaba	ibinababa	ibababa
give back	sauli	isauli	isinauli	isinasauli	isasauli
hide or *keep*	tago	itago	itinago	itinatago	itatago
toss	hagis	ihagis	inihagis	inihahagis	ihahagis
put	lagay	ilagay	inilagay	inilalagay	ilalagay
put away	ligpit	iligpit	iniligpit	inililigpit	ililigpit
bring out	labas	ilabas	inilabas	inilalabas	ilalabas
*cook** (*-in*)	Luto	iluto	iniluto	iniluluto	iluluto
*boil** (*-in*)	laga	ilaga	inilaga	inilalaga	ilalaga
*close** (*-an*)	sara	isara	isinara	isinasara	isasara
*open** (*-an*)	bukas	ibukas	ibinukas	ibinubukas	ibubukas

Word formation rules:

Infinitive: add the affix ***i-*** **at the beginning of the root word**.

bigay + ***i-*** = **i**bigay

Completed: (1) add the affix ***-in-*** **before the first vowel of the root word**

bigay + ***-in-*** = b**in**igay

and (2) add the affix ***-i*** **at the beginning**.

binigay + ***i-*** = **i**binigay

Incompleted: (1) **repeat the first CV** of the root,

bigay + rep1stCV = **bi**bigay

(2) add the affix ***-in-*** **before the first vowel of the stem**,

bibigay + ***-in-*** = b**in**ibigay

and (3) add the affix ***i-*** **at the beginning**.

bibigay + ***i-*** = **i**binibigay

Contemplated: (1) **repeat the first CV** of the root

bigay + **rep1stCV** = **bi**bigay

and (2) add the affix ***i-*** **at the beginning**.

bibigay + ***i-*** = **i**bibigay

Note on reduplication of first CV: repeat only the first vowel if the word starts with a vowel.

Additional notes:

(1) An incompleted verb stem is the resultant form after applying the initial but not all word formation rules.

(2) Root words that start with the sounds /l/, /r/, and /h/ undergo metathesis or reordering of sounds when the infix /-in-/ is attached to it for the completed and incompleted forms.

(3) Some verb roots can take other OF affixes. Examples of these are marked by an asterisk (*) and an alternative OF affix for them in the preceding table.

-An verbs

English	*Root*	Neutral/ *infinitive*	Completed/ *perfective*	Incompleted/ *progressive*	*Contemplated/ imperfective*
wipe	punas	punasan	pinunasan	pinupunasan	pupunasan
wash	hugas	hugasan	hinugasan	hinuhugasan	huhugasan
*laundry**	laba	labhan	nilabhan	nilalabhan	lalabhan
*cover**	takip	takpan	tinakpan	tinatakpan	tatakpan
open or *turn on**	bukas	buksan	binuksan	binubuksan	bubuksan
close or *turn off**	sara	sarhan	sinarhan	sinasarhan	sasarhan
*beautify***	ganda	gandahan	ginandahan	ginagandahan	gagandahan
*shorten***	ikli	iklian	iniklian	iniiklian	iiklian
*lengthen***	haba	habaan	hinabaan	hinahabaan	hahabaan
*strengthen***	lakas	lakasan	nilakasan	nilalakasan	lalakasan
*weaken***	hina	hinaan	hininaan	hinihinaan	hihinaan

Word formation rules:

Infinitive: add the affix ***-an*** **at the end of the root word.**

hugas + ***-an*** = hugas**an**

Completed: (1) add the affix ***-in-*** **before the first vowel of the root word**

hugas + ***-in-*** = h**in**ugas

and (2) add the affix ***-an*** **at the end.**

hinugas + ***-an*** = hinugas**an**

Incompleted: (1) **repeat the first CV** of the root,

hugas + rep1stCV = **hu**hugas

(2) add the affix ***-in-*** **before the first vowel**,

huhugas + ***-in-*** = h**in**uhugas

and (3) add the affix ***-an*** **at the end.**

hinuhugas + ***-an*** = hinuhugas**an**

Contemplated: (1) **repeat the first CV** of the root

hugas + **rep1stCV** = **hu**hugas

and (2) add the affix ***-an*** **at the end.**

huhugas + ***-an*** = huhugas**an**

Note on reduplication of first CV: repeat only the first vowel if the word starts with a vowel.

Additional notes:

(1) An incompleted verb stem is the resultant form after applying the initial but not all word formation rules.

(2) Root words that start with the sounds /l/, /r/, and /h/ undergo metathesis or reordering of sounds when the infix /-in-/ is attached to it for the completed and incompleted forms.

(3) Some verb roots drop the vowel in the final syllable of the root when the suffix /-an/ is attached to it. Examples of these are marked by an asterisk (*) in the preceding table.

(4) There is a set OF *an-* verbs that are derived from adjective roots. The examples in the preceding table are marked by a double asterisk (**). Their AF sentence counterparts are expressed in the causative mood (see section on verbal mood).

The different aspectual forms of OF verbs have the same uses and functions as the aspectual forms of the AF verbs. Here are some illustrative OF verbal sentences. To show the distinct case roles of each noun phrase, their equivalent AF verbal sentences are also provided here. The sentences contain verbs that are inflected for both focus and aspect. The affix on the verb and the subject of the sentence are in bold.

OF verbal sentence	***Equivalent AF verbal sentence***
Babasah**in** ko **ang artikulo** sa Linggo. *OF.Will read–gen.I–**subjmark.article** – on Sunday* *I will read **the article** on Sunday.*	Babasa **ako** ng artikulo sa Linggo. *AF.Will read–**subj.I** –genmark. article–on Sunday* ***I** will read the article on Sunday.*
Itinapon ni Anna **ang basura**. *Threw away–genmark.Anna–**subjmark.trash*** *Anna threw away **the trash**.*	**Nag**tapon **si Anna** ng basura. *AF.Threw away–**subjmark.Anna**–genmark.trash* ***Anna** threw away the trash.*
Punas**an** mo **ang mesa**. *Wipe clean–gen.you–**subjmark. table*** *(You) Wipe **the table**.*	**Mag**punas **ka** ng mesa. *AF.Wipe clean–subj.you–**genmark. table*** *(**You**) Wipe the table.*

6.3 Location/direction-focus (LDF) **verbs** indicate that the location or direction of the action expressed by the verb is the subject or focus of the sentence. In the indicative mood, there are two affixes associated with this focus form: the suffix /-an/, usually indicating direction; and the circumfix /pag – an/, usually indicating location. Some verb roots can take both /-an/ and /pag – an/ affixes interchangeably, but most LDF verbs are either *-an* **verbs** or *pag – an* **verbs**. The following is a table of commonly used LDF verbs with their complete aspectual forms.

Direction-focus an- verbs

English	***Verb root***	*Neutral/* ***infinitive***	*Completed/* ***perfective***	*Incompleted/* ***progressive***	***Contemplated/ imperfective***
*give to**	bigay	bigyan	binigyan	binibigyan	bibigyan
*put in**	lagay	lagyan	linagyan	linalagyan	lalagyan
*bring to**	dala	dalhan	dinalhan	dinadalhan	dadalhan
*look at**	tingin	tingnan	tiningnan	tinitingnan	titingnan
go to	punta	puntahan	pinuntahan	pinupuntahan	pupuntahan
pour on	buhos	buhusan	binuhusan	binubuhusan	bubuhusan
look at	tingin	tingnan	tiningnan	tinitingnan	titingnan
stare at	titig	titigan	tinitigan	tinititigan	tititigan
sing to	awit	awitan	inawitan	inaawitan	aawitan
read to	basa	basahan	binasahan	binabasahan	babasahan
write to	sulat	sulatan	sinulatan	sinusulatan	susulatan
step on	tapak	tapakan	tinapakan	tinatapakan	tatapakan
go with	sama	samahan	sinamahan	sinasamahan	sasamahan
make a call to	tawag	tawagan	tinawagan	tinatawagan	tatawagan
give help to	tulong	tulungan	tinulungan	tinutulungan	tutulungan
object to	tutol	tutulan	tinutulan	tinututulan	tututulan
fight against	laban	labanan	nilabanan	nilalabanan	lalabanan

Word formation rules:

Infinitive: add the affix ***-an*** **at the end of the root word**.

hugas + ***-an*** = hugas**an**

Completed: (1) add the affix ***-in-*** **before the first vowel of the root word**

hugas + ***-in-*** = h**in**ugas

and (2) add the affix ***-an*** **at the end**.

hinugas + ***-an*** = hinugas**an**

Incompleted: (1) **repeat the first CV** of the root,

hugas + rep1stCV = **hu**hugas

(2) add the affix ***-in-* before the first vowel**,

huhugas + ***-in-*** = h**in**uhugas

and (3) add the affix ***-an* at the end**.

hinuhugas + ***-an*** = hinuhugas**an**

Contemplated: (1) **repeat the first CV** of the root

hugas + **rep1stCV** = **hu**hugas

and (2) add the affix ***-an* at the end**.

huhugas + ***-an*** = huhugas**an**

Note on reduplication of first CV: repeat only the first vowel if the word starts with a vowel.

Additional notes:

(1) An incompleted verb stem is the resultant form after applying the initial but not all word formation rules.

(2) Root words that start with the sounds /l/, /r/, and /h/ undergo metathesis or reordering of sounds when the infix /-in-/ is attached to it for the completed and incompleted forms.

(3) Some verb roots drop the vowel in the final syllable of the root when the suffix /-an/ is attached to it. Examples of these are marked by an asterisk (*) in the preceding table.

Location-focus pag – an verbs

English	***Verb root***	Neutral/ ***infinitive***	Completed/ ***perfective***	Incompleted/ ***progressive***	***Contemplated/ imperfective***
dance at	sayaw	pagsayawan	pinagsayawan	pinagsasayawan	pagsasayawan
write on	sulat	pagsulatan	pinagsulatan	pinagsusulatan	pagsusulatan
sleep on	tulog	pagtulugan	pinagtulugan	pinagtutulugan	pagtutulugan
swim in	langoy	paglanguyan	pinaglanguyan	pinaglalanguyan	paglalanguyan
strive for	sikap	pagsikapan	pinagsikapan	pinagsisikapan	pagsisikapan
*give in to**	bigay	pagbigyan	pinagbigyan	pinagbibigyan	pagbibigyan
*cover for**	takip	pagtakpan	pinagtakpan	pinagtatakpan	pagtatakpan
cook in	luto	paglutuan	pinaglutuan	pinaglulutuan	paglulutuan
put on top of	patong	pagpatungan	pinagpatungan	pinagpapatungan	pagpapatungan
take from	kuha	pagkunan	pinagkunan	pinagkukunan	pagkukunan
put effort in	hirap	paghirapan	pinaghirapan	pinaghihirapan	paghihirapan
put blame on	bintang	pagbintangan	pinagbintangan	pinagbibintangan	pagbibintangan
keep in or *hide from*	tago	pagtaguan	pinagtaguan	pinagtataguan	pagtataguan

Word formation rules:

Infinitive: add the circumfix ***pag– an* to the root word**.

sayaw + ***pag– an*** = **pag**sayaw**an**

Completed: add the affix ***-in-* before the first vowel of the infinitive form**.

pagsayawan + ***-in-*** = p**in**agsayawan

Incompleted: (1) **repeat the first CV** of the root,

sayaw + rep1stCV = **sa**sayaw

(2) add the circumfix ***pag– an* to the stem**,

sasayaw + ***pag– an*** = **pag**sasayaw**an**

and (3) add the infix ***-in* before the first vowel of the stem**.

pagsasayawan + ***-in*** = p**in**agsasayawan

Contemplated: (1) **repeat the first CV** of the root

sayaw + rep1stCV = **sa**sayaw

and (2) add the circumfix ***pag– an* to the stem**.

sasayaw + ***pag– an*** **-** = **pag**sasayaw**an**

Note on reduplication of first CV: repeat only the first vowel if the word starts with a vowel.

Additional notes:

(1) An incompleted verb stem is the resultant form after applying the initial but not all word formation rules.

(2) Some verb roots drop the vowel in the final syllable of the root when the suffix /-an/ is attached to it. Examples of these are marked by an asterisk (*) in the preceding table.

The different aspectual forms of LDF verbs have the same uses and functions as the aspectual forms of the AF verbs. Here are some illustrative LDF verbal sentences. To show the distinct case roles of each noun phrase, their equivalent AF verbal sentences are also provided here. The sentences contain verbs that are inflected for both focus and aspect. The affix on the verb and the subject of the sentence are in bold.

Examples indicating direction of the action

DF verbal sentence	***Equivalent AF verbal sentence***
Puputah**an** niya **ang lola niya**. *Will go–gen.he/she–**subjmark.his/her grandmother*** *He/she will go **to his/her grandmother**.*	Pupunta **siya** sa lola niya. *Will go–subj.**he/she** –oblmark.his/her grandmother* ***He/she** will go to his/her grandmother.*

DF verbal sentence	***Equivalent AF verbal sentence***
Tatawag**an** ni Juan **si Maria**. *Will call–genmark.Juan–**subjmark. Maria*** *Juan will make a call **to Maria**.*	Tatawag **si Juan** kay Maria. *Will call–**subjmark.Juan** –oblmark. Maria* ***Juan** will make a call **to Maria**.*
Susulat**an** ng estudyante **ang guro niya**. *Will write–genmark.student–**subjmark.his/her teacher.*** *The student will write **to his/her teacher**.*	Susulat **ang estudyante** sa guro niya. *Will write–**subjmark.student**–oblmark.his/her teacher.* ***The student** will write to his/her teacher.*

Examples indicating location

LF verbal sentence	***Equivalent AF verbal sentence***
Paglalagy**an** ko ng mga sapatos **ang kartong iyan**. *Will put–gen.I–genmark. shoes–**subjmark.that box*** *I will put (the) shoes **in that box**.*	**Mag**lalagay **ako** ng mga sapatos sa kartong iyan. *Will put–**subj.I** –genmark.shoes–oblmark.that box* ***I** will put (the) shoes **in that box**.*
Paglulutu**an** ni Juan **ang kawaling iyan**. *Will cook–genmark.Juan–**subjmark. that frying pan*** *Juan will cook (the food) **in that frying pan**.*	**Mag**luluto **si Juan** sa kawaling iyan. *Will cook–**subjmark.Juan** –oblmark. that frying pan* ***Juan** will cook (the food) in that frying pan.*
Pagsusulat**an** niya **ang papel**. *Will write–gen.he/she–**subjmark. child*** *He/she will write **on the paper**.*	**Mag**susulat **siya** sa papel. *Will write–subj.he/she–**oblmark. child*** ***He/she** will write on the paper.*

6.4 **Beneficiary-focus (BF) verbs** indicate that the noun benefiting from the actor performing the action expressed by the verb is the subject or focus of the sentence. In the indicative mood, the affix associated with this focus form is the prefix /ipag-/. For a number of verbs, the affix is shortened to /i-/, especially for verb roots that take the affix /-in/ in their OF form. Thus, BF forms are mostly ***ipag-* verbs** and some ***i-* verbs**. The following is a table of commonly used BF verbs with their complete aspectual forms.

BF *ipag- and i- verbs*					
English	**Root word**	Neutral/ ***infinitive***	*Completed/* ***perfective***	*Incompleted/* ***progressive***	***Contemplated/ imperfective***
cook – for	luto	ipagluto	ipinagluto	ipinagluluto	ipagluluto
do laundry for	laba	ipaglaba	ipinaglaba	ipinaglalaba	ipaglalaba
clean – for	linis	ipaglinis	ipaglilinis	ipinaglilinis	ipaglilinis
wash – for	hugas	ipaghugas	ipinaghugas	ipinaghuhugas	ipaghuhugas
write – for	sulat	ipagsulat	ipinagsulat	ipinagsusulat	ipagsusulat
prepare – for	handa	ipaghanda	ipinaghanda	ipinaghahanda	ipaghahanda
paint – for	pinta	ipagpinta	ipinagpinta	ipinagpipinta	ipagpipinta
lift – for	buhat	ipagbuhat	ipinagbuhat	ipinagbubuhat	ipagbubuhat
throw away – for	tapon	ipagtapon	ipinagtapon	ipinagtatapon	ipagtatapon
bring – for	dala	ipagdala	ipinagdala	ipinagdadala	ipagdadala
pay – for	bayad	ipagbayad	ipinagbayad	ipinagbabayad	ipagbabayad
make – for	gawa	igawa	iginawa	iginagawa	igagawa
get or *take – for*	kuha	ikuha	ikinuha	ikinukuha	ikukuha
buy – for	bili	ibili	ibinili	ibinibili	ibibili
borrow – for	hiram	ihiram	inihiram	inihihiram	ihihiram
find – for	hanap	ihanap	inihanap	inihahanap	ihahanap

Word formation rules for *ipag-* verbs:

Infinitive: add the prefix ***ipag-* to the root word.**

luto + ***ipag-*** = **ipag**luto

Completed: add the affix ***-in-* after the first consonant of the infinitive form.**

ipagluto + ***-in-*** = ip**in**agluto

Incompleted: (1) **repeat the first CV** of the root,

luto + rep1stCV = **lu**luto

(2) add the prefix ***ipag-* to the stem,**

luluto + ***ipag-*** = **ipag**luluto

and (3) add the infix ***-in-* after the first consonant of the stem.**

ipagluluto + ***-in-*** = ip**in**agluluto

Contemplated: (1) **repeat the first CV** of the root

luto + rep1stCV = **lu**luto

and (2) add the prefix ***ipag-* to the stem.**

luluto + ***ipag-*** = **ipag**luluto

<u>Word formation rules for *i-* verbs:</u>

Infinitive: add the affix ***i-*** **at the beginning of the root word**.

gawa + ***i-*** = **i**gawa

Completed: (1) add the affix ***-in-*** **before the first vowel of the root word**

\+ ***-in-*** = g**in**awa

and (2) add the affix ***-i*** **at the beginning**.

ginawa + ***i-*** = **i**ginawa

Incompleted: (1) **repeat the first CV** of the root,

gawa + rep1stCV = **ga**gawa

(2) add the affix ***-in-*** **before the first vowel of the stem**,

gagawa + ***-in-*** = g**in**agawa

and (3) add the affix ***i-*** **at the beginning**.

gagawa + ***i-*** = **i**ginagawa

Contemplated: (1) **repeat the first CV** of the root

gawa + **rep1stCV** = **ga**gawa

and (2) add the affix ***i-*** **at the beginning**.

gagawa + ***i-*** = **i**gagawa

Note on reduplication of first CV: repeat only the first vowel if the word starts with a vowel.

Additional notes:

(1) An incompleted verb stem is the resultant form after applying the initial but not all word formation rules.

(2) Root words that start with the sounds /l/, /r/, and /h/ undergo metathesis or reordering of sounds when the infix /-in-/ is attached to it for the completed and incompleted forms.

Here are some illustrative BF verbal sentences. To show the distinct case roles of each noun phrase, their equivalent AF verbal sentences are also provided here. The sentences contain verbs that are inflected for both focus and aspect. The affix on the verb and the subject of the sentence are in bold.

BF verbal sentence	***Equivalent AF verbal sentence***
Ipagluluto ni Ben ng pansit **ang mga kaibigan niya**. *Will cook–genmark.Ben–genmark. noodles.**subjmark–his friends*** *Ben will cook noodles **for his friends**.*	**Mag**luluto **si Ben** ng pansit para sa mga kaibigan niya. *Will cook–**subjmark.Ben** –genmark. noodles.for–oblmark–his friends* ***Ben** will cook noodles for his friends.*
Igagawa niya ng ensalada **ang kapit-bahay niya**.	Gagawa **siya** ng ensalada para sa kapitbahay niya.

Will make–gen.he/she–gen.salad– ***subjmark.his/her neighbor.*** *He/she will make a salad* ***for his/her neighbor.***	*Will make–**subj.he/she** –gen.salad–for–oblmark.his/her neighbor.* ***He/she*** *will make a salad for his/her neighbor.*
Ipaglalaba ko ng mga damit **ang lola ko.** *Will launder–gen.I–gen. clothes–**subjmark.grandmother. genmark*** *I will wash clothes **for my grandmother.***	**Mag**lalaba **ako** ng mga damit para sa lola ko. *Will launder–**subj.I** –gen. clothes–for–oblmark.my grandmother* ***I*** *will wash clothes for my grandmother.*
Ibibili ng tatay ng kompyuter **ang anak niya.** *Will buy–genmark.father–genmark. computer–**subjmark.his child*** *The dad will buy a computer **for his son/daughter.***	Bibili **ang tatay** ng kompyuter para sa anak niya. *Will buy–**subjmark.father** –genmark. computer–for–oblmark.his child* ***The dad*** *will buy a computer for his son/daughter.*

6.5 **Instrumental-focus (IF) verbs** indicate that the noun used in performing the action expressed by the verb is the subject or focus of the sentence. In the indicative mood, the affix associated with this focus form is the prefix /ipang-/. Thus, the shorthand for this set of verbs can be ***ipang-*** **verbs.** Remember that the sound /-ng/ assimilates to the place of articulation of the initial sound of the root word to which it attached. The following is a table of commonly used IF verbs with their complete aspectual forms.

IF ipang- verbs					
English	***Root word***	*Neutral/* ***infinitive***	*Completed/* ***perfective***	*Incompleted/* ***progressive***	***Contemplated/ imperfective***
paint with	pinta	ipampinta	ipinampinta	ipinampipinta	ipampipinta
lift with	buhat	ipambuhat	ipinambuhat	ipinambubuhat	ipambubuhat
pay with	bayad	ipambayad	ipinambayad	ipinambabayad	ipambabayad
buy with	bili	ipambili	ipinambili	ipinambibili	ipambibili
cook with	luto	ipanluto	ipinanluto	ipinanluluto	ipanluluto
do laundry with	laba	ipanlaba	ipinanlaba	ipinanlalaba	ipanlalaba
clean with	linis	ipanlinis	ipanlilinis	ipinanlilinis	ipanlilinis
write with	sulat	ipansulat	ipinansulat	ipinansusulat	ipansusulat

wash with	hugas	ipanghugas	ipinanghugas	ipinanghuhugas	ipanghuhugas
prepare with	handa	ipanghanda	ipinanghanda	ipinanghahanda	ipanghahanda
draw with	guhit	ipangguhit	ipinangguhit	ipinangguguhit	ipangguguhit
make with	gawa	ipanggawa	ipinanggawa	ipinanggagawa	ipanggagawa
get or take with	kuha	ipangkuha	ipinangkuha	ipinangkukuha	ipangkukuha
remove with	alis	ipang-alis	ipinang-alis	ipinang-aalis	ipang-aalis

Word formation rules:

Infinitive: add the prefix ***ipang-* to the root word**.

guhit + ***ipang-*** = **ipang**guhit

Completed: add the affix ***-in-* after the first consonant of the infinitive form**.

ipangguhit + ***-in-*** = ip**in**angguhit

Incompleted: (1) **repeat the first CV** of the root,

guhit + rep1stCV = **gu**guhit

(2) add the prefix ***ipag-* to the stem**,

guguhit + ***ipang-*** = **ipang**guguhit

and (3) add the infix ***-in-* after the first consonant of the stem.**

ipangguguhit+ ***-in-*** = ip**in**angguguhit

Contemplated: (1) **repeat the first CV** of the root

guhit + rep1stCV = **gu**guhit

and (2) add the prefix ***ipag-* to the stem**.

guguhit + ***ipang-*** = **ipang**guguhit

Note on reduplication of first CV: repeat only the first vowel if the word starts with a vowel.

Additional notes:

(1) An incompleted verb stem is the resultant form after applying the initial but not all word formation rules.

(2) The final /-ng/ sound of the prefix /ipang-/ assimilates to the place of articulation of the initial labial and dento-alveolar consonant sounds of the root. The sound changes are reflected in the spelling of the words: /ipang/ + /p or b/ → /ipam/; /ipang-/ + /t, d, l, r, s/ → /ipan/.

Here are some illustrative IF verbal sentences. To show the distinct case roles of each noun phrase, their equivalent AF verbal sentences are also provided here. The sentences contain verbs that are inflected for both focus and aspect. The affix on the verb and the subject of the sentence are in bold.

IF verbal sentence	*Equivalent AF verbal sentence*
Ipambabayad ni Jim ng utang **ang suweldo niya**. *Will pay–genmark.Jim–genmark.debt–* ***subjmark.his salary*** *Jim will pay for his debt* ***with his salary****.*	**Mag**babayad **si Jim** ng utang sa pamamagitan ng suweldo niya. *Will pay–****subjmark.Jim*** *–genmark. debt–oblmark.with his salary* ***Jim*** *will pay for his debt with his salary.*
Ipangkulay mo ng buhok **ang tinang ito**. *Color–gen.you–genmark.hair–* ***subjmark.this dye*** *(You) Color (your) hair* ***with this dye****.*	**Mag**kulay **ka** ng buhok sa pamamagitan ng tinang ito. *Color–****subj.you****–genmark.hair– oblmark.with this dye* *(****You****) Color (your) hair with this dye.*
Ipambili mo ng pagkain ang perang ito. *Buy–gen.you–genmark. food–****subjmark.this money*** *(You) Buy food* ***with this money****.*	**Bum**ili ka ng pagkain sa pamamagitan ng perang ito. *Buy–****subj.you****–genmark. food–oblmark.with this money* *(****You****) Buy food with this money.*

The five aforementioned focus forms can be said to express roughly the same message, but they have different functions in the language. Generally, AF forms are used when introducing a topic or starting a conversation regarding topics about which the speaker assumes little or no previous contextual background knowledge on the part of the interlocutor or listener. The other focus forms, OF, LDF, BF, and IF, are used once the discourse universe and elements of the narrative or conversation have been established to bring attention to or focus on the other elements or specific details. Communication exchanges may be started with non-AF forms if the speaker assumes that the listener or interlocutor has enough contextual background knowledge about the topic of conversation (e.g., prior communication exchanges, general, conventional, or widely known facts and information).

The last two sections of this chapter will discuss two focus forms that are not universally accepted to be part verbal focus. However, they merit attention and inclusion in this book because these forms are widely used when talking about a wide range of familiar everyday topics.

6.6 **Experiencer-focus (EF) verbs** indicate that the noun experiencing the event or action expressed by the verb is the subject or focus of the sentence. These verbs often indicate the experiencing of an emotion or physical sensation. The structure of the EF verbal sentence looks like the AF sentence, and this is the reason why these *ma-* verbs of this category are sometimes mislabeled as AF verbs. The distinction is important because these verbs are the only ones that figure in verbal sentences that look to their equivalent reason-focus (RF) sentences for clear case role marking.

6.6.1 The following table lists some of the more commonly used **EF** *ma-* verbs.

EF ma- verbs					
English	***Root word***	*Neutral/ **infinitive***	*Completed/ **perfective***	*Incompleted/ **progressive***	***Contemplated/ imperfective***
get scared	takot	matakot	natakot	natatakot	matatakot
be shocked	gulat	magulat	nagulat	nagugulat	magugulat
get bored	inip	mainip	nainip	naiinip	maiinip
get annoyed	inis	mainis	nainis	naiinis	maiinis
experience loss	talo	matalo	natalo	natatalo	matatalo
go bankrupt	lugi	malugi	nalugi	nalulugi	malulugi
get dizzy	hilo	mahilo	nahilo	nahihilo	mahihilo
be saddened	lungkot	malungkot	nalungkot	nalulungkot	malulungkot
be elated	tuwa	matuwa	natuwa	natutuwa	matutuwa
be worried	bahala	mabahala	nabahala	nababahala	mababahala
to die	matay	mamatay	namatay	namamatay	mamamatay
be driven to tears	iyak	maiyak	naiyak	naiiyak	maiiyak
be induced to laughter	tawa	matawa	natawa	natatawa	matatawa

Word formation rules:

Infinitive: add the affix ***ma-* at the beginning of the root word**.

nood + *ma-* = **ma**nood

Completed: change the /m/ of the affix to /n/, and add the prefix ***na-* to the root word**.

nood + *na-* = **na**nood

Incompleted: (1) **repeat the first CV** of the root

nood + rep1stCV = **no**nood

and (2) add the affix ***na-* at the beginning**.

nonood + ***na-*** = **na**nonood

Contemplated: (1) **repeat the first CV** of the root

nood + rep1stCV = **no**nood

and (2) add the affix ***ma-* at the beginning**.

nonood + ***ma-*** = **ma**nonood

Note on reduplication of first CV: repeat only the first vowel if the word starts with a vowel.

6.6.2 Another set of EF verbs that are often confused for AF forms are **deadjectival *um-* verbs** (i.e., verbs that are derived from adjective roots). These verbs express the meaning *to become whatever quality the adjective root expresses*. Here are some examples.

Deadjectival EF um- verbs

English	***Root word***	Neutral/ ***infinitive***	Completed/ ***perfective***	Incompleted/ ***progressive***	***Contemplated/ imperfective***
become tall	tangkad	tumangkad	tumangkad	tumatangkad	tatangkad
become small	Liit	lumiit	lumiit	lumiliit	liliit
become high	Taas	tumaas	tumaas	tumataas	tataas
become fat	Taba	tumaba	tumaba	tumataba	tataba
become thin	payat	pumayat	pumayat	pumapayat	papayat
become short	Ikli	umikli	umikli	umiikli	iikli
become cold	lamig	lumamig	lumamig	lumalamig	Lalamig
become hot	init	uminit	uminit	umiinit	Iinit
become slow	bagal	bumagal	bumagal	bumabagal	Babagal
become beautiful	ganda	gumanda	gumanda	gumaganda	gaganda
become delicious	sarap	sumarap	sumarap	sumasarap	Sasarap

Word formation rules:

Infinitive: add the affix ***-um*** **before the first vowel of the root word**.

takbo + *-um-* = **tum**akbo

Completed: add the affix ***-um-*** **before the first vowel of the root word**.

takbo + *-um-* = **tum**akbo

Incompleted: (1) **repeat the first CV** of the root word

takbo + rep1stCV = **ta**takbo

and (2) add the affix ***-um-*** **before the first vowel**.

tatakbo + *-um-* = **tum**atakbo

Contemplated: repeat the first CV of the root word.

takbo + rep1stCV = **ta**takbo

Note on reduplication of first CV: repeat only the first vowel if the word starts with a vowel.

6.6.3 While the majority of EF verbs take the affix /ma-/ and /-um-/, there is a small set of verbs that take the affix *-in*. Often, these verbs indicate infestation or affliction. The following table lists some of the more commonly used **EF *-in* verbs.**

EF *-in* verbs

English	***Root word***	*Neutral/* ***infinitive***	*Completed/* ***perfective***	*Incompleted/* ***progressive***	***Contemplated/ imperfective***
be termite infested	anay	anayin	inanay	inaanay	Aanayin
be swarmed by flies	langaw	langawin	nilangaw	nilalangaw	lalangawin
be swarmed by ants	langgam	langgamin	nilanggam	nilalanggam	lalanggamin
be bug infested	surot	surutin	sinurot	sinusurot	Susurutin
be infested with lice	kuto	kutuhin	kinuto	kinukuto	kukutuhin
be afflicted with cough	ubo	ubuhin	inubo	inuubo	Uubuhin
be afflicted with the flu	trangkaso	trangkasuhin	tinrangkaso	tinatrangkaso	tatrangkasuhin
have an asthma attack	hika	hikain	hinika	hinihika	Hihikain
experience gas pain	kabag	kabagin	kinabag	kinakabag	kakabagin
be infected with scabies	galis	galisin	ginalis	ginagalis	Gagalisin

Word formation rules:

Infinitive: add the affix ***-in /-hin*** **at the end of the root word.**

kain + ***-in*** = kain**in**/basa + *-hin* = basa**hin**

Completed: add the affix ***-in-*** **before the first vowel of the root word.**

kain + ***-in-*** = k**in**ain

Incompleted: (1) **repeat the first CV** of the root

kain + **rep1stCV** = **ka**kain

and (2) add the affix ***-in-*** **before the first vowel.**

kakain + ***-in-*** = k**in**akain

Contemplated: (1) **repeat the first CV** of the root

kain + **rep1stCV** = **ka**kain

and (2) add the affix ***-in*** **at the end.**

kakain + ***-in*** = kakain**in**

Note on reduplication of first CV: repeat only the first vowel if the word starts with a vowel.

Additional notes:

(1) For root words that end in a vowel sound (i.e., there is no glottal stop following the vowel), use the suffix /-hin/ instead of /-in/.

(2) Root words that start with the sounds /l/, /r/, and /h/ undergo metathesis or reordering of sounds when the infix /-in/ is attached to it for the completed and incompleted forms.

As these affixes overlap with other focus forms, learners may find it rather confusing or daunting to memorize. But, a reliable test is to look at the subject of the sentence. For *ma-* verbs, if the *ang* phrase of the sentence is not a volitional actor or doer of the action expressed by a *ma-* verb, then the verb is not an AF form. For *um-* verbs, if the root word expresses a quality rather than an action or event, it is a deadjectival verb, and therefore also an experiencer verb form. In the sentences, the *ang* phrase is also not a volitional actor or doer of the action. In the case of *in-* verbs, if the actor is incorporated in the verb itself, then the verb is not an OF form.

Here are some examples showing the contrast between EF *ma-* verbs and AF *ma-* verbs. Under the EF verbs column, the subject (*ang* phrase in bold) of the sentence is a non-volitional noun referent experiencing the event or action expressed by the verb. On the other hand, under the AF verbs column, the subject (*ang* phrase in bold) is a volitional actor who is the doer of the action expressed by the verb.

EF ma- verbs	***AF ma- verbs***
Nalungkot **si Pedro** dahil sa balita. ***Pedro****was saddened because of the news.*	**Na**nood ng sine **si Pedro**. ***Pedro*** *watched a movie.*
Natuwa **ang tiya ko** dahil sa pagbisita ko. ***My aunt*** *was elated because of my visit.*	**Na**kinig sa radyo **ang tiya ko**. ***My aunt*** *listened to the radio.*
Nahilo **siya** dahil sa gutom. ***He/she*** *felt dizzy because of hunger.*	**Nat**ulog **siya** sa kuwarto. ***He/she*** *slept in the room.*

Here are some examples providing contrast between EF *um-* verbs and adjectival sentences containing the adjectives from which the example verbs are derived. Under the EF verbs column, the subject (*ang* phrase in bold) of the sentence is a non-volitional noun referent experiencing the event or action expressed by the verb. On the other column, the subject (*ang* phrase in bold) is the noun being described by the adjective contained in the predicate.

EF um- verbs	*Adjectival sentences*
B**um**agal **ang daloy ng trapik sa EDSA**. ***Traffic along EDSA*** *slowed down.*	Mabagal **ang daloy ng trapik sa EDSA**. ***Traffic along EDSA*** *is slow.*
B**um**aba **ang presyo ng tiket sa eroplano**. ***Plane fares*** *have gone down.*	Mababa **ang presyo ng tiket sa eroplano**. ***Plane fares*** *are low.*
P**um**ayat **ang kaibigan ko**. ***My friend*** *became skinny.*	Payat **ang kaibigan ko**. ***My friend*** *is skinny.*

Here are some examples providing contrast between OF *in-* verbs and EF *in-* verbs. Note that in the sentences under the EF *in-* verbs column, there is no *ng* phrase actor but rather a causer of the action or event incorporated into the verb itself. In contrast, the OF *in-* verbs figure in sentences where the actor or doer of the action expressed by the verb is overtly expressed as a *ng* phrase (shown in bold in the examples). These verbs often express meanings that indicate either infestation or affliction.

EF in- verbs	*OF in- verbs*
In**anay** ang mesa sa labas. *The table outside was infested with* ***termites***.	Pinatay **niya** ang mga anay sa mesa. ***He/she*** *exterminated the termites in the table.*
Ni**langgam** ang mga pagkain sa piknik. *The food at the picnic was infested by* ***ants***.	Inalis **nila** ang mga langgam sa pagkain. ***They*** *removed the ants from the food.*
Tinat**rangkaso** ang bata. *The child is afflicted with* ***the flu***.	Ginamot **ng doktor** ang trangkaso ng bata. ***The doctor*** *treated the child's flu.*

6.7 **Reason-focus or resultative verbs** indicate that the reason for the experiencer feeling the emotion or sensation or having the quality expressed by the verb is the subject or focus of the sentence. The affix associated with the EF- verbs is the prefix /ika-/. Reason-focus sentences have equivalent EF *ma-* verbal sentence forms. The following is a table of commonly used ***ika-*** **verbs** with their complete aspectual forms.

RF ika- verbs					
English	***Root word***	Neutral/ ***infinitive***	*Completed/* ***perfective***	*Incompleted/* ***progressive***	***Contemplated/ imperfective***
cause death	matay	ikamatay	ikinamatay	ikinamamatay	ikamamatay
cause sadness	lungkot	ikalungkot	ikinalungkot	ikinalulungkot	ikalulungkot
cause joy	tuwa	ikatuwa	ikinatuwa	ikinatutuwa	ikatutuwa
cause worry	bahala	ikabahala	ikinabahala	ikinababahala	ikababahala
cause boredom	inip	ikainip	ikinainip	ikinaiinip	ikaiinip
cause anger	galit	ikagalit	ikinagalit	ikinagagalit	ikagagalit
cause tiredness	pagod	ikapagod	ikinapagod	ikinapapagod	ikapapagod
cause fear	takot	ikatakot	ikinatakot	ikinatatakot	ikatatakot
cause anxiety	balisa	ikabalisa	ikinabalisa	ikinababalisa	ikababalisa
cause annoyance	inis	ikainis	ikinainis	ikinaiinis	ikaiinis
result in beauty	ganda	ikaganda	ikinaganda	ikinagaganda	ikagaganda
result in wealth	yaman	ikayaman	ikinayaman	ikinayayaman	ikayayaman
result in difficulty	hirap	ikahirap	ikinahirap	ikinahihirap	ikahihirap
result in goodness	buti	ikabuti	ikinabuti	ikinabubuti	ikabubuti
result in happiness	saya	ikasaya	ikinasaya	ikinasasaya	ikasasaya

Word formation rules for *ika-* verbs:

Infinitive: add the prefix ***ika-* to the root word.**

tuwa + ***ika-*** = **ika**tuwa

Completed: add the affix ***-in-* after the first consonant of the infinitive form.**

ikatuwa + ***-in-*** = ik**in**atuwa

Incompleted: (1) **repeat the first CV** of the root,

tuwa + rep1stCV = **tu**tuwa

(2) add the prefix ***ipag-* to the stem**,

tutuwa + ***ika-*** = **ika**tutuwa

and (3) add the infix ***-in-* after the first consonant of the stem.**

ikatutuwa + ***-in-*** = ik**in**atutuwa

Contemplated: (1) **repeat the first CV** of the root

tuwa + rep1stCV = **tu**tuwa

and (2) add the prefix ***ika-* to the stem.**

tutuwa + ***ika-*** = **ika**tutuwa

Note on reduplication of first CV: repeat only the first vowel if the word starts with a vowel.

Here are some illustrative RF verbal sentences with their equivalent EF verbal sentences. The verbs are inflected for both focus and aspect. The affix on the verb and the subject of the sentence are in bold.

RF verbal sentences	***Equivalent EF verbal sentences***
Ikin**a**matay niya **ang sakit na kanser**. *He/she died **from cancer**.*	**Na**matay **siya** dahil sa sakit na kanser. ***He/she** died because of cancer.*
Ikin**a**takot nila **ang malakas na bagyo**. *They were scared **of the powerful typhoon**.*	**Na**takot **sila** dahil sa malakas na bagyo. ***They** felt scared because of the powerful typhoon.*
Ikinabahala ng nanay **ang balita**. *The mother was bothered **by the news**.*	**Na**bahala **ang nanay** dahil sa balita. ***The mother** felt anxiety because of the news.*
Ikayayaman mo **ang pagsisikap** sa trabaho. ***Perseverance** at work **will result in wealth**.*	**Yaya**man **ka** dahil sa pagsisikap mo sa trabaho. ***You** will get rich because of your perseverance.*
Ikin**a**hirap nila **ang pagsusugal ni Ben**. ***Ben's gambling resulted in** their **difficulties**.*	H**um**irap **sila** dahil sa pagsusugal ni Ben. ***They** became poor because of Ben's gambling.*
Ikin**a**saya ng mga tao **ang pagbisita ng pangulo**. **The president's visit made** the people **happy**.	S**um**aya **ang mga tao** dahil sa pagbisita ng pangulo. ***The people** felt happy because of the president's visit.*

Chapter 7

Verbal mood

Verbal mood is a marking in the verb, through affixation, that indicates the mode or manner in which the speaker's thought is expressed. It may also include the speaker's attitude about the information being provided. In addition to indicative mood, which is the default setting of verbs, covered in the discussion of verbal focus, Filipino verbs can also be marked for the following grammatical mood: distributive, reciprocal, abilitative, accidental, social, social-participative, and causative. Like the indicative forms, in addition to mood, these verbs also inflect for focus and aspect.

7.1 **Distributive mood** implies plural objects of the action and repeated action by the actor or doer of the action. It is always in the actor-focus (AF) form (i.e., the subject of the sentence of a distributive verb is the actor). The affix associated with the actor-focus distributive mood is /mang-/; thus, these verbs are also referred to as ***mang-* verbs**. The final /-ng/ sound of the affix assimilates to the place of articulation of the initial sound of the verb root to which it is attached, and the phonological change is reflected in the spelling of the verbs (see chapter on phonology and spelling). The table here lists some examples of commonly used distributive mood verbs with their complete aspectual forms. Following the list are some examples showing contrast between AF distributive and AF indicative sentences.

AF distributive mood mang- verbs

English	***Root word***	*Neutral/* ***infinitive***	*Completed/* ***perfective***	*Incompleted/* ***progressive***	*Contemplated/* ***imperfective***
pick up some	pulot	mamulot	namulot	namumulot	mamumulot
go picking	pitas	mamitas	namitas	namimitas	mamimitas

DOI: 10.4324/9781315739427-8

AF distributive mood mang- verbs					
English	***Root word***	*Neutral/* ***infinitive***	*Completed/* ***perfective***	*Incompleted/* ***progressive***	*Contemplated/* ***imperfective***
take several	kuha	manguha	nanguha	nangunguha	mangunguha
gather wood	kahoy	mangahoy	nangahoy	nangangahoy	mangangahoy
go shopping	bili	mamili	namili	namimili	mamimili
cause trouble	gulo	manggulo	nanggulo	nanggugulo	manggugulo
to deceive	loko	manloko	nanloko	nanloloko	manloloko
go fishing	isda	mangisda	nangisda	nangingisda	mangingisda
go for a stroll	pasyal	mamasyal	namasyal	namamasyal	mamamasyal
to cheat	daya	mandaya	nandaya	nandadaya	mandadaya

Word formation rules:

Infinitive: add the prefix ***mang-* to the root word**.

gulo + ***mang-*** = **mang**gulo

Completed: change the /m/ of the affix to /n/, and add the prefix ***nang-* to the root word**.

gulo + ***nang-*** = **nang**gulo

Incompleted: (1) **repeat the first consonant–vowel (CV)** of the root

gulo + rep1stCV = **gu**gulo

and (2) add the prefix ***nang-* to the stem**.

gugulo + ***nang-*** = **nang**gugulo

Contemplated: (1) **repeat the first CV** of the root

gulo + rep1stCV = **gu**gulo

and (2) add the prefix ***mang-* to the stem**.

gugulo + ***mang-*** = **mang**gugulo

Note on reduplication of first CV: repeat only the first vowel if the word starts with a vowel.

Additional notes:

(1) An incompleted verb stem is the resultant form after applying the initial but not all word formation rules.

(2) The final /-ng/ sound of the prefix /mang-/ assimilates to the place of articulation of the initial labial and dento-alveolar consonant sounds of the root. The sound changes are reflected in the spelling of the words: /mang/ + /p or b/ → /mam/; /mang-/ + /t, d, l, r, s/ → /man/. Usually, assimilation to voiceless obstruents is total, and the word formation rules apply after complete assimilation.

Distributive AF verbs	*Indicative AF verbs*
Nanguha ng bato sa tabing-dagat **si Fe**. ***Fe*** *went pebble-picking on the beach.*	K**um**uha ng bato sa tabing-dagat **si Fe**. ***Fe*** *took a pebble on the beach.*
Namili ng damit **si Mara**. ***Mara*** *went shopping for clothes.*	B**um**ili ng damit **si Mara**. ***Mara*** *bought a dress.*
Namitas ng mangga **ang lalaki**. ***The man*** *went mango-picking.*	P**um**itas ng mangga **ang lalaki**. ***The man*** *picked a mango (from the tree).*

7.2 **Reciprocal mood** implies plural actor sharing the same action. It is always in the AF form (i.e., the subject of the sentence of a reciprocal verb is the plural actor). The affix associated with this mood is the circumfix /mag – an/; thus, these verbs are also referred to as ***mag – an*** **verbs**. However, there are some AF *mag-* verbs that are inherently reciprocal (e.g., mag-usap *converse*, mag-away *quarrel*, and magtalo *argue*). They are not included in this category. The table here lists some examples of commonly used reciprocal mood verbs with their complete aspectual forms. Following the list are some examples showing contrast between AF distributive and AF/object-focus (OF) indicative sentences.

AF reciprocal mood mag – an verbs

English	***Root word***	*Neutral/* ***infinitive***	*Completed/* ***perfective***	*Incompleted/* ***progressive***	*Contemplated/* ***imperfective***
tease each other	biro	magbiruan	nagbiruan	nagbibiruan	magbibiruan
love each other	mahal	magmahalan	nagmahalan	nagmamahalan	magmamahalan
call each other	tawag	magtawagan	nagtawagan	nagtatawagan	magtatawagan
help each other	tulong	magtulungan	nagtulungan	nagtutulungan	magtutulungan
tell each other	sabi	magsabihan	nagsabihan	nagsasabihan	magsasabihan
collide	bangga	magbanggaan	nagbanggaan	nagbabanggaan	magbabanggaan
fight or compete with each other	labanan	maglabanan	naglabanan	naglalabanan	maglalabanan
blame each other	sisi	magsisihan	nagsisihan	nagsisisihan	magsisisihan
talk to each other	kuwento	magkuwen-tuhan	nagkuwen-tuhan	nagkukuwen-tuhan	magkukuwen-tuhan
write to each other	sulat	magsulatan	nagsulatan	nagsusulatan	magsusulatan
have an argument	sagot	magsagutan	nagsagutan	nagsasagutan	magsasagutan
make a promise to each other	sumpa	magsumpaan	nagsumpaan	nagsusumpaan	magsusumpaan

Word formation rules:

Infinitive: add the circumfix ***mag* – *an* to the root word**.

sulat + ***mag* – *an*** = **mag**sulat**an**

Completed: change the /m/ of the affix to /n/, and add the circumfix ***nag* – *an* to the root word**.

sulat + ***nag* – *an*** = **nag**sulat**an**

Incompleted: (1) **repeat the first CV** of the root

sulat + rep1stCV = **su**sulat

and (2) add the circumfix ***nag* – *an* to the stem**.

susulat + ***nag* – *an*** = **nag**susulat**an**

Contemplated: (1) **repeat the first CV** of the root

sulat + rep1stCV = **su**sulat

and (2) add the circumfix ***mag* – *an* to the stem**.

susulat + ***mag* – *an*** = **mag**susulat**an**

Note on reduplication of first CV: repeat only the first vowel if the word starts with a vowel.

Additional notes:

(1) An incompleted verb stem is the resultant form after applying the initial but not all word formation rules.

(2) The /o/ sound in the final syllable of verb roots is raised to /u/ when the suffix /-an/ is attached to it.

Reciprocal AF verbs	***Indicative AF/OF verbs***
Nagkuwentu**han sina Mark at Lisa**. ***Mark and Lisa*** *exchanged stories.*	**Nag**kuwento **si Mark** kay Lisa. ***Mark*** *told Lisa a story.*
Nagtawag**an ang estudyante at guro**. ***The student and the teacher*** *called each other.*	T**um**awag **ang estudyante** sa guro. ***The student*** *called the teacher.*
Nagsuntuk**an ang mga bata**. ***The children*** *had a fistfight with each other.*	S**in**untok ng isang bata **ang ibang bata**. [OF] *A kid hit* ***another kid****.*

7.3 **Social mood** indicates that the actor is sharing the resources or action of another noun (a *sa* phrase when overtly expressed in the sentence) with the implied permission, with or without reservation, of that other noun. It is always in the AF form (i.e., the subject of the sentence of a social verb is the doer of the action expressed by the verb). The somewhat unequal relationship between the actor and the noun whose resources or action are being shared is implied, with the actor being the dependent entity. The affix associated with this mood is the prefix /maki-/; thus, these verbs are also referred to as ***maki-* verbs**. The table here lists some examples of commonly used social mood verbs with their complete aspectual forms. Following the list are some examples showing contrast between AF social sentences and AF indicative sentences.

AF social mood maki- verbs					
English	***Root word***	*Neutral/* ***infinitive***	*Completed/* ***perfective***	*Incompleted/* ***progressive***	*Contemplated/* ***imperfective***
eat at	kain	makikain	nakikain	nakikikain	makikikain
sleep at	tulog	makitulog	nakitulog	nakikitulog	makikitulog
get along with	sama	makisama	nakisama	nakikisama	makikisama
have a drink at	inom	makiinom	nakiinom	nakikiinom	makikiinom
cook at	luto	makiluto	nakiluto	nakikiluto	makikiluto
shower at	ligo	makiligo	nakiligo	nakikiligo	makikiligo
watch – at	nood	makinood	nakinood	nakikinood	makikinood
join in singing	kanta	makikanta	nakikanta	nakikikanta	makikikanta
join in the fun	saya	makisaya	nakisaya	nakikisaya	makikisaya
condole with	damay	makiramay	nakiramay	nakikiramay	makikiramay
take shelter at	silong	makisilong	nakisilong	nakikisilong	makikisilong
leave something with	iwan	makiiwan	nakiiwan	nakikiiwan	makikiiwan

Word formation rules:

Infinitive: add the prefix ***maki-* to the root word.**

kain + ***maki-*** = **maki**kain

Completed: change the /m/ of the affix to /n/, and add the prefix ***naki-* to the root word.**

kain + ***naki-*** = **naki**iwan

Incompleted: (1) **repeat the second CV** of the prefix ***naki-***

naki- + rep2ndCV = naki**ki-**

and (2) add the affix to the root.

nakiki- + kain = **nakiki**kain

Contemplated: (1) **repeat the second CV** of the prefix ***maki-***

maki- + rep2ndCV = maki**ki-**

and (2) add the affix to the root.

makiki- + kain = **makiki**kain

Social AF verbs	***Indicative AF verbs***
Nakikain **ako** sa kaibigan ko. *I ate at my friend's.* *(Implied: My friend let me share his/her food.)*	K**um**ain **ako** sa bahay ng kaibigan ko. ***I** ate at my friend's house.*
Nakitawag **ako** sa kaklase ko. *I made a call using my classmate's telephone.* *(Implied: My classmate gave me permission.)*	T**um**awag **ako** sa kaklase ko. ***I**called my classmate.*

Makikinood **sila** ng telebisyon.
***They** will watch television at someone else's place or using someone else's device. (Implied: with the owner's permission)*

Manonood **sila** ng telebisyon.
They will watch television.

7.4 **Social-participative mood** indicates that the actor is in a reciprocal social relationship with another noun (a *sa* phrase when overtly expressed in the sentence) that shares the resources and action expressed by the verb. The somewhat equal sharing of resources and full participation in the activity of the other noun are implied. It is always in the AF form (i.e., the subject of the sentence of a social verb is the doer of the action expressed by the verb). The affix associated with this mood is the circumfix /makipag – an/; thus, these verbs are also referred to as ***makipag – an* verbs**. The table here lists some examples of commonly used social-participative mood verbs with their complete aspectual forms. Following the list are some examples showing contrast between AF social-participative sentences and AF indicative sentences.

AF social-participative mood makipag – an verbs

English	***Root word***	*Neutral/* ***infinitive***	*Completed/* ***perfective***	*Incompleted/* ***progressive***	*Contemplated/* ***imperfective***
joke with	biro	makipagb-iruan	nakipagb-iruan	nakikipagb-iruan	makikipagb-iruan
flirt with	landi	makipa-glandian	nakipa-glandian	nakikipa-glandian	makikipa-glandian
kiss with	halik	makipagha-likan	nakipagha-likan	nakikipagha-likan	makikipagha-likan
argue with	sagot	makipagsa-gutan	nakipagsa-gutan	nakikipagsa-gutan	makikipagsa-gutan
drink together with	inom	makipag-inuman	nakipag-inuman	nakikipag-inuman	makikipag-inuman
correspond with	sulat	makipagsu-latan	nakipagsu-latan	nakikipagsu-latan	makikipagsu-latan
be in a fistfight with	suntok	makipagsun-tukan	nakipagsun-tukan	nakikipagsun-tukan	makikipagsun-tukan
make a vow with	sumpa	makipag-sumpaan	nakipag-sumpaan	nakikipag-sumpaan	makikipag-sumpaan
race with	una *first*	makipag-unahan	nakipag-unahan	nakikipag-unahan	makikipag-unahan
exchange with	palit	makipagpali-tan	nakipagpali-tan	nakikipagpali-tan	makikipag-palitan
*converse with**	usap	makipag-usap	nakipag-usap	nakikipag-usap	makikipag-usap

*quarrel with**	away	makipag-away	nakipag-away	nakikipag-away	makikipag-away
*argue with**	talo	makipagtalo	nakipagtalo	nakikipagtalo	makikipagtalo

Word formation rules:

Infinitive: add the circumfix ***makipag – an* to the root word**.

halik + ***makipag – an*** = **makipag**halik**an**

Completed: change the /m/ of the affix to /n/, and add the circumfix ***nakipag – an* to the root word**.

halik + ***nakipag – an*** = **nakipag**halik**an**

Incompleted: (1) **repeat the second CV** of the circumfix ***nakipag – an***

makipag – an + rep2ndCV = maki**ki**pag – an

and (2) add the affix to the root.

nakikipag – an + kain = **nakikipag**halik**an**

Contemplated: (1) **repeat the second CV** of the circumfix ***makipag – an***

makikipag – an + rep2ndCV = maki**ki**pag – an

and (2) add the affix to the root.

makikipag – an + kain = **makikipag**halik**an**

Additional notes:

(1) The /o/ sound in the final syllable of verb roots is raised to /u/ when the suffix /-an/ is attached to it.
(2) The /o/ sound in the final syllable of a root word is raised to /u/ when the circumfix /makipag – an/ or /nakipag – an/ is attached.
(3) Actor-focus indicative mood verbs that are inherently reciprocal take only the affix /makipag-/. The examples in the preceding table are marked by an asterisk (*).

Social-participative AF verbs	***Indicative AF verbs***
Nakipag-inum**an si Max** sa mga kaopisina niya. ***Max*** *went drinking with his coworkers.*	**Um**inom **si Max** kasama ng mga kaopisina niya. ***Max*** *drank with his coworkers.*
Nakipagkuwentu**han ako** sa kapatid ko. ***I*** *exchanged stories with my brother/sister.*	**Nag**kuwento **ako** sa kapatid ko. ***I*** *told a story to my brother/sister.*
Nakipagsagut**an** si Mila kay Jim. ***Mila*** *argued with Jim.*	S**um**agot **si Mila** kay Jim. ***Mila*** *replied to Jim.*

7.5 **Abilitative mood** indicates that the actor is able to perform the action expressed by the verb because he/she has either time, means, opportunity, or skill to do it. The interpretation is largely dependent on the context in which the verb occurs. The affixes associated with this verbal mood are the prefixes /maka-/ and /makapag-/ for AF forms and the prefix /ma-/ for the focus forms object focus (OF), location–direction focus (LDF), benefactive focus (BF), and instrumental focus (IF). Like other verbs, these also inflect for aspect.

7.5.1 **Actor-focus abilitative mood** verbs are formed with the affix /maka-/ or /makapag-/. Hence, the shorthand for this set is ***maka*** **(*pag*)- verbs**. The affix /maka-/ is used for verb roots associated with the AF indicative affix /-um/ or *um-* verbs. The affix /makapag-/ is used for verb roots associated with the AF indicative affix /mag-/ or *mag-* verbs.

AF abilitative maka- verbs

English	***um- Verb***	*Neutral/* ***infinitive***	*Completed/* ***perfective***	*Incompleted/* ***progressive***	***Contemplated/ imperfective***
make	gumawa	makagawa	nakagawa	nakakagawa nakagagawa	makakagawa makagagawa
dance	sumayaw	makasayaw	nakasayaw	nakakasayaw nakasasayaw	makakasayaw makasasayaw
go out	lumabas	makalabas	nakalabas	nakakalabas nakalalabas	makakalabas makalalabas
reply	sumagot	makasagot	nakasagot	nakakasagot nakasasagot	makakasagot makasasagot
buy	bumili	makabili	nakabili	nakakabili nakabibili	makakabili makabibili

Word formation rules:

Infinitive: add the prefix ***maka-*** **to the root word**.

bili + ***maka-*** = **maka**bili

Completed: change the /m/ of the affix to /n/, and add the prefix ***naka-*** **to the root word**.

bili + ***naka-*** = **naka**bili

Incompleted I: (1) **repeat the second CV** of the prefix ***naka-***

naka- + rep2ndCV = naka**ka**-

and (2) add the affix to the root.

nakaka- + bili = **nakaka**bili

Incompleted II: (1) **repeat the first CV** of the root

bili + rep1stCV = **bi**bili

and (2) add the *naka-* to the stem.

naka- + bibili = **naka**bibili

Contemplated I: (1) **repeat the second CV** of the prefix ***maka-***

maka- + rep2ndCV = maka**ka**-

and (2) add the affix to the root.

makaka- + bili = **makaka**bili

Contemplated II: (1) **repeat the first CV** of the root

bili + rep1stCV = **bi**bili

and (2) add the affix *maka-* to the stem.

maka- + bibili = **maka**bibili

AF abilitative makapag- verbs

English	***mag-Verb***	*Neutral/* ***infinitive***	*Completed/* ***perfective***	*Incompleted/* ***progressive***	***Contemplated/ imperfective***
wash	hugas	makapa-ghugas	nakapaghugas	nakakapaghugas nakapaghuhugas	makakapaghugas makapaghuhugas
clean	maglinis	makapa-glinis	nakapaglinis	nakakapaglinis nakapaglilinis	makakapaglinis makapaglilinis
cook	magluto	makapa-gluto	nakapagluto	nakakapagluto nakapagluluto	makakapagluto makapagluluto
give	magbigay	makapag-bigay	nakapagbigay	nakakapagbigay nakapagbibigay	makakapagbigay makapagbibigay
bring	magdala	makapag-dala	nakapagdala	nakakapagdala nakapagdadala	makakapagdala makapagdadala

Word formation rules:

Infinitive: add the prefix ***maka-*** **to the root word**.

bili + ***makapag-*** = **makapag**bigay

Completed: change the /m/ of the affix to /n/, and add the prefix ***naka-*** **to the root word**.

bigay + ***nakapag-*** = **nakapag**bigay

Incompleted I: (1) **repeat the second CV** of the prefix ***nakapag-***

nakapag- + rep2ndCV = naka**ka**pag-

and (2) add the affix to the root.

nakakapag- + bigay = **nakakapag**bigay

Incompleted II: (1) **repeat the first CV** of the root

bigay + rep1stCV = **bi**bigay

and (2) add the affix *naka-* to the stem.

nakapag- + bibigay = **nakapag**bibigay

Contemplated I: (1) **repeat the second CV** of the prefix ***makapag-***

makapag- + rep2ndCV = maka**ka**pag-

and (2) add the affix to the root.

makakapag- + bigay = **makakapag**bigay

Contemplated II: (1) **repeat the first CV** of the root

bigay + rep1stCV = **bi**bigay

and (2) add the affix *makapag-* to the stem.

makapag- + bibigay = **makapag**bibigay

The choice between options I and II for the incompleted and contemplated forms is up to individual speakers, although some teachers of Filipino insist on option II as the proper way of conjugating the verbs. However, some speakers feel that option II is a more conservative form.

The following are examples of sentences with AF abilitative mood verbs. Their indicative mood counterparts are provided to show contrast. The mood and focus affixes and the subject are in bold.

Abilitative AF verbs	***Indicative AF verbs***
Nakapunta **si Jun** sa Davao noong Mayo. ***Jun*** *was able to go to Davao in May.*	P**um**unta **si Jun** sa Davao noong Mayo. ***Jun*** *went to Davao in May.*
Nakakapaglaba **ako** tuwing Sabado. ***I*** *am able to do laundry every Saturday.*	**Nag**lalaba **ako** tuwing Sabado. ***I*** *do laundry every Saturday.*
Makakapag-aral **ang mga estudyante** sa kapihan. ***The students*** *will be able to study at the coffee shop.*	**Mag**-aaral **ang mga estudyante** sa kapihan. ***The students*** *will study at the coffee shop.*

7.5.2 **Non-AF abilitative mood** verbs are formed by attaching the prefix / ma-/ to their **OF, LDF, BF, or IF** indicative forms, with the exception of forms derived from OF *in*- verbs, which require attaching the prefix / ma-/ only to the root word. This is yet another set of ***ma*- verbs**.

OF abilitative mood ma- verbs					
English	***Indicative in- verbs***	*Neutral/* ***infinitive***	*Completed/* ***perfective***	*Incompleted/* ***progressive***	***Contemplated/ imperfective***
make	gawin	magawa	nagawa	nagagawa	magagawa
play	tugtugin	matugtog	natugtog	natutugtog	matutugtog
finish	tapusin	matapos	natapos	natatapos	matatapos
watch	panoorin	mapanood	napanood	napapanood	mapapanood
bring	dalhin	madala	nadala	nadadala	madadala
English	*Indicative* ***i- verbs***	*Neutral/* ***infinitive***	*Completed/* ***perfective***	*Incompleted/* ***progressive***	***Contemplated/ imperfective***
give	ibigay	maibigay	naibigay	naibibigay	maibibigay
prepare	ihanda	maihanda	naihanda	naihahanda	maihahanda
teach	ituro	maituro	naituro	naituturo	maituturo
write	isulat	maisulat	naisulat	naisusulat	maisusulat
put away	iligpit	mailigpit	nailigpit	naililigpit	maililigpit

English	*Indicative* **an- verbs**	*Neutral/* **infinitive**	*Completed/* **perfective**	*Incompleted/* **progressive**	**Contemplated/ imperfective**
wash	hugasan	mahugasan	nahugasan	nahuhugasan	mahuhugasan
wipe	punasan	mapunasan	napunasan	napupunasan	mapupunasan
cover	takpan	matakpan	natakpan	natatakpan	matatakpan
open	buksan	mabuksan	nabuksan	nabubuksan	mabubuksan
close	sarhan	masarhan	nasarhan	nasasarhan	masasarhan

LDF abilitative mood ma- verbs

English	***Indicative pag – an verbs***	*Neutral/* ***infinitive***	*Completed/* ***perfective***	*Incompleted/* ***progressive***	***Contemplated/ imperfective***
dance at	pagsayawan	Mapagsay-awan	napagsayawan	napagsasay-awan	mapagsasayawan
cook in	paglulutuan	mapaglutuan	napaglutuan	napaglulutuan	mapaglulutuan
keep in	pagtaguan	mapagtaguan	napagtaguan	napagtataguan	mapagtataguan
sleep on	pagtulugan	mapagtulugan	napagtulugan	napagtutulugan	mapagtutulugan
pass through	pagdaanan	mapagdaanan	napagdaanan	napagdadaanan	mapagdadaanan
English	*Indicative* ***-an verbs***	*Neutral/* ***infinitive***	*Completed/* ***perfective***	*Incompleted/* ***progressive***	***Contemplated/ imperfective***
call	tawagan	matawagan	natawagan	natatawagan	matatawagan
go to	puntahan	mapuntahan	napuntahan	napupuntahan	mapupuntahan
help	tulungan	matulungan	natulungan	natutulungan	matutulungan
give	bigyan	mabigyan	nabigyan	nabibigyan	mabibigyan
look at	tingnan	matingnan	natingnan	natitingnan	matitingnan

BF abilitative mood ma- verbs

English	***Indicative ipag-verbs***	*Neutral/* ***infinitive***	*Completed/* ***perfective***	*Incompleted/* ***progressive***	***Contemplated/ imperfective***
cook for	ipagluto	maipagluto	naipagluto	naipagluluto	maipagluluto
bring for	ipagdala	maipagdala	naipagdala	naipagdadala	maipagdadala
write for	ipagsulat	maipagsulat	naipagsulat	naipagsusulat	maipagsusulat
prepare for	ipaghanda	maipaghanda	naipaghanda	naipaghahanda	maipaghahanda
do laundry for	ipaglaba	maipaglaba	naipaglaba	naipaglalaba	maipaglalaba

English	***Indicative i- verbs***	*Neutral/ **infinitive***	*Completed/ **perfective***	*Incompleted/ **progressive***	***Contemplated/ imperfective***
buy for	ibili	maibili	naibili	naibibili	maibibili
make for	igawa	maigawa	naigawa	naigagawa	maigagawa
get for	ikuha	maikuha	naikuha	naikukuha	maikukuha
find for	ihanap	maihanap	naihanap	naihahanap	maihahanap

IF abilitative mood ma- verbs					
English	***Indicative ipang-verbs***	*Neutral/ **infinitive***	*Completed/ **perfective***	*Incompleted/ **progressive***	***Contemplated/ imperfective***
kill with	ipampatay	maipam-patay	naipampatay	naipampapatay	maipampapatay
clean with	ipanlinis	maipanlinis	naipanlinis	naipanlilinis	maipanlilinis
cut with	ipamputol	maipam-putol	naipamputol	naipampuputol	maipampuputol
open with	ipambukas	maipam-bukas	naipambukas	naipambubukas	maipambubukas
wash with	ipanghugas	maipang-hugas	naipanghugas	naipanghuhu-gas	maipanghuhugas

Word formation rules for these verbs follow those of the indicative OF forms. With the exception of *in-* verbs, which follow the same conjugation pattern as OF *ma-* verb indicative mood forms, all other non-AF abilitative mood forms simply attach the prefix /ma-/ to the full indicative mood form. The rest of the conjugation patterns follow the word formation rules of OF indicative mood verbs (see section on OF indicative mood verbs).

The following are examples of sentences with non-AF abilitative mood verbs. Their indicative mood counterparts are provided to show contrast. The mood and focus affixes and the subject are in bold.

Abilitative mood OF verbs	***Indicative mood OF verbs***
Magagawa ni Ana **ang proyekto niya**. *Ana will be able to do **her project**.*	Gagaw**in** ni Ana **ang proyekto niya**. *Ana will do **her project**.*
Naibigay niya **ang pera** sa simbahan. *He/she was able to give **the money** to the church.*	**I**binigay niya **ang pera** sa simbahan. *He/she gave **the money**to the church.*
Nahuhugasan ng kasambahay **ang mga plato**. *The maid is able to wash **the dishes**.*	Hinuhugas**an** ng kasambahay **ang mga plato**. *The maid washes **the dishes**.*

Abilitative mood LDF verbs	*Indicative mood LDF verbs*
Natawagan ng estudyante **ang guro**. *The student was able to call **the teacher**.*	Tinawag**an** ng estudyante **ang guro**. *The student called **the teacher**.*
Mapagtutulugan niya **ang sopa**. *He/she will be able to sleep **on the sofa** .*	**Pag**tutulug**an** niya **ang sopa**. *He/she will sleep **on the sofa**.*
Abilitative mood BF verbs	***Indicative mood BF verbs***
Naipaghanda ng nanay ng meryenda **si Ben**. *(The) mother was able to prepare a snack **for Ben**.*	**Ipinag**handa ng nanay ng meryenda **si Ben**. *(The) mother prepared a snack **or Ben**.*
Maibibili ko ng kamiseta **ang kapatid ko**. *I will be able to buy a shirt **for my brother***	**I**bibili ko ng kamiseta **ang kapatid ko**. *I will buy a shirt **for my brother** .*
Abilitative mood IF verbs	***Indicative mood IF verbs***
Naipambayad ko ng utang **ang regalo mo**. *I was able to pay my debt **with your gift**.*	**Ipinam**bayad ko ng utang **ang regalo mo**. *I paid my debt **with your gift**.*
Maipanggagamot mo ng sugat **ang dahon ng bayabas**. *You can treat a wound **with guava leaves**.*	**Ipang**gagamot mo ng sugat **ang dahon ng bayabas**. *You will treat a wound **with guava leaves**.*

7.5.3 **Object-focus abilitative perception–cognition** verbs are a special class of potential verbs that generally do not have AF counterparts. These are often, but not exclusively, used in sentences that contain an embedded clause as subject. The two affixes associated with this form are the prefix /ma-/ and the circumfix /ma – an/.

OF perception–cognition ma- (-an) verbs

English	***Root word***	*Neutral/* ***infinitive***	*Completed/* ***perfective***	*Incompleted/* ***progressive***	***Contem-plated/ imperfective***
to see	kita	makita	nakita	nakikita	makikita
to hear	rinig	marinig	narinig	naririnig	maririnig
to remember	alala	maalala	naalala	naaalala	maaalala
to realize	tanto	matanto	natanto	natatanto	matatanto
come to mind	isip	maisip	naisip	Naiisip	maiisip
notice	pansin	mapansin	napansin	napapansin	mapapansin
to forget	kalimot	makalimutan	nakalimutan	nakakalimutan	makakalimutan
to learn to do	tuto	matutunan	natutunan	natututunan	matututunan
to find out	alam	malaman	nalaman	nalalaman	malalaman
to feel	ramdam	maramdaman	naramdaman	nararamdaman	mararamdaman

Word formation rules:

Infinitive: add the affix ***ma- (-an)* to the root word**.

rinig + *ma-* = **ma**rinig
ramdam + *ma – an* = **ma**ramdam**an**

Completed: change the /m/ of the affix to /n/, and add the prefix ***na-* to the word**.

rinig + *ma-* = **ma**rinig
ramdam + *ma – an* = **ma**ramdam**an**

Incompleted: (1) **repeat the first CV** of the root

rinig + rep1stCV = **ri**rinig
ramdam + rep1stCV = **ra**ramdam

and (2) add the affix ***na- (-an)* to the stem**.

ririnig + ***na-*** = **na**ririnig
raramdam + ***na – an*** = **na**raramdam**an**

Contemplated: (1) **repeat the first CV** of the root

rinig + rep1stCV = **ri**rinig
ramdam + rep1stCV = **ra**ramdam

and (2) add the affix ***ma- (-an)* to the stem**.

ririnig + ***ma-*** = **na**ririnig
raramdam + ***ma – an*** = **na**raramdam**an**

Note on reduplication of first CV: repeat only the first vowel if the word starts with a vowel.

The following are examples illustrating the use of perception–cognition verbs in sentences with an *ang* phrase and sentences with an embedded clause as subject.

OF abilitative perception–cognition verbs with *ang* phrase subject

Nakita nila **ang mga buwaya** sa ilog.
*They saw **the crocodiles** in the river.*

Nalam**an** ni Minda **ang sikreto ni Hilda**.
*Minda found out **Hilda's secret**.*

OF abilitative perception–cognition verbs with embedded sentential subject

Narinig namin **kung kailan ang pagdiriwang sa bahay ninyo**.
*We heard about **when the celebration at your house will be**.*

Natutun**an** ng mga bata **na hindi dapat lumakad sa burol sa gabi**.
*The children learned **that they should not walk on the hill at night.***

7.6 **Accidental mood** indicates that the actor accidentally or unintentionally did the action expressed by the verb. Like the abilitative mood, the interpretation is highly context-dependent. The affixes associated with this verbal mood are spelled exactly the same as the abilitative mood affixes (i.e., they are homographs). In some dialects of Tagalog, they are homonyms (i.e., they have the same pronunciation). In others, there is a difference in pronunciation. Although this book follows the latter analysis, many speakers of Filipino do not make this distinction. This is why some linguists conflate the abilitative and accidental mood forms into one mood inflection called the aptative or potential mood. The accidental mood affixes are the prefix /maka:-/ for AF forms and the prefix /ma:-/ for the focus forms OF, LDF, and IF. The symbol /:/ represents vowel length here. However, standard Filipino orthography does not have a symbol representing vowel length, so learners will have to keep in mind that there is this slight difference in pronunciation between the abilitative and accidental mood affixes. Like other verbs, these also inflect for aspect.

7.6.1 **Actor-focus accidental mood** verbs are formed with the affix /maka:-/. Hence, the shorthand for this set is ***maka*:- verbs**.

AF accidental maka:- verbs

English	***um- Verb***	*Neutral/* ***infinitive***	*Completed/* ***perfective***	*Incompleted/* ***progressive***	***Contemplated/ imperfective***
kill	pumatay	maka:patay	naka:patay	naka:kapatay naka:papatay	maka:kapatay maka:papatay
hit	bumundol	maka:bundol	naka:bundol	naka:kabundol naka:bubundol	maka:kabundol maka:bubundol
take	kumuha	maka:kuha	naka:kuha	naka:kakuha naka:kukuha	maka:kakuha maka:kukuha
burn	magsunog	maka:sunog	naka:sunog	naka:kasunog naka:susunog	maka:kasunog maka:susunog
throw	magtapon	maka:tapon	naka:tapon	naka:katapon naka:tatapon	maka:katapon maka:tatapon

7.6.2 **Non-AF accidental mood** verbs are formed by attaching the prefix /ma:-/ to their **OF, LDF, or IF** indicative forms, with the exception of OF *in-* verbs, which require attaching the prefix /ma:-/ only to the root word. Thus, in this book, these are referred to as ***ma*:- verbs**. Note that there are no beneficiary-focus (BF) accidental mood forms.

OF accidental mood ma:- verbs					
English	*Indicative* ***in- verbs***	*Neutral/* ***infinitive***	*Completed/* ***perfective***	*Incompleted/* ***progressive***	***Contemplated/ imperfective***
eat	kainin	ma:kain	na:kain	na:kakain	ma:kakain
drink	inumin	ma:inom	na:inom	na:iinom	ma:iinom
kick	sipain	ma:sipa	na:sipa	na:sisipa	ma:sisipa
hit	banggain	ma:bangga	na:bangga	na:babangga	ma:babangga
bite	kagatin	ma:kagat	na:kagat	na:kakagat	ma:kakagat
English	***Indicative i- verbs***	*Neutral/* ***infinitive***	*Completed/* ***perfective***	*Incompleted/* ***progressive***	***Contemplated/ imperfective***
toss	itapon	ma:itapon	na:itapon	na:itatapon	ma:itatapon
include	isama	ma:isama	na:isama	na:isasama	ma:isasama
drop	ihulog	ma:ihulog	na:ihulog	na:ihuhulog	ma:ihuhulog
give	ibigay	ma:ibigay	na:ibigay	na:ibibigay	ma:ibibigay
put away	iligpit	ma:iligpit	na:iligpit	na:ililigpit	ma:ililigpit
English	***Indicative -an verbs***	*Neutral/* ***infinitive***	*Completed/* ***perfective***	*Incompleted/* ***progressive***	***Contemplated/ imperfective***
wash	hugasan	ma:hugasan	na:hugasan	na:huhugasan	ma:huhugasan
guess	hulaan	ma:hulaan	na:hulaan	na:huhulaan	ma:huhulaan
cover	takpan	ma:takpan	na:takpan	na:tatakpan	ma:tatakpan
open	buksan	ma:buksan	na:buksan	na:bubuksan	ma:bubuksan
close	sarhan	ma:sarhan	na:sarhan	na:sasarhan	ma:sasarhan

LDF abilitative mood ma:- verbs					
English	***Indicative -an verbs***	*Neutral/* ***infinitive***	*Completed/* ***perfective***	*Incompleted/* ***progressive***	***Contemplated/ imperfective***
step on	tapakan	ma:tapakan	na:tapakan	na:tatapakan	ma:tatapakan
sit on	upuan	ma:upuan	na:upuan	na:uupuan	ma:uupuan
left behind	iwanan	ma:iwanan	na:iwanan	na:iiwanan	ma:iiwanan
forget	kalimutan	ma:kalimutan	na:kalimutan	na:kakalimutan	ma:kakalimutan
put	paglagyan	ma:paglagyan	na:paglagyan	na:paglalagyan	ma:paglalagyan

IF abilitative mood ma:- verbs					
English	***Indicative ipang- verbs***	*Neutral/* ***infinitive***	*Completed/* ***perfective***	*Incompleted/* ***progressive***	***Contemplated/ imperfective***
kill with	ipampatay	ma:ipampatay	na:ipampatay	na:ipampapatay	ma:ipampapatay
clean with	ipanlinis	ma:ipanlinis	na:ipanlinis	na:ipanlilinis	ma:ipanlilinis
cut with	ipamputol	ma:ipamputol	na:ipamputol	na:ipampuputol	ma:ipampuputol

open with	ipambukas	ma:ipambukas	na:ipambukas	na:ipambubukas	ma:ipambubukas
wash with	ipanghugas	ma:ipanghugas	na:ipanghugas	na:ipanghuhugas	ma:ipanghuhugas

Word formation rules for these verbs follow those of the non-AF abilitative forms. With the exception of forms derived from OF *in-* verbs, which require attaching the prefix /ma:-/ only to the root word, all other non-AF abilitative mood forms simply attach the prefix /ma:-/ to the full indicative mood form (see section on OF indicative mood verbs).

The following are examples of sentences with non-AF accidental mood verbs. Their indicative mood counterparts are provided to show contrast. The mood and focus affixes and the subject are in bold.

Accidental mood OF verbs	***Indicative mood OF verbs***
Na:kain ni Pedro **ang pagkain ni Jim**. *Pedro accidentally ate **Jim's food.***	K**in**ain ni Pedro **ang pagkain ni Jim**. *Pedro ate **Jim's food.***
Na:itapon niya **ang papel ko**. *He/she accidentally threw away **my paper***	**I**tinapon niya **ang papel ko**. *He/she threw away **my paper**.*
Na:tatakpan ng babae **ang bata**. *The woman is unintentionally blocking **the child**.*	Tinatakp**an** ng babae **ang bata**. *The woman is (deliberately) blocking **the child**.*
Accidental mood LDF verbs	***Indicative mood LDF verbs***
Na:tapakan ng lalaki **ang pusa**. *The man accidentally stepped **on the cat**.*	Tinapak**an** ng lalaki **ang pusa**. *The man stepped **on the cat**.*
Ma:uupuan ni Mila **ang lobo**. *Mila will accidentally sit **on the balloon**.*	Uupu**an** ni Mila **ang lobo**. *Mila will sit **on the balloon**.*
Accidental mood IF verbs	***Indicative mood IF verbs***
Na:ipampunas niya ng mesa **ang panyo ko**. *He/she accidentally wiped the table **with my hankie**.*	**Ipinam**punas niya ng mesa **ang panyo ko**. *He/she wiped the table **with my hankie**.*
Na:ipambili ko ng pagkain **ang pera mo**. ***I unintentionally used your money to buy food.***	**Ipinam**bili ko ng pagkain **ang pera mo**. *I used **your money** to buy food.*

7.7 **Causative mood** indicates that one actor is causing another actor to perform the action expressed by the verb. The causative mood affix /pa-/ interacts with indicative mood affixes to create different focus forms. Therefore, instead of using only the cover term ***pa-* verbs**, in this section each focus form in the causative mood will be discussed separately. Like other verbs, these also inflect for aspect. Causatives inherently imply involvement of **two actors: (1) a causer,** the noun causing another actor to perform the action expressed by the verb, and (2) **a causee,** the noun actually performing the action expressed by the verb. Due to this fact, this verbal mood has two AF forms.

7.7.1 Actor-focus 1 causative mood indicates that the subject (i.e., the *ang* phrase) of the sentence is the causer. The affix associated with this is / magpa-/. In a sentence, the causee may or may not be overtly expressed. When it is present, it is in the oblique case. Here are some examples of commonly used ***magpa-*** **verbs** and their aspectual forms.

AF-1 causative magpa- verbs

English	*AF* ***indicative***	*Neutral/* ***infinitive***	*Completed/* ***perfective***	*Incompleted/* ***progressive***	***Contemplated/ imperfective***
Make	gumawa	magpagawa	nagpagawa	nagpapagawa	magpapagawa
Help	tulong	magpatulong	nagpatulong	nagpapatulong	magpapatulong
accompany	sumama	magpasama	nagpasama	nagpapasama	magpapasama
Cook	magluto	magpaluto	nagpaluto	nagpapaluto	magpapaluto
study	mag-aral	magpaaral	nagpaaral	nagpapaaral	magpapaaral

<u>Word formation rules:</u>

Infinitive: add the prefix ***magpa-*** **to the root word**.

bili + ***magpa-*** = **magpa**bili

Completed: change the /m/ of the affix to /n/,and add the prefix ***nagpa-*** **to the root word**.

bili + ***nagpa-*** = **nagpa**bili

Incompleted: (1) **repeat the second CV** of the prefix ***nagpa-***

nagpa- + rep2ndCV = nagpa**pa-**

and (2) add the affix to the root

nagpapa- + bili = **nagpapa**bili

Contemplated: (1) **repeat the second CV** of the prefix ***maka-***

magpa- + rep2ndCV = magpa**pa-**

and (2) add the affix to the root.

magpapa- + bili = **magpapa**bili

The following are illustrative sentences with AF-1 causative verbs. The mood and focus affixes as well as the subject are in bold.

Magpakain **ka** ng almusal sa bata.
*AF1 caus.eat–**subj.you(causer)** –genmark.breakfast–oblmark.child(causee).*
*(**You**) Make the child eat./(**You**) Feed the child.*

Nagpaluto **si Maria** ng pagkain kay Juan.
*AF I caus.cooked–**subjmark.Maria(causer)** –genmark.food–oblmark.Juan (causee)*
***Maria** requested Juan to cook (for her).*

Magpapatayo ng bahay sa probinsya **ang lolo ko**.
*AF I caus.will build–genmark.house–oblmark.province–**subjmark.my grandfather (causer)***
***My grandfather** will have a house built in the province.*

7.7.2 **Actor-focus 2 causative mood** indicates that the subject (i.e., the *ang* phrase) of the sentence is the causee. The affix associated with this is /pa – in/, for verbs that are either *um-* or *ma-* verbs in the indicative mood, and /papag – in/, for verbs that are *mag-* verbs in the indicative mood. In a sentence, the causer may or may not be overtly expressed. When it is present, it is in the genitive case. Here are some examples of commonly used ***pa – in* verbs and *pag – in* verbs** and their aspectual forms. The choice between options I and II for the incompleted and contemplated forms is up to individual speakers, although some teachers of Filipino insist on option II as the proper way of conjugating the verbs.

AF-2 causative pa – in verbs

English	*AF* ***indicative***	*Neutral/* ***infinitive***	*Completed/* ***perfective***	*Incompleted/* ***progressive***	***Contemplated/ imperfective***
make … eat (feed)	kumain	pakainin	pinakain	pinapakain pinakakain	papakainin pakakainin
make … sleep	matulog	patulugin	pinatulog	pinapatulog pinatutulog	papatulugin patutulugin
let inside	Pumasok	papasukin	pinapasok	pinapapasok pinapapasok	papapasukin pinapapasok
send away	umalis	paalisin	pinaalis	pinapaalis pinaaalis	papaalisin paaalisin
let … sit	umupo	paupuin	pinaupo	pinapaupo pinauupo	papaupuin pauupuin

<u>Word formation rules:</u>

Infinitive: add the circumfix ***pa – in* to the root word**.
alis + ***pa – in*** = **pa**alis**in**

Completed: (1) add the prefix ***pa-* to the root word**
alis + ***pa-*** = **pa**alis

and (2) add the infix ***-in-*** before the first vowel of the stem.

-in- + paalis = p**in**aalis

Incompleted I: (1) **repeat the first CV** of the prefix ***pa-***,

pa- + rep1stCV = ***papa-***

(2) add the affix to the root,

papa- + alis = **papa**alis

and (3) add the infix ***-in-*** before the first vowel of the stem.

-in- + papaalis = p**in**apaalis

Incompleted II: (1) **repeat the first CV** of the root,

alis + rep1stCV = **aa**lis

(2) add the prefix ***pa-*** to the stem,

pa- + aalis = **pa**aalis

and (3) add the infix ***-in-*** before the first vowel of the second stem.

-in- + papaalis = p**in**aaalis

Contemplated: (1) **repeat the first CV** of the circumfix ***pa – in***

pa – in + rep1stCV = ***papa – in***

and (2) add the affix to the root.

papa – in + alis = **papa**alis**in**

Contemplated II: (1) **repeat the first CV** of the root

alis + rep1stCV = **aa**lis

and (2) add the circumfix ***pa – in*** to the stem.

pa – in + aalis = **pa**aalis**in**

AF-2 causative pag – in verbs

English	***AF indicative***	*Neutral/* ***infinitive***	*Completed/* ***perfective***	*Incompleted/* ***progressive***	***Contemplated/ imperfective***
make … clean	maglinis	paglinisin	pinaglinis	pinapaglinis pinaglilinis	papaglinisin paglilinisin
send to school	mag-aral	pag-aralin	pinag-aral	pinapag-aral pinag-aaral	papag-aralin pag-aaralin
request to cook	magluto	paglutuin	pinagluto	pinapagluto pinagluluto	papaglutuin paglulutuin
ask to bring	magdala	pagdalhin	pinagdala	pinapagdala pinagdadala	papagdalhin pagdadalhin
assign to collect	magkolekta	pagkolek-tahin	pinagkolekta	pinapagkolekta pinagkokolekta	papagkolektahin pagkokolektahin

Word formation rules:

Infinitive: add the circumfix ***pag – in*** **to the root word**.

linis + ***pag – in*** = **pag**linis**in**

Completed: (1) add the prefix ***pa-*** **to the root word**

linis + ***pag-*** = **pag**linis

and (2) add the infix ***-in-*** before the first vowel of the stem.

-in- + paglinis = p**in**aglinis

Incompleted I: (1) **repeat the first CV** of the prefix ***pag-***,

pag- + rep1stCV = **papag-**

(2) add the affix to the root,

papag- + linis = **papag**linis

and (3) add the infix ***-in-*** before the first vowel of the stem.

-in- + papaalis = p**in**apaglinis

Incompleted II: (1) **repeat the first CV** of the root,

linis + rep1stCV = **li**linis

(2) add the prefix ***pa-*** to the stem,

pag- + lilinis = **pag**lilinis

and (3) add the infix ***-in-*** before the first vowel of the second stem.

-in- + paglilinis = p**in**aglilinis

Contemplated: (1) **repeat the first CV** of the circumfix ***pag – in***

pag – in + rep1stCV = ***papa**g – in*

and (2) add the affix to the root.

papag – in + linis = **papag**linis**in**

Contemplated II: (1) **repeat the first CV** of the root

linis + rep1stCV = **li**linis

and (2) add the circumfix ***pag – in*** to the stem.

pag – in + lilinis = **pag**lilinis**in**

The following are examples of sentences with AF-2 causative mood verbs. The mood and focus affixes and the subject are in bold.

Pakain**in** mo ng almusal **ang bata**.
*AF2caus.eat–gen.you(causer)–genmark.breakfast–**subjmark.child(causee)**.*
*(You) Make **the child** eat./(You) Feed **the child**.*

Pinagluto ni Maria ng pagkain **si Juan**.
*AF2caus.cooked–genmark.Maria(causer)–genmark.food–**subjmark.Juan(causee)***
*Maria made **Juan** cook (for her).*

Pagtatayu**in** ng lolo ko ng bahay **ang tiyo ko**.
*AF2caus.will build–genmark.my grandfather(causer)–genmark.house–**subjmark.my uncle(causee)***
***My grandfather** will have my uncle build a house.*

7.7.3 **Object-focus causative mood** indicates that the subject (i.e., the *ang* phrase) of the sentence is the object on which the action of the verb is performed. The affix associated with this is /ipa-/. In a sentence, both causer and causee may or may not be overtly expressed. When they are present, the causer is in the genitive case, while the causee is in the oblique case. Generally, at least one actor is overtly expressed. Here are some examples of commonly used *ipa-* **verbs** and their aspectual forms. The choice between options I and II for the incompleted and contemplated forms is up to individual speakers, although some teachers of Filipino insist on option II as the proper way of conjugating the verbs.

OF causative ipa- verbs

English	***OF indicative***	*Neutral/ infinitive*	*Completed/ perfective*	*Incompleted/ progressive*	***Contemplated/ Imperfective***
make ... clean	linisin	ipalinis	ipinalinis	ipinapalinis ipinalilinis	ipapalinis ipalilinis
make ... eat (feed)	kainin	ipakain	ipinakain	ipinapakain ipinakakain	ipapakain ipakakain
request to put	ilagay	ipalagay	ipinalagay	ipinapalagay ipinalalagay	ipapalagay ipalalagay
ask to give	ibigay	ipabigay	ipinabigay	ipinapabigay ipinabibigay	ipapabigay ipabibigay
ask to do laundry	labhan	ipalaba	ipinalaba	ipinapalaba ipinalalaba	ipapalaba ipalalaba

Word formation rules:

Infinitive: add the prefix ***ipa-* to the root word.**

kain + ***ipa-*** = **ipa**kain

Completed: (1) add the prefix ***pa-* to the root word**

kain + ***ipa-*** = **ipa**kain

and (2) add the infix ***-in-*** after the first consonant of the stem.

-in- + ipakain = ip**in**akain

Incompleted I: (1) **repeat the second syllable** of the prefix ***ipa-***,

ipa- + rep1stCV = ***ipa*** *pa-*

(2) add the affix to the root,

ipapa- + kain = **ipapa**kain

and (3) add the infix ***-in-*** before the first vowel of the stem.

-in- + ipapakain = ip**in**apakain

Incompleted II: (1) **repeat the first CV** of the root,

kain + rep1stCV = **ka**kain

(2) add the prefix ***ipa-*** to the stem,

ipa- + kakain = **ipa**kakain

and (3) add the infix ***-in-*** before the first vowel of the second stem.

-in- + ipakakain = ip**in**akakain

Contemplated I: (1) **repeat the second syllable** of the prefix ***ipa-***

ipa- + rep1stCV = ***ipapa-***

and (2) add the affix to the root.

ipapa- + kain = **ipapa**kain

Contemplated II: (1) **repeat the first CV** of the root

kain + rep1stCV = **ka**kain

and (2) add the prefix ***ipa-*** to the stem.

ipa- + kakain = **ipa**kakain

Here are some examples of sentences with OF causative mood verbs. The mood and focus affixes and the subject are in bold.

Ipakain mo **ang tinapay** sa bata.
*OFcaus.eat–gen.you(causer)–**subjmark.bread** –oblmark.child(causee).*
*(You) Make the child eat **the bread.** /(You) Feed **the bread** to the child.*

Ipinaluto ni Maria **ang manok** kay Juan.
*OFcaus.cooked–genmark.Maria(causer)–**subjmark.chicken** –oblmark.Juan (causee)*
*Maria made Juan cook **the chicken** (for her).*

Ipapaayos ng nanay ko ang kotse sa talyer.
*OFcaus.will fix–genmark.my mother(causer)–**subjmark.car** –oblmark.shop (causee)*
*My mother will have **the car** fixed at the shop.*

7.7.4 **Location/direction-focus causative mood** indicates that the subject (i.e., the *ang* phrase) of the sentence is the location or direction of the action expressed by the verb. The affixes associated with this are / pa – an/, for direction-focus verbs, and /papag – an/ for location-focus verbs. In a sentence, both causer and causee may or may not be overtly expressed. When they are present, the causer is in the genitive case, while the causee is in the oblique case. Generally, at least one actor is overtly expressed. Here are some examples of commonly used ***pa – an*** **and** ***papag – an*** **verbs** and their aspectual forms. The choice between options I and II for the incompleted and contemplated forms is up to individual speakers, although some teachers of Filipino insist on option II as the proper way of conjugating the verbs.

LDF causative pa – an verbs

English	***LDF indicative***	*Neutral/* ***infinitive***	*Completed/* ***perfective***	*Incompleted/* ***progressive***	***Contemplated/ imperfective***
have ... checked	tingnan	patingnan	pinatingnan	pinapatingnan pinatitingnan	papatingnan patitingnan
have ... helped	tulungan	patulungan	pinatulungan	pinapatulungan pinatutulungan	papatulungan patutulungan
have ... called	tawagan	patawagan	pinatawagan	pinapatawagan pinatatawagan	papatawagan patatawagan
have ... given	bigyan	pabigyan	pinabigyan	pinapabigyan pinabibigyan	papabigyan pabibigyan
have ... written to	sulatan	pasulatan	pinasulatan	pinapasulatan pinasusulatan	papasulatan pasusulatan

Word formation rules:

Infinitive: add the circumfix ***pa – an* to the root word**.

tawag + ***pa – an*** = **pa**tawag**an**

Completed: (1) add the circumfix ***pa – an* to the root word**

tawag + ***pa – an*** = **pa**tawag**an**

and (2) add the infix ***-in-*** before the first vowel of the stem.

-in- + patawagan = p**in**atawagan

Incompleted I: (1) **repeat the first CV** of the circumfix ***pa – an***,

pa – an + rep1stCV = ***pa****pa – an*

(2) add the affix to the root,

papa – an + tawag = **papa**tawag**an**

and (3) add the infix ***-in-*** before the first vowel of the stem.

-in- + papatawagan = p**in**apatawagan

Incompleted II: (1) **repeat the first CV** of the root,

tawag + rep1stCV = **ta**tawag

(2) add the circumfix ***pa – an*** to the stem,

pa – an + tatawag = **pa**tatawag**an**

and (3) add the infix ***-in-*** before the first vowel of the second stem.

-in- + papatawagan = p**in**apatawagan

Contemplated: (1) **repeat the first CV** of the circumfix ***pa – in***

pa – in + rep1stCV = ***papa – in***

and (2) add the affix to the root.

papa – in + alis = **papa**alis**in**

Contemplated II: (1) **repeat the first CV** of the root

tawag + rep1stCV = **ta**tawag

and (2) add the circumfix ***pa – an*** to the stem.

pa – an + tatawag = **pa**tatawag**an**

LDF causative papag – an verbs

English	***LDF indicative***	*Neutral/* ***infinitive***	*Completed/* ***perfective***	*Incompleted/* ***progressive***	***Contem-plated/ imperfective***
have … written on	pagsulatan	papagsu-latan	pinapagsu-latan	pinapapagsulatan pinapagsusulatan	papapagsulatan papagsusulatan
have … cooked in	paglutuan	papaglu-tuan	pinapaglutuan	pinapapaglutuan pinapaglulutuan	papapaglutuan papaglulutuan
have … danced on	pagsayawan	papagsay-awan	pinapagsay-awan	pinapapagsayawan pinapagsasayawan	papapagsayawan papagsasayawan
have … given	pagbigyan	papag-bigyan	pinapag-bigyan	pinapapagbigyan pinapagbibigyan	papapagbigyan papagbibigyan
have … swum in	paglanguyan	papaglan-guyan	pinapaglan-guyan	pinapapaglanguyan pinapaglalanguyan	papapaglanguyan papaglalanguyan

Word formation rules:

Infinitive: add the circumfix ***papag – an* to the root word**.

sulat + ***papag – an*** = **papag**sulat**an**

Completed: add the circumfix ***papag – an* to the root word**

sulat + ***papag – an*** = **papag**sulat**an**

and (2) add the infix ***-in-*** before the first vowel of the stem.

-in- + patawagan = p**in**apagsulatan

Incompleted I: (1) **repeat the first CV** of the circumfix ***papag – an***,

papag – an + rep1stCV = ***pa**papag – an*

(2) add the affix to the root,

papapag – an + sulat = **papapag**sulat**an**

and (3) add the infix ***-in-*** before the first vowel of the stem.

-in- + papatawagan = p**in**apapagsulatan

Incompleted II: (1) **repeat the first CV** of the root,

sulat + rep1stCV = **su**sulat

(2) add the circumfix ***papag – an*** to the stem,

papag – an + susulat = **papag**susulat**an**

and (3) add the infix ***-in-*** before the first vowel of the second stem.

-in- + papagsusulatan = p**in**apagsusulatan

Contemplated I: (1) **repeat the first CV** of the circumfix ***papag – an***

papag – an + rep1stCV = ***pa**papag – an*

and (2) add the affix to the root.

papapag – an + sulat = **papapag**sulat**an**

Contemplated II: (1) **repeat the first CV** of the root

sulat + rep1stCV = **su**sulat

and (2) add the circumfix ***papag – an*** to the stem.

papag – an + susulat = **papag**susulat**an**

Here are some examples of sentences with LDF causative mood verbs. The mood and focus affixes and the subject are in bold.

Palagy**an** mo ng bulaklak **ang mesa** sa kapatid mo.
*LDFcaus.put–gen.you(causer)–genmark.flower–**subjmark.table** –oblmark.your sibling(causee).*
*(You) Have your sibling put flowers **on the table**.*

Pinatawag**an** ng prinsipal **ang mga estudyante**.
*LDFcaus.called–genmark.principal(causer)–**subjmark.students***
*The principal ordered that calls be made **to the students**.*

Papaglutu**an** mo ng manok kay Ben **ang kaserolang iyan**.
*OFcaus.cooked–gen.you(causer)–genmark.chicken–oblmark.Ben(causee)–**subjmark.that pot***
*(You) Have Ben cook chicken **in that pot**.*

Pinapaglangguyan nila sa bisita **ang bagong languyan.**
*LDFcaus.swam–gen.they(causer)–oblmark.guest(causee)–**subjmark.new swimming pool***
*They made the guest swim **in the new swimming pool.***

7.7.5 **Benefactive-focus causative mood** indicates that the subject (i.e., the *ang* phrase) of the sentence is the beneficiary of the action expressed by the verb. The affix associated with this is /ipagpa-/. In a sentence, both causer and causee may or may not be overtly expressed, although usually at least one actor is overtly expressed. When they are present, the causer is in the genitive case, while the causee is in the oblique case. Here are some examples of commonly used ***ipagpa-* verbs** and their aspectual forms.

BF causative ipagpa- verbs

English	*BF indicative*	*Neutral/ infinitive*	*Completed/ perfective*	*Incompleted/ progressive*	***Contemplated/ imperfective***
have ... made for	igawa	ipagpagawa	ipinagpagawa	ipinagpapagawa	ipagpapagawa
have ... bought for	ibili	ipagpabili	ipinagpabili	ipinagpapabili	ipagpapabili
have ... cooked for	ipagluto	ipagpaluto	ipinagpaluto	ipinagpapaluto	ipagpapaluto
have ... built for	ipagtayo	ipagpatayo	ipinagpatayo	ipinagpapatayo	ipagpapatayo
have ... cleaned for	ipaglinis	ipagpalinis	ipinagpalinis	ipinagpapalinis	ipagpapalinis

Word formation rules:

Infinitive: add the prefix ***ipagpa-* to the root word.**
gawa + ***ipagpa-*** = **ipagpa**gawa
Completed: add the prefix ***ipagpa-* to the root word**
gawa + ***ipagpa-*** = **ipagpa**gawa
and (2) add the infix ***-in-*** after the first consonant of the stem.
-in- + ipagpagawa = ip**in**agpagawa
Incompleted: (1) **repeat the third syllable** of the prefix ***ipagpa-***,
ipagpa- + rep3rdCV = ipagpa**pa**-
(2) add the affix to the root,
ipagpapa- + gawa = **ipagpapa**gawa
and (3) add the infix ***-in-*** before the first vowel of the stem.
-in- + ipagpapagawa = ip**in**agpapagawa
Contemplated: (1) **repeat the third syllable** of the prefix ***ipagpa-***
ipagpa- + rep3rdCV = *ipagpa**pa**-*
and (2) add the affix to the root.
ipagpapa- + gawa = **ipagpapa**gawa

Here are some examples of sentences with BF causative mood verbs. The mood and focus affixes and the subject are in bold.

Ipagpabili mo ng prutas sa kasambahay **ang lola**.
BFcaus.buy–gen.you(causer)–genmark.fruits–oblmark.maid(causee)– ***subjmark.grandmother***
(You) Have the maid buy fruits ***for grandmother.***

Ipinagpatayo niya ng bahay **ang mga magulang niya**.
*BFcaus.built–gen.he/she.genmark.house–****subjmark.his/her parents***
He/she had a house built ***for her parents.***

Ipagpapaluto ni Mara ng pansit **si Bob**.
*BFcaus.willcook–genmark.Mara(causer)–genmark.noodles–****subjmark.Bob***
Mara will have noodles cooked (by someone else) ***for Bob.***

7.7.6 **Instrumental-focus causative mood** indicates that the subject (i.e., the *ang* phrase) of the sentence is the instrument used to perform the action expressed by the verb. The affix associated with this is /ipapang-/. In a sentence, both causer and causee may or may not be overtly expressed, although usually at least one actor is overtly present. When they are present, the causer is in the genitive case, while the causee is in the oblique case. Here are some examples of commonly used *ipapang-* verbs and their aspectual forms.

IF causative ipapang- verbs

English	***IF indicative***	*Neutral/* ***infinitive***	*Completed/* ***perfective***	*Incompleted/* ***progressive***	***Contemplated/ imperfective***
have ... use in cooking	ipanluto	ipapanluto	ipinapanluto	ipinapapanluto	ipapapanluto
have ... use at home	ipambahay	ipapamba-hay	ipinapamba-hay	ipinapapam-bahay	ipapapambahay
have ... use in the office	ipang-opisina	ipapang-opisina	ipinapang-opisina	ipinapapang-opisina	ipapapang-opisina
have ... use in cleaning	ipanlinis	ipapanlinis	ipinapanlinis	ipinapapanlinis	ipapapanlinis
have ... use for cutting	ipanggupit	ipapang-gupit	ipinapang-gupit	ipinapapang-gupit	ipapapanggupit

Word formation rules:

Infinitive: add the prefix ***ipapang-* to the root word**.
gawa + ***ipapang-*** = **ipapang**gawa
Completed: add the prefix ***ipapang-* to the root word**
gawa + ***ipapang-*** = **ipapang**gawa

and (2) add the infix ***-in-*** after the first consonant of the stem.

-in- + ipagpagawa = ip**in**apanggawa

Incompleted: (1) **repeat the second syllable** of the prefix **ipapang-**,

ipapang- + rep2ndCV = *i**pa** papang-*

(2) add the affix to the root,

ipapapang- + gawa = **ipapapang**gawa

and (3) add the infix ***-in-*** before the first vowel of the stem.

-in- + ipapapanggawa = ip**in**apapanggawa

Contemplated: (1) **repeat the second syllable** of the prefix ***ipapang-***

ipapang- + rep2ndCV = *i**pa** papang-*

and (2) add the affix to the root.

ipapapang- + gawa = **ipapapang**gawa

Here are some examples of sentences with IF causative mood verbs. The mood and focus affixes and the subject are in bold.

Ipapambili mo ng meryenda sa kasambahay **ang perang ito**.
*IFcaus.buy–gen.you(causer)–genmark.snack–oblmark.maid(causee)–**subjmark.this money***
*(You) Have the maid buy dinner **with this money**.*

Ipinapapanlinis niya sa akin ng bakuran **ang walis na iyan**.
*IFcaus.clean–gen.he/she(causer).obl.I(causee)–genmark.yard–**subjmark. that broom***
*He/she makes me clean the yard **with that broom**.*

Ipapapanghugas ni Rita ng mga plato **ang sabon**.
*IFcaus.willwash–genmark.Rita(causer)–genmark.dishes–**subjmark.soap***
*Rita will (have someone) wash the dishes **with the soap**.*

The last three verbal mood forms to be covered in this section are **limited derived forms**. These appear to encode meanings that combine at least two verbal moods. These all inflect for AF.

7.8 *Magka-* **verbs** are denominal forms (i.e., verbs **derived from nouns**) that encode the idea that the *ang* phrase actor acquired the noun expressed by the root with some help or influence from outside factors in precipitating the event, such as luck or (in)opportune timing. Refer to the following verb list and similar verb forms discussed in earlier sections for word formation rules. The following are commonly used *magka-* verbs in all their aspectual forms and some illustrative sentences.

Denominal magka- verbs meaning to acquire X					
English	***Source noun***	*Neutral/* ***infinitive***	*Completed/* ***perfective***	*Incompleted/* ***progressive***	***Contemplated/ imperfective***
have a child	anak	magkaanak	nagkaanak	Nagkakaanak	magkakaanak
acquire money	pera	magkapera	nagkapera	Nagkakapera	magkakapera
acquire a house	bahay	magkaba-hay	nagkabahay	Nagkakabahay	magkakabahay
have a scar	peklat	magkape-klat	nagkapeklat	Nagkakapeklat	magkakapeklat
have a spouse	asawa	magkaa-sawa	nagkaasawa	Nagkakaasawa	magkakaasawa
have a job or *work*	trabaho	magkatra-baho	nagkatrabaho	nagkakatrabaho	magkakatrabaho
acquire a car	kotse	magkako-tse	nagkakotse	Nagkakakotse	magkakakotse
have a cold	sipon	magka-sipon	nagkasipon	Nagkakasipon	magkakasipon

Examples:

Nagkaanak ng kambal **sina Mina at Bong**.
Had *child–genmark.twins–**subjmark.Mina and Bong***
Mina and Bong *had twins.*

Magkakatrabaho na **ang kuya ko** sa susunod na buwan.
Will get *a job–finally–**subjmark.my older brother** –next month*
My older brother *will finally get a job next month.*

Nagkakasipon ako tuwing tag-ulan.
Get a *cold–**subj.I** –every rainy season*
I *get a cold every rainy season.*

7.9 *Magpaka-* **verbs** comprise a small set of de-adjectival forms (i.e., verbs **derived from adjectives**). They encode the meaning that the *ang* phrase on his/her/their own volition chooses to engage in behavior resulting in the condition expressed by the root word. Refer to the following verb list and similar verb forms discussed in earlier sections for word formation rules. The following are commonly used *magpaka-* verbs in all their aspectual forms and some illustrative sentences.

De-adjectival magpaka- verbs meaning to engage in behavior resulting in X					
English	***Source adjective***	*Neutral/* ***infinitive***	*Completed/* ***perfective***	*Incompleted/* ***progressive***	***Contemplated/ imperfective***
be drunk	lasing	magpakalas-ing	nagpakalasing	nagpapakalas-ing	magpapakalasing
be true	totoo	magpak-atotoo	nagpakatotoo	nagpapak-atotoo	magpapakatotoo
be happy	saya	magpaka-saya	nagpakasaya	nagpapakasaya	magpapakasaya
be stupid	tanga	magpaka-tanga	nagpakatanga	nagpapaka-tanga	magpapakatanga
be nice	bait	magpakabait	nagpakabait	nagpapakabait	magpapakabait
be crazy	baliw	magpakab-aliw	nagpakabaliw	nagpapakab-aliw	magpapakabaliw
be lazy	tamad	magpakata-mad	nagpakatamad	nagpapakata-mad	magpapakatamad
be skilled	husay	magpaka-husay	nagpakahusay	nagpapaka-husay	magpapakahusay
be martyr-like	martir	magpaka-martir	nagpakamartir	nagpapaka-martir	magpapakamartir
be deador kill one's self	matay	magpaka-matay	nagpakamatay	nagpapaka-matay	magpapakamatay

<u>Examples:</u>

> **Magpa**kabait kayo.
> ***Be*** *nice*–***subj.you all***
> ***You all*** be nice.
>
> **Nagpaka**lasing na naman ang tiyo ko kahapon.
> ***Got*** *drunk–again*–***subjmark.my uncle*** *yesterday*
> ***My uncle*** *got drunk again yesterday.*
>
> **Magpapaka** saya kami sa bakasyon namin sa probinsya.
> ***Will have*** *fun*–***subj.we*** *–oblmark.our vacation–oblmark.province*
> ***We will*** *have fun on our vacation in the province.*

7.10 *Mapa-* **verbs** comprise a small set of de-verbal forms (i.e., verbs **derived from other verbs**). These words encode the meaning that the *ang* phrase, with volition, performed the action expressed by the root word due to circumstances that forced, persuaded, induced, or put pressure on him/her/them to do it. Refer to the following verb list and similar verb forms discussed in earlier sections for word formation rules. The following are commonly used *mapa-* verbs in all their aspectual forms and some illustrative sentences.

De-verbal *mapa-* verbs meaning *to be induced/forced into doing X*					
English	***Source verb***	*Neutral/* ***infinitive***	*Completed/* ***perfective***	*Incompleted/* ***progressive***	***Contemplated/ imperfective***
forced to run	takbo	mapatakbo	napatakbo	Napapatakbo	mapapatakbo
forced to jump	lundag	mapalun-dag	napalundag	Napapalundag	mapapalundag
induced to laughter	tawa	mapatawa	napatawa	Napapatawa	mapapatawa
induced to sing	kanta	mapakanta	napakanta	Napapakanta	mapapakanta
induced to scream	sigaw	mapasigaw	napasigaw	Napapasigaw	mapapasigaw
forced to look up	tingala	mapatin-gala	napatingala	Napapatingala	mapapatingala
forced to cook	luto	mapaluto	napaluto	Napapaluto	mapapaluto
forced to drive	drayb	mapadrayb	napadrayb	Napapadrayb	napapadrayb
forced to fight	laban	mapalaban	napalaban	Napapalaban	mapapalaban
induced to cough	ubo	mapaubo	napaubo	Napapaubo	mapapaubo

Chapter 8

Pseudo-verbs and other verb forms

This chapter will discuss verb forms that generally do not inflect for aspect and, except in very rare cases, have only one form.

8.1 **Pseudo-verbs** function as helping verbs that indicate modality. Hence, they may sometimes also be referred to as modal verbs, expressing either desire, obligation, want, or need. The sentence in which a pseudo-verb occurs must have a main verb in the infinitive form. In addition, a linker must come immediately before the main verb. The linker is usually dropped when the main verb follows a word that ends in a consonant. When enclitics and pronouns occur in a sentence with pseudo-verbs, they have to immediately follow the pseudo-verb, except when a pronoun is used to express possession. In the examples provided, the pseudo-verb, linker, and main verb will be in bold. A linker enclosed in parenthesis is often dropped, especially in spoken Filipino.

8.1.1 **Dapat** indicates obligation. It is roughly equivalent to the English modal verb *must*. Here are some examples.

Dapat ako**ng** **pumunta** sa opisina bukas.
Must–subj.I.lnk–to go–oblmark.office–tomorrow
I ***must go*** *to the office tomorrow.*

Dapat (na) linisin ng lalaki ang kotse niya.
Must–lnk–to clean–genmark.man–subjmark.his car
The man ***must clean*** *his car.*

8.1.2 **Puwede** indicates ability or possibility. It is roughly equivalent to the English modal verb *can*. **Maaari** is a synonym of /puwede/, but it is deemed more formal. Here are some examples.

Puwede siya**ng** **tumugtog** ng gitara.
Can–subj.he/she.lnk–to play–oblmark.guitar
He ***can play*** *the guitar.*

DOI: 10.4324/9781315739427-9

Puwedeng dalhin ng kaibigan ko ang kompyuter niya.
Can.lnk–to bring–genmark.my friend–subjmark.his/her computer
My friend ***can bring*** *his/her computer.*

8.1.3 **Bawal** indicates restriction. It translates into English as *not allowed* or *forbidden*. Here are some examples.

Bawal kayo**ng pumarada** sa harap ng gusali.
Not allowed–subj.youPl.lnk–to park–oblmark.front–genmark.building
You ***are not allowed to park*** *in front of the building.*

Bawal (na) kumain ang mga bisita sa museyo.
Forbidden–(lnk)–to eat–subjmark.visitors–oblmark.museum
Visitors are ***forbidden to eat*** *at the museum.*

The pseudo-verbs /dapat/, /puwede/ or /maaari/, and /bawal/ require an infinitive form main verb when it functions as a helping verb. This main verb determines the case marking on the noun phrases (NPs) in the sentence. For example, if the main verb is actor focus (AF), the actor NP must have a nominative case marking, and if the main verb is object focus (OF), the actor NP must have genitive case marking.

The pseudo-verbs /kailangan/, /gusto/ or /nais/, and /bawal/ also require an infinitive main verb form. However, unlike the previous three helping verbs, these auxiliary verbs trigger the obligatory use of genitive case marking on the actor NP, regardless of the focus form of the main verb.

8.1.4 **Kailangan** indicates need. It translates into English as *should* or *need*. Here are some examples.

Kailangan mo**ng magpatingin** sa doktor.
Should–gen.youSg.lnk–to get checked–oblmark.doctor
You ***should consult*** *a doctor.*

Kailangan(g) ibigay ni Ben ang pera sa kapatid niya.
Need.(lnk)–to give–genmark.Ben–subjmark.money–oblmark.his sibling
Ben ***needs to give*** *the money to his brother/sister.*

8.1.5 **Gusto** indicates desire, wanting, or liking. It translates into English as *like* or *want*. **Nais** is a synonym of /gusto/, but it is deemed more formal. Here are some examples.

Gusto namin**g manood** ng sine mamaya.
Want–gen.we.lnk–to watch–genmark.movie–later
We ***want to watch*** *a movie later.*

Gustong kumuha ng mga turista ng mga litrato ng bundok.
Like.lnk–to take–genmark.tourists–genmark.pictures–genmark.mountain
*Tourists **like to take** pictures of the mountain.*

8.1.6 **Ayaw** indicates dislike, not wanting, or liking. It translates into English as *not like* or *not want*. Here are some examples.

Ayaw naming **manood** ng sine mamaya.
Not want–gen.we.lnk–to watch–genmark.movie–later
*We **do not want to watch** a movie later.*

Ayaw (na) umakyat ng mga turista sa bundok kapag tag-ulan.
Not like–(lnk)–to climb–genmark.tourists–oblmark.mountain–when–rainy season
*Tourists **do not like to climb** the mountain during rainy season.*

Some pseudo-verbs can take focus affixes and function as main verbs. When they do, they can also be inflected for aspect. Some examples are shown here. (For inflection, see chapter on verbs.)

AF	***OF***	***Location–direction focus (LDF)***
umayaw *change one's mind after initially agreeing*	gustuhin *want*	ayawan *reject*
magkagusto *develop a liking*	kailanganin *need*	pagbawalan *forbid*
	ipagbawal *to forbid*	magustuhan *find to one's liking*

8.1.7 Other verbs that function like pseudo-verbs are the following: **alam** *know* (*something*), **marunong** *be knowledgeable* (*about something*), and **mahilig** *be fond* (*of doing something*). /Alam/ has the same sentence structure as /gusto, ayaw, kailangan/ in that the actor or doer of the action is always a *ng* phrase. /Marunong/ and /mahilig/ always have the actor or doer as the *ang* phrase. Here are some examples.

Alam naming **gawin** ang parol.
Know–gen.we.lnk–to make–subjmark.Christmas lantern
*We **know how to make** a Christmas lantern.*

Marunong silang **magsaka** at **mangisda**.
Know–sub.they.lnk–to farm–and–to fish
*They **know how** to farm and to fish.*

Mahilig (na) magtanim ng mga bulaklak ang tiya ko.
Fond of–(lnk)–to plant–genmark.flowers–subjmark.my aunt
*My aunt **is fond of** planting flowers (in the garden).*

Pseudo-verbs are magnets for enclitics and pronouns. That is, when occurring in the same clause with enclitics and/or GEN and NOM pronouns, pseudo-verbs pull or attract these clitic forms so that a strict word ordering rule is established. In the competition for the position immediately following the pseudo-verb, the rule is enclitics + GEN pronoun + NOM pronoun, except with the pronouns /ko/, /mo/, and /ka/, which are stronger and precede enclitic adverbs. In the following examples, this strict word order in sentences containing pseudo-verbs, enclitics, and pronouns is demonstrated.

Pumasok sa kuwarto si Mario.
Mario went inside the room.

Pumasok **daw** sa kuwarto si Mario.
***I heard** that Mario went inside the room.*

Pumasok **daw siya** sa kuwarto.
***I heard** that **he** went inside the room.*

Pumasok **ka raw** sa kuwarto.
***They say** that **you** (should) go inside the room.*

<u>**Puwede**</u> **ka raw** pumasok sa kuwarto.
***They say** that **you** <u>**can**</u> go inside the room.*

Dinala ni Amy ang kompyuter sa labas.
Amy brought the computer outside.

Dinala **niya ito** sa labas.
***She** brought **it** outside.*

Dinala **pala niya ito** sa labas.
***I am surprised to hear** that **she** brought **it** outside.*

Dinala **mo pala ito** sa labas.
***I am surprised to hear** that **you** brought **it** outside.*

Kailangan mo pala itong dalhin sa labas.
***I am surprised to hear** that **you need to** bring **it** outside.*

8.2 *Paki-* **verbs** are used to express request or ask a favor. The meaning of the affix /paki-/ is very similar to the word *please* in English. The structure of the sentence in which this verb occurs is non-AF. The verb is formed by simply attaching the prefix /paki-/ to a root word of an OF verb or a verb stem of LDF verbs (see chapter on verbs for focus inflection). The object may be marked by **ang** when it is definite, or **ng** when it is indefinite. Here are some examples.

Pakikuha mo **ng pagkain** sa kusina.
***OFPlease.get**–gen.youSg–**genmark.food** –oblmark.kitchen*
(*Will you*) ***Please get food** from the kitchen.*

Pakilagay mo **ang bag mo** sa mesa.
OFPlease.put–*gen.youSg*–***subjmark.your bag*** –*oblmark.table*
(Would you) ***Please put your bag*** *on the table.*

Pakilagyan mo ng bulaklak **ang plorera**.
LDFPlease.put–*gen.youSg*–*genmark.flower*–***subjmark.flower vase***
(Would you) ***Please put*** *flowers* ***in the vase****.*

8.3 Verbs of sense and emotion

A small set of stative verbs that indicate feelings and sensation behave differently from other verb forms, although they may also inflect for aspect, focus, and mood like other verbs. Their bare root or uninflected forms are often used to express current or present state or condition. These bare forms can also function as helping verbs co-occurring with infinitive forms of other verbs. Some frequently used forms are provided here with their AF and OF forms.

magmahal (AF)/mahalin (OF) *to love*
magnais (AF)/naisin (OF) *to want*
magnasa (AF)/nasain (OF) *to desire*
mangarap (AF)/pangarapin (OF) *to dream of* or *to fantasize about*
gustuhin (OF) *to like/to want*
ayawan (I/DF) *to dislike/to reject*

Mahal ka namin.
We ***love*** *you.*

Ako ang **nagmamahal** sa iyo.
I am the one who ***loves*** *you.*

Mamahalin kita magpakailanman.
I will love *you forever.*

Pangarap kong maglakbay sa buong mundo.
I ***dream*** *of traveling around the world.*

Inayawan nila ang pagkaing dinala ko sa salusalo.
They ***disliked*** *the food that I brought to the celebration.*

Gustuhin ko mang mamili, hindi puwede dahil wala akong pera.
Even if I ***wanted*** *to go shopping, I could not because I have no money.*

8.4 Verbs of perception and cognition

Another set of stative verbs that behave differently are associated with states of perceiving or recognizing an object or event. Many of these verbs are used almost exclusively as OF forms, and the object of the sentence can be an *ang* marked noun or an embedded complement clause.

The following chart lists some of the most frequently used perception–cognition verbs and some examples of their use in sentences.

OF perception–cognition verbs	Completed	Incompleted	Contemplated
maisip *think of*	naisip	naiisip	maiisip
maalala *remember*	naalala	naaalala	maaalala
makita see	nakita	nakikita	makikita
marinig *hear*	narinig	naririnig	maririnig
mapansin *notice*	napansin	napapansin	mapapasin
madiskubre *find out* or *discover*	nadiskubre	nadidiskubre	madidiskubre
matuklasan *find out* or *discover*	natuklasan	natutuklasan	matutuklasan
maramdaman *feel*	naramdaman	nararamdaman	mararamdaman
mabalitaan *hear about*	nabalitaan	nababalitaan	mababalitaan
matutunan *learn*	natutunan	natututunan	matututunan
makalimutan *forget*	nakalimutan	nakakalimutan	makakalimutan
malaman *learn* or *find out*	nalaman	nalalaman (alam)	malalaman
maintindihan *understand*	naintindihan	naiintindihan	maiintindihan
mapagtanto *realize*	napagtanto	napapagtanto	mapapagtanto

Naalala ko ang mga kuwento ng aking lola.
*I **remember** my grandmother's stories.*

Naalala ko na may bisitang darating bukas.
*I (just) **remembered** that we have a guest coming tomorrow.*

Naiisip ko ang mga problema sa aming bayan tuwing nagbabasa ako ng balita.
*I **think** about the problems in our town every time I watch the news.*

Naiisip ko kung bakit marami ang mga OFW na nawalan ng trabaho.
*I **think** about why many OFWs lost their jobs.*

Matututunan ng mga estudyante ang iba't-ibang paraan ng katutubong paghahabi.
*The students **will learn** different techniques of traditional weaving.*

Matututunan din nila kung paano gawin ang mga bagong disenyo.
*They **will** also **learn** how to make new designs.*

Nalaman ng kaklase ni Minda ang kanyang sikreto.
*Minda's classmate **found out** her secret.*

Nalaman ng kaklase ni Minda na aalis na siya sa kanyang trabaho.
*Minda's classmate **learned** that she is leaving her job very soon.*

Yet another set of perception–cognition verbs are expressed as syntactically intransitive AF forms. Some take the infix /-um/, others take the prefix /mag-/, and some the prefix /mang-/. Because this AF verb form is syntactically intransitive, the clause in which it occurs cannot have a GEN-marked object, but instead have an OBL-marked NP or an embedded clause object. As such, these forms have locative/directional-focus (L/DF) form counterparts. The following chart provides some of the more frequently used verbs of this type and a few illustrative sentences.

AF perception–cognition verbs	***Completed***	***Incompleted***	***Contemplated***
maniwala (AF) paniwalaan (LF) *believe*	naniwala pinaniwalaan	naniniwala pinaniniwalaan	maniniwala paniniwalaan
magtiwala (AF) pagkatiwalaan (LF) *trust*	nagtiwala pinagkatiwalaan	nagtitiwala pinagkakatiwalaan	magtitiwala pagkakatiwalaan
magduda (AF) pagdudahan (LF) *doubt*	nagduda pinagdudahan	nagdududa pinagdududahan	magdududa pagdududahan
mainggit (AF) kainggitan (LF) *jealous*	nainggit kinainggitan	naiinggit kinaiinggitan	maiinggit kaiinggitan
sumang-ayon (AF) sang-ayunan (LF) *agree to or with*	sumang-ayon sinang-ayunan	sumasang-ayon sinasang-ayunan	sasang-ayon sasang-ayunan
tumutol (AF) tutulan (LF) *object to*	tumutol tinutulan	tumututol tinututulan	tututol tututulan
magmunimuni (AF) pagmunimunihan (LF) *mull over*	nagmunimuni pinagmunimunihan	nagmumunimuni pinagmumunimunihan	magmumunimuni pagmumunimunihan
mag-isip (AF) pag-isipan (LF) *consider*	nag-isip pinag-isipan	nag-iisip pinag-iisipan	mag-iisip pag-iisipan

maawa (AF)	naawa	naaawa	maaawa
kaawaan (LF)	kinaawaan	kinaaawaan	kaaawaan
take pity on			
magsisi (AF)	nagsisi	nagsisisi	magsisisi
pagsisihan (LF)	pinagsisihan	pinagsisisihan	pagsisisihan
regret			

Naniniwala siya sa himala.
*He/she **believes in** miracles.*

Naniniwala siya na magbabago rin ang kanyang asawa.
*He/she **believes that** his/her spouse will eventually change.*

Pinaniniwalaan niya ang mga kuwentong-multo.
*He/she **believes in** ghost stories.*

Sumasang-ayon si Lina sa iyong pananaw.
*Lina **agrees with** your opinion.*

Sumasang-ayon kami na dapat magkaroon ng batas ng dibosryo sa Pilipinas.
*We **agree that** the Philippines should have a divorce law.*

Sinasang-ayunan ng maraming tao ang panukalang batas na ito.
*Many people **agree with** this proposed bill.*

8.5 Verbs of becoming, existing, and possession

There is a small set of stative verbs that indicate existence/non-existence, becoming, accompanying, having, or possessing an object or a quality. These verbs behave differently than canonical verb forms, as illustrated by the following examples.

AF existential verbs	***Completed***	***Incompleted***	***Contemplated***
magkaroon *to have or acquire*	nagkaroon	nagkakaroon	magkakaroon
maging *to become*	naging	nagiging	magiging
mawalan *to experience loss*	nawalan	nawawalan	mawawalan
magmukhang-N/adj. *to look like N/adj.*	nagmukhang-X	nagmumukhang-X	magmumukhang-X
magmay-ari *to own*	nagmay-ari	nagmamay-ari	magmamay-ari

magkasama *be together*	nagkasama	nagkakasama	magkakasama

Nagkaroon ng magandang buhay sa siyudad ang kanyang kapatid.
*His/her sibling **had** a good life in the city.*

Nagiging mainit na ang panahon ngayon.
*The weather is **becoming** warmer now.*

Mawawalan tayo ng kuryente bukas dahil sa bagyo.
*We are **going to lose electricity** tomorrow due to the hurricane.*

8.6 Impersonal verbs

There is a small class of verbs in Filipino, mostly associated with weather-related events, called impersonal verbs. The infix /-um/ is attached to root words that are commonly nouns referring to naturally occurring weather events. The most frequently used forms are listed in the following chart. These verbs can often stand on their own as full sentences.

Impersonal verbs	***Completed***	***Incompleted***	***Contemplated***
umulan *to rain*	umulan	umuulan	uulan
bumagyo *to have a storm*	bumagyo	bumabagyo	babagyo
lumindol *have an earthquake*	lumindol	lumilindol	lilindol
kumidlat *have lightning*	kumidlat	kumikidlat	kikidlat
kumulog *have thunder*	kumulog	kumukulog	kukulog
bumaha *have a flood*	bumaha	bumabaha	babaha
umaraw *be sunny*	umaraw	Umaaraw	aaraw
humangin *be windy* or *breezy*	humangin	humahangin	hahangin
gumabi *turn nighttime*	gumabi	gumagabi	gagabi
dumilim *turn dark*	dumilim	dumidilim	didilim
lumiwanag *turn bright*	lumiwanag	lumiliwanag	liliwanag

guminaw *get cold*	guminaw	gumiginaw	giginaw
uminit *get warm*	uminit	Umiinit	iinit

Umuulan.
(It is) raining.

Bumabagyo sa aming probinsya ngayon.
***There is a hurricane** in our province currently.*

Ayon sa balita, **aaraw** na raw bukas.
*According to the news, **it will** finally **be sunny** tomorrow.*

Umuwi na kayo dahil **gumagabi** na.
*You better go home now because **it is getting late**.*

Lumiliwanag na.
*It is **getting bright** now.*

8.7 **Intermittent action verbs** are AF forms that indicate frequent action expressed by the root word. The verb is formed by attaching the prefix /pa-/ to a reduplicated verb root (i.e., ***pa-* + reduplication of the root word**). Here are some examples.

Palakad-lakad si Pedro sa *mall* habang naghihintay sa kaibigan niya.
***Walking about**–subjmark.Pedro–oblmark.mall–while–waiting–oblmark.his friend*
*Pedro **walked about** while waiting for his friend at the mall.*

Patingin-tingin ang bata sa mga bisita sa salusalo.
***Cast glances**–subjmark.child–oblmark.guests–oblmark.party*
*The child **cast glances** at the guests at the party.*

Palaboy-laboy sa kalye ang mga estudyante kahapon.
***Loiter**–oblmark.street–subjmark.students–yesterday*
*The students **were loitering** on the streets.*

8.8 **Nearly started action verbs** are AF forms that indicate nearly started action expressed by the root word. In a sentence, it is often followed by the adverbial enclitic **na** *already*. The verb is formed by attaching the prefix /pa-/ or /papa-/ to a verb root (i.e., **(*pa*)*pa-* + root word**). Here are some examples.

Papaalis na ako ngayon.
***About to leave**–already.subj.I–now*
*I am **about to leave** now.*

Papatulog na kami nang dumating ang mga pulis.
***About to sleep**–already–subjmark.we–when–came–subjmark.police*
*We were **about to sleep** when the police came.*

Papalabas na si Pedro nang umulan.
***About to go out**–already–subjmark.Pedro–when–rained*
*Pedro was **about to go out** when it rained.*

8.9 **Upon completion of action verbs** are non-AF forms that express the meaning *immediately after performing the action* expressed by the verb root. When overtly expressed in a sentence, the actor or doer of the action is in the genitive case. The verb is formed by attaching the prefix /pagka-/ to a verb root (i.e., ***pagka-*** **+ root word**). Here are some examples.

Pagkaluto ni Maria, dumating ang kaibigan niya.
***Upon finishing cooking**–genmark.Maria–arrived–subjmark.her friend*
***After** Maria **finished cooking**, her friend arrived.*

Pagkakain nila, nanood sila ng sine.
***Soon after eating**–gen.they–watched–subjmark.they–genmark.movie*
***(Soon) after eating**, they watched a movie.*

Pagkagradweyt ng ate ko, pumunta siya sa Amerika.
***After graduation**–genmark.my older sister–went–subj.she–oblmark.America*
***After**my older sister **graduated**, she went to America.*

8.10 **Recent perfective verbs** are non-AF forms that the action expressed by the verb root has *just been completed*. The actor or doer of the action is always in the genitive case. The verb is formed by attaching the prefix /ka-/ to a verb root with a reduplicated first (C)V (i.e., ***ka-*** **+ reduplication of first (C)V of the root + root word**). Alternatively, the prefix may be reduplicated (*ka-* + *kaka-*) instead of the first CV of the root. In a sentence, the verb is often followed by the adverbial enclitic **lang** *just* or *only*, but without it the sentence would still be grammatical. Here are some examples.

Katatapos lang ng klase namin.
***Just finished**–lang–genmark.our class*
*Our class just **ended**.*

Kalilinis ko ng bahay kahapon.
***Just cleaned**–gen.I–genmark.house–yesterday*
*I **just cleaned** the house yesterday.*

Kakagising lang ng kuya ko.
***Just awoke**–lang–genmark.my older brother*
*My older brother **just woke up**.*

Kakaayos niya ng kotse.
***Just fixed**–gen.he/she–genmark.car*
*He/she **just fixed** the car.*

Chapter 9

Adverbs

In this chapter, the discussion of adverbs, words used to modify action or events, is divided into four sections: adverbs of time; adverbs of manner using prepositions; adverbs of manner using adjectives; and enclitic adverbs, some of which are temporal and most of which are modal.

9.1 **Temporal adverbs** are words that can be thought of as providing tense to Filipino sentences because verbs in the language inflect for aspect but not tense.

9.1.1 The **adverbs of time associated with past events** are listed in the following table along with examples of their use.

English	***Filipino***	***Sentences***
previously or *formerly*	dati	Dati, nakatira kami sa Quezon City. *Previously, we lived in Quezon City.*
back then	noon	Noon, nagtuturo ang nanay ko sa Science High School. *Back then, my mother was teaching at the Science High School.*
in + point or *period in time*	noong +	Nagbiyahe ang pamilya ko sa Canada noong isang taon. *My family went on a trip to Canada last year.*
yesterday	kahapon	Pumunta ako sa palengke kahapon. *I went to the market yesterday.*
two days ago	kamakalawa	Dumating ang tiya ko galing sa probinsya kamakalawa. *My aunt came from the province two days ago.*

DOI: 10.4324/9781315739427-10

English	Filipino	Sentences
recently	kamakailan	Ipinasa ng kongreso ang panukalang batas kamakailan. *Congress passed the proposed bill recently.*
earlier today	kanina	Nagbigay ng pahayag ang pangulo kaninang umaga. *The president issued a statement earlier this morning.*
when	nang/noong	Nang nag-aaral ako sa unibersidad, nagtatrabaho ako sa kapeterya. *When I was studying at the university, I used to work in the cafeteria.*

The adverb **noon** can be made more specific by adding a particular period or point in time. A linker is necessary in this context; hence, the form becomes *noong* + **specific point in time**. Here are some examples.

English	Filipino	English	Filipino
the other day	noong isang araw	*last Christmas*	noong Pasko
last week	noong isang lingo	*last summer*	noong tag-init
last month	noong isang buwan	*last Monday*	noong Lunes
last year	noong isang taon	*last May*	noong Mayo
a long time ago	noong unang panahon	*in 1950*	noong 1950
back in the day	noong araw	*in the past*	noong nakaraan

The adverb **kanina** is often translated into English as *earlier*. However, it can only be an earlier time within the 24-hour period a particular utterance is spoken or to which it is referring. The time can be made more specific by using kanina as a modifier for a particular point or period in the day, like **kaninang umaga** *earlier today in the morning*, **kaninang tanghali** *earlier today at noon*, etc.

9.1.2 The **adverbs of time associated with present or ongoing action and recurring or habitual action or events** are listed in the following table along with examples of their use.

English	Filipino	Sentences
today, presently, at this time, or these days	ngayon	May klase kami ngayon *We have a class today.* Nagluluto si Pedro ngayon. *Pedro is cooking right now.* Mahirap humanap ng trabaho ngayon. *It is hard to find a job these days.*

this + point or *period in time*	ngayong + point or period in time	May konsiyerto sa parke ngayong gabi. *There is a concert at the park tonight.* Mas mataas ang presyo ng gasolina ngayong buwan. *The price of oil is higher this month.*
every + point or *period in time*	tuwing + point or period in time	Tumatakbo si Anna sa parke tuwing alas sais ng umaga. *Anna runs in the park every morning at 6:00.* Umuuwi ako sa probinsya tuwing Disyembre. *I go home to the province every December.*
every hour	oras-oras	Kailangan mong uminom ng tubig oras-oras. *You need to drink water every hour.*
every day	araw-araw	Araw-araw, nagmemeryenda si Mark sa kapihan. *Mark eats a snack at the coffee shop every day.*
every night	gabi-gabi	Nagbabasa siya ng balita sa internet gabi-gabi. *He/she reads news on the internet every night.*
every week	linggu-linggo	Nagtatanghalian kami ng mga kaibigan ko linggu-linggo. *My friends and I eat lunch* (*together*) *every week.*
every year	taun-taon	Binibisita ko ang lolo at lola ko taun-taon. *I visit my grandparents every year.*
whenever	kapag	Kapag nagbabasa ako, nakikinig din ako ng musika. *Whenever I am reading, I also listen to music.*

9.1.3 The **adverbs of time associated with future events** are listed in the following table along with examples of their use.

English	*Filipino*	*Sentences*
later today	mamaya	Manonood kami ng sine mamayang gabi. *We are watching a movie later tonight.*
tomorrow	bukas	Papasok ako sa klase bukas. *I am going to class tomorrow.*
two days from now	sa makalawa	Darating ang mga pinsan ko sa makalawa. *My cousins are coming two days from now.*
in the future	sa hinaharap	Magpapatayo ang alkalde ng klinika sa kinabukasan. *The mayor will have a clinic built in the future.*
in + point or period in time	sa + point or period in time	Bibisita ang presidente sa aming bayan sa susunod na buwan. *The president will visit our town next month.*
when or if	kung	Pupunta ako sa salusalo kung pupunta ka. *I will go to the party if you would go.*

The adverb **sa** can be made more specific by adding a particular period or point in time. Here are some examples.

English	*Filipino*	*English*	*Filipino*
next week	sa susunod na linggo	*this coming Christmas*	sa Pasko
next month	sa susunod na buwan	*this coming January*	sa Enero
next year	sa susunod na taon	*this coming Monday*	sa Lunes
next summer	sa susunod na tag-init	*this coming vacation*	sa bakasyon
next vacation	sa susunod na bakasyon	*in 2050*	sa 2050

The adverb **mamaya** is often translated into English as *later*. However, it can only be a later time within the 24-hour period a particular utterance is spoken or to which it is referring. The time can be made more specific by using kanina as a modifier for a particular point or period in the day, like **mamayang hapon** *later this afternoon*, **mamayang alas singko ng hapon** *later today at 5:00 pm*, etc.

9.2 **Adverbs of manner** are used to describe the way in which an action is performed or the manner in which an event occurs. In Filipino, these adverbs can be grouped into two types based on their derivation and morphological structure, namely, (1) de-verbal and (2) de-adjectival.

9.2.1 De-verbal adverbs of manner are adverbs that are derived from verbs. These are formed by attaching the prefix /pa-/ to a verb root. Here are some common examples.

English	*De-verbal adverbs*	*Source verbs*
facing forward	paharap	humarap *to face*
with back turned	patalikod	tumalikod *to turn one's back*
leftward	pakaliwa	kumaliwa *to turn left*
rightward	pakanan	kumanan *to turn right*
upward	pataas	itaas *to raise*
downward	pababa	ibaba *to lower*
toward the outer part	palabas	ilabas *to bring out*
toward the inner part	papasok	ipasok *to bring inside*
toward the direction of . . .	papunta	pumunta *to go*
in a kneeling manner	paluhod	lumuhod *to kneel*
secretly	patago	itago *to hide*
in a traitorous manner	patraydor	traydorin *to betray*
in a standing manner	patayo	tumayo *to stand*

9.2.2 De-adjectival adverbs of manner are adverbs that are derived from adjectives. These words are morphologically identical to their adjective counterparts. The only difference is in the way that they are used as modifiers. Adjectives modify nouns while adverbs modify verbs and sentences. Here are some common examples.

English	*De-adjectival adverb*	*Source adjective*
frequently	madalas	madalas *frequent*
beautifully	maganda	maganda *beautiful*
promptly or *early*	maaga	maaga *early*
quietly	tahimik	tahimik *quiet*
politely or *respectfully*	magalang	magalang *respectful* or *polite*
peacefully	mapayapa	mapayapa *peaceful*
loudly	malakas	malakas *loud*
quickly	mabilis	mabilis *fast* or *quick*
greatly	magaling	magaling *good*
scarily	nakakatakot	nakakatakot *scary*
annoyingly	nakakainis	nakakainis *annoying*
disgustingly	nakakasuka	nakakasuka *disgusting*
in an animal-like manner	malahayop	malahayop *animal-like*

In a sentence, there are two ways in which adverbs can be used to describe specific actions or events. It can either come before the verb or after the verb. When it comes before the verb, a linker is used to link the word immediately preceding the verb, which must be inflected for aspect. When it comes after the verb, the word **nang** must immediately precede the adverb. The following are examples demonstrating the different sentence structures. Adverbs modifying an action or event attract clitics (enclitic adverbs and pronouns) so that these words have to immediately follow the adverb in a sentence.

Structure 1: adjective + linker + finite verb

Paluhod na lumakad sa simbahan si Mario.
*Mario **walked** inside the church **on his knees**.*

Mabilis siyang **nagdrayb** kanina para maiwasan niya ang trapik.
*He **drove fast** earlier so he can avoid the (rush hour) traffic.*

Masayang nagluluto si Maria habang nakikinig ng musika.
*Maria **is happily cooking** while listening to music.*

Tahimik kaming **magbabasa** sa aklatan.
*We **will quietly read** in the library.*

Structure 2: nang + adjective

Lumakad nang paluhod sa simbahan si Mario.
*Mario **walked** inside the church **on his knees**.*

Nagdrayb siya **nang mabilis** kanina para maiwasan niya ang trapik.
*He **drove fast** earlier so he can avoid the (rush hour) traffic.*

Nagluluto nang masaya si Maria habang nakikinig ng musika.
*Maria **is happily cooking** while listening to music.*

Magbabasa kami **nang tahimik** sa aklatan.
*We **will quietly read** in the library.*

When adverbs are used in sentences that express general statements, the adverb comes before an infinitive verb, and there is no linker required before the verb. However, some speakers prefer to add a linker, especially when the word immediately preceding the verb ends in a vowel. As in the preceding examples, adverbs modifying an action or event attract clitics (enclitic adverbs and pronouns) so that these words have to immediately follow the adverb in a sentence.

Structure: adjective + infinitive verb

Mabilis lumakad si Pedro.
*Pedro **walks fast**./Pedro is a fast walker.*

Mabagal siya **magdrayb**.
*He/she **drives slowly**./He/she is a slow driver.*

Magaling na magluto si Gina.
*Gina **cooks well**./Gina is a good cook.*

Tahimik silang **magtrabaho** sa pabrika.
*They **work quietly** in the factory./They are quiet workers.*

9.3 Enclitic adverbs

There is a closed class of adverbs in Filipino called enclitic particles that indicate either temporality, specifying time frame or sequencing of events, or modality, indicating the attitude of the speaker about the information he/she is expressing. The meanings of these enclitic adverbs are hard to pin down because by themselves they are uninterpretable. They have to be part of a clause to have meaning, and some enclitics can have multiple meanings that are largely determined by the context. These adverbs have inherent clitic property, which attracts them to the highest predicate so that in a sentence, they have to immediately follow the predicate. Pronouns also have clitic properties, but because enclitic adverbs are stronger clitics, except for the monosyllabic pronouns **ko**, **mo**, and **ka**, enclitic adverbs come before pronouns when they occur together in a sentence or clause. If there are multiple enclitics in a sentence, monosyllabic ones come before longer ones. Generally, only a maximum of three or four enclitics can occur in the same clause. Because most of them are either mono- or disyllabic, here is the general order in which they come.

na	pa	nga	lang	din	daw	po	ba	muna	naman	yata	kaya	sana	pala

9.3.1 Na indicates that an expected outcome has already happened. It usually translates into English as *already*. Here are some examples.

Umuwi **na** ang mga bata.
*The children have gone home **(as expected)**.*

Kumain ka **na** ba?
*Have you **already** eaten?*

Nakapagluto **na** ng hapunan si Minda.
*Minda **is (already)** done cooking dinner.*

9.3.2 Pa indicates that an expected outcome has not happened yet. It usually translates into English as *still* or *yet*. It is semantically the opposite of **na**, so **na** and **pa** cannot occur in the same clause together. Here are some examples.

Hindi **pa** natatapos ang klase.
Class is not over ***yet****.*

Nag-aaral **pa** ang mga anak niya.
His/her children are ***still*** *studying.*

Maglilinis **pa** ako ng banyo.
I ***still*** *have to clean the bathroom.*

9.3.3 Nga is used to emphasize or confirm the information expressed by a sentence. A close equivalent of this function in English can be expressed by the word *indeed*, *certainly*, or *surely*. Here are some examples.

Maganda **nga** ang parke sa bayan.
The park in town is ***indeed*** *beautiful.*

Darating **nga** sila sa Sabado.
They are ***indeed*** *coming on Saturday.*

Nakakatuwa **nga** ang konsiyerto.
The concert is ***certainly*** *enjoyable.*

9.3.4 Lang/lamang is used to minimize the perceived importance of a referent. A close equivalent in English is the word *only* or *just*. The longer form **lamang** is generally deemed more formal. Here are some examples.

Kakain **lang** kami sa mall.
We are ***only*** *going to eat at the mall.*

Maliit **lang** ang apartment namin.
Our apartment is ***rather*** *small.*

Napulot ko **lang** ito sa daan.
I ***just*** *picked this up from the road.*

9.3.5 Din/rin is used to indicate additional or similar information. It is roughly equivalent to the English words *also* and *too*. The variants follow the old Tagalog phonological rule on the sound /d/, which changes /d/ to /r/ in intervocalic position. Thus, **din** is used when the adverb follows a word that ends in a consonant, and **rin** is used when the adverb follows a word that ends in a vowel. Here are some examples.

Pupunta si Mario sa konsiyerto at pupunta **rin** si Ben.
Mario is going to the concert and Ben is going ***too****.*

Mahaba ang eksamen at mahirap **din** ito.
*The exam is long and difficult **too**.*

Gusto ko **ring** magbakasyon sa Zamboanga.
*I **also** want to go on vacation in Zamboanga.*

9.3.6 **Daw/raw** indicates that the information being provided is secondhand (i.e., the speaker is not the direct source of information but merely relaying information from someone or somewhere else). There is not one word in English that can be considered a close equivalent of the adverb. However, a few English expressions would be appropriate translations in some contexts, namely, *it is said*, *according to sources*, and *unconfirmed reports say*. The variants follow the old Tagalog phonological rule on the sound /d/, which changes /d/ to /r/ in intervocalic position. Thus, **daw** is used when the adverb follows a word that ends in a consonant, and **raw** is used when the adverb follows a word that ends in a vowel. Here are some examples.

Hindi **raw** mag-eeroplano si Mila.
(I heard) *Mila is not traveling by plane.*

May dayaan **daw** na nangyari noong eleksyon.
Unconfirmed reports say *that there was cheating during the election.*

Nakatira **raw** ang isang mangkukulam sa bahay na iyan.
Some say *that a witch lives in that house.*

9.3.7 **Po/ho** indicates deference, respect, or politeness toward the addressee or interlocutor, often used when talking to an older person, a superior at work, a person of authority, or an adult stranger. The second person plural pronoun is used even when there is only one addressee. The variant /ho/ is deemed to be less formal or more intimate. Often, sentences with this adverb are translated into English with the addition of the form address *sir* or *madame/ma'am*. Here are some examples.

Saan **po** kayo pupunta?
*Where are you going, **sir/ma'am**?*

Ipinabibigay **po** ito ng aking nanay.
*My mother asked me to give this (to you), **sir/ma'am**.*

Puwede **po** bang magtanong?
*May I ask a question, **sir/ma'am**?*

9.3.8 **Ba** is used to ask a yes/no question. It has no English equivalent because the addition of this adverb simply turns a declarative sentence into an interrogative one. Here are some examples.

Taga-Baguio ka **ba**?
Are you from Baguio?

Nagtatrabaho **ba** si Jim sa bangko?
Does Jim work at the bank?

Malayo **ba** ang bahay ninyo?
Is your house far?

9.3.9 **Muna** indicates that an action or event being qualified takes precedence over other actions or events. Its close English equivalents are *first of all* and *before anything else*. Here are some examples.

Magsisimba **muna** sina Jun at Lisa.
Before they do anything else, *Jun and Lisa will go to church* ***first***.

Kakain **muna** kami bago manood ng sine.
We will eat ***(first)*** *before watching a movie.*

Magluluto **muna** ako.
I am going to cook ***first***.

9.3.10 **Naman** is the enclitic adverb whose semantic content is most difficult to pin down because it can mean different things in different contexts. Some of its most common uses are (1) to indicate contrast from previously stated information, (2) to indicate a turn in a sequentially ordered turn-taking situation, and (3) to express a gentle admonishment. Here are some examples.

Masipag si Mario at matalino **naman** si Maria.
Mario is diligent **while** Maria is intelligent.

Pagkatapos niyang maligo, ako **naman** ang gagamit ng banyo.
After he/she is done (with the shower), ***then*** *I will use the bathroom.*

Maglinis **naman** kayo ng kuwarto.
Why don't you *clean your room?*

9.3.11 **Yata** indicates uncertainty about the information being expressed. There is no equivalent English word for it, but the expressions *I think but I am not sure* and *maybe/perhaps* approximate the meaning expressed by the adverb. Here are some examples.

Wala **yata** kaming klase sa Lunes.
I think (but I am not sure about this information) *that we do not have a class on Monday.*

Magpapaparti **yata** si Josie sa bagong taon.
I think (but this information is unconfirmed) *that Josie will throw a party on New Year's Day.*

Lilipat **yata** sa Maynila ang pamilya nila.
I ***think (but I am not certain)****that their family is moving to Manila.*

9.3.12 Kaya indicates curiosity and uncertainty about the information being expressed. There is no equivalent English word for it, but the expression *I wonder* can approximate the meaning expressed by the adverb. The sentence in which it occurs is always interrogative in Filipino. Here are some examples.

Hindi **kaya** masyadong matagal ang biyahe?
I wonder *if the trip is really long.*

Magpapakain **kaya** si Lorna sa kaarawan niya?
I wonder *if Lorna will treat us (to dinner) on her birthday.*

Magbabago **kaya** ang kalagayan sa aming bayan?
I wonder *if the situation in our town will change.*

9.3.13 Sana indicates a hope, wish, or desire. Semantically, it is close to the English words *hopefully*, *with hope*, and *I wish*. Unlike other enclitic adverbs, /sana/ can be used in sentence-initial position, as shown in the last example.

Magbabakasyon **sana** kami sa Sagada sa tag-init.
We were ***hoping*** *to go to Sagada for a vacation in the summer.*

Tahimik **sana** sa kapihan para makapag-aral ako.
I hope *that it is quiet at the coffee shop so I can study.*

Manalo **sana** ako sa lotto. or Sana manalo ako sa lotto.
I wish *to win the lottery.* ***I wish*** *to win the lottery.*

9.3.14 Pala indicates surprise at the unexpected turn of events. No single word in English can capture the meaning of the adverb, but there are some expressions that can carry the same meaning, such as *what a surprise* and *surprisingly*. Here are some examples.

Magbibigay **pala** ng malaking donasyon sa simbahan ang kapitbahay ko.
It is surprising, but apparently *my neighbor is giving a large donation to the church.*

Bumili **pala** ng hapunan si Dan para sa ating lahat.
What a surprise! *Dan bought dinner for everybody.*

Nakakatuwa **pala** ang palabas.
The show was ***surprisingly*** *enjoyable.*

Chapter 10

Connectors or conjunctions

Conjunctions join clauses together and are generally divided into two groups, coordinating conjunctions, which connect two independent clauses, and subordinating conjunctions, which connect a subordinate or dependent clause to the main or independent clause.

10.1 **Coordinating connectors** join together words, phrases, and independent clauses that are of equal syntactic weight. The most important ones and examples of their usage are provided in the following table.

English	*Filipino*	*Sentences*
and	at	Masipag **at** matalino ang kaibigan ko. *My friend is diligent* ***and*** *smart.*
		Nagluto ng tanghalian si Mario **at** naglinis ng banyo si Lina. *Mario cooked lunch* ***and*** *Lina cleaned the bathroom.*
or	o	Magdadala ako ng gulay **o** prutas sa piknik. *I will bring (either) vegetables* ***or*** *fruits to the picnic.*
		Magluluto ba tayo ng hapunan **o** kakain tayo sa labas? *Are we cooking dinner* ***or*** *are we eating out?*
but	pero/ ngunit	Marunong **pero** tamad si Juan. *Juan is smart* ***but*** *lazy.*
		Masakit ang ulo ni Gina **ngunit** pumasok pa rin siya sa trabaho. *Gina has a headache,* ***but*** *she still went to work.*
for	kasi/ dahil	Mura **kasi** luma ang kotseng nabili niya. *The car that he bought was cheap* ***for*** *it was old.*

DOI: 10.4324/9781315739427-11

		Natapos niya agad ang eksamen **dahil** hindi ito mahirap. *He/she finished the exam early* ***for*** *it was not difficult.*
so	kaya	Matao **kaya** maingay sa salusalo. *It was crowded,* ***so*** *it was loud at the party.*
		Darating si Linda bukas **kaya** lilinisin ko ang kuwarto niya. *Linda is arriving tomorrow* ***so*** *I will clean her room (now).*

10.2 **Subordinating conjunctions** join an independent or main clause and a dependent or subordinate clause to express one of the following: cause, effect, sequence, contrast, comparison, reason, or condition.

10.2.1 Subordinating conjunctions indicating cause and effect

English	*Filipino*	*Sentences*
because	dahil/ sapagkat	Maraming taong lumipat sa lungsod **dahil** wala silang mahanap na trabaho sa nayon. *Many people moved to the city* ***because*** *they could not find jobs in the village.*
		Sapagkat nakalbo na ang kabundukan, mas madalas nang bumaha sa aming bayan. ***Because*** *highland forests have been decimated, our town has become vulnerable to more flooding.*
that is why or *therefore*	kaya naman/ samakatuwid	Mataas ang presyo ng mga bilihin **kaya naman** humihingi ng karagdagang sahod ang mga manggagawa. *Commodity prices are high,* ***that is why*** *workers are demanding higher wages.*
		Ayaw pakinggan ng administrasyon ang hinaing ng mga manggagawa tungkol sa masamang kundisyon sa pabrika. **Samakatuwid** naghain sila ng reklamo sa Departamento ng Paggawa. *The workers' complaints about the unsafe working conditions at the factory were ignored by the administration.* ***Therefore****, they had to file a formal complaint at the Department of Labor.*
in order to or *so that*	para/upang	**Para** matupad mo ang iyong pangarap, kailangan mong mag-aral nang mabuti. ***In order to*** *achieve your goal, you need to study hard.*

Nagtrabaho siya sa ibayong dagat **upang** makatulong sa kanyang pamilya.
He/she worked overseas ***so that*** *he/she can help her family.*

10.2.2 Subordinating conjunctions indicating sequence of events

English	***Filipino***	***Sentences***
(back) when	nang/ noong	Nagtatrabaho sa bangko ang tatay ko **nang** nakatira pa siya sa Canada. *My father used to work at a bank* ***(back) when*** *he was still living in Canada.* **Noong** nag-aaral si Ana sa unibersidad, nakatira siya sa bahay ng tiya niya sa Quezon City. ***(Back) when*** *Ana was studying at the university, she was living at her aunt's house in Quezon City.*
before	bago	**Bago** umuwi si Allen, namili muna siya sa groseri. ***Before*** *Allen went home, he went grocery-shopping first.* Tumira kami sa Cebu **bago** kami lumipat sa Maynila. *We lived in Cebu* ***before*** *we moved to Manila.*
while	habang	Nag-uusap ang mga estudyante sa labas **habang** hinihintay nilang magsimula ang klase. *The students are talking outside* ***while*** *(they are) waiting for the class to start.* **Habang** nanonood ng telebisyon si Lito, ginagawa niya ang kanyang takdang proyekto. ***While*** *Lito is watching television, he is working on his project.*
(mean)while	samantala	Abala sa paghahanda ng pagkain para sa piyesta ang mga tiya ni Ben. **Samantala**, naglalagay naman ng mga ilaw at dekorasyon sa loob at labas ng bahay ang mga kapatid niya. *Ben's aunts are busy with the food preparations for the fiesta.* ***Meanwhile****, (for their part) his siblings are installing decorations inside and outside the house.*

		Samantalang nanonood ng palabas sa plasa ang mga matandang bisita, naglalaro naman ang mga bata sa perya. ***While*** *the grown-ups are watching the show at the plaza, the kids are enjoying the games at the fair.*
after	matapos na	**Matapos na** salantain ng bagyo ang aming bayan noong isang linggo, niyanig naman ito ng lindol kahapon. ***After*** *our town was devastated by a typhoon last week, it was struck by an earthquake yesterday.* Nagsimula na ang proyektong pabahay sa aming baranggay **matapos na** ibigay ng pamahalaan ang badyet para dito. *The housing project in our neighborhood commenced* ***after*** *the government released the budget.*
when(ever)	kapag	**Kapag** may mga kaibigan akong bumibisita mula sa ibang bansa, ipinapasyal ko sila sa Fort Santiago. ***Whenever*** *friends from abroad come to visit, I take them on a sightseeing tour at Fort Santiago.* Sumasakay ako ng bus **kapag** nagbibiyahe ako papunta sa Pangasinan. *I take the bus* ***whenever*** *I go on a trip to Pangasinan.*

10.2.3 Subordinating conjunctions indicating contrast, reason, or condition

English	*Filipino*	*Sentences*
but *however*	ngunit subalit	Maagang umalis si Pina, **ngunit** nahuli pa rin siya sa klase. *Pina left early,* ***but*** *she was still late for class.* Maganda at tahimik ang aming baryo, **subalit** madalas itong tamaan ng bagyo. *Our village is nice and quiet.* ***However,*** *it is frequently hit by a typhoon.*
nevertheless	gayunpaman gayunman	Matagal nang nakatira ang pamilya ni Luisa sa Amerika. **Gayunpaman**, madalas pa rin siyang bumisita sa Pilipinas. *Luisa's family has lived in the United States for a long time.* ***Nevertheless,*** *she still visits the Philippines frequently.*

		Malaki ang kontribusyon ng turismo sa aming ekonomiya. **Gayunman**, nananatiling mahirap ang maraming tao sa aming lugar. *Tourism contributes a great deal to our economy.* ***Nevertheless****, many people in our town remain poor.*
even though	kahit na	**Kahit na** malungkot ang buhay na malayo sa pamilya, maraming Pilipino pa rin ang pumipiling magtrabaho sa ibang bansa. ***Even though*** *life away from one's family is lonely, many Filipinos still choose to work abroad.*
		Naglalakad pa rin ang aking lola papuntang simbahan araw-araw **kahit na** medyo mahina na ang tuhod niya. *My grandmother still walks to church every day* ***even though*** *her knees are now a little weak.*
instead of	sa halip na	Nagpasiya siyang magbukas ng klinika sa aming baryo **sa halip na** magtrabaho sa ibang bansa. *She decided to open a clinic in our village* ***instead of*** *working abroad.*
		Sa halip na manood ka ng telebisyon buong araw, bakit hindi ka magbasa ng libro? ***Instead of*** *watching television all day, why don't you read a book?*
except when or *unless*	maliban kung	Ayaw kong pumunta sa mall **maliban kung** may kailangan akong bilhin doon. *I do not like going to the mall* ***except when*** *I need to buy something there.*
		Hanggat maaari, hindi ako sumasakay ng taksi **maliban kung** walang dyip na nagbibiyahe sa lugar na gusto kong puntahan. *As much as possible, I do not take a taxi* ***unless*** *there are no jeepneys plying the route to a place where I would like to go.*
(*rather*) *than*	kaysa	Mas gusto kong pumunta sa tabing-dagat **kaysa** umakyat sa bundok. *I like going to the beach* (*more*) ***than*** *hiking up the mountain.*
		Kaysa matulog ka diyan, bakit hindi ka lumakad sa labas? ***Rather than*** (*you*) *sleeping in, why don't you take a walk outside?*

if (only), counterfactual or *if, conditional*	kung (. . . sana)/ kung	**Kung** natapos nang maaga ang pulong, nakapanood **sana** tayo ng palabas sa teatro. ***If (only)*** *the meeting had ended early, we could have watched a theater show.* Magdadala ako ng karaoke **kung** mangangako kang kakanta ka. *I will bring a karaoke machine **if** you promise that you will sing.*
as long as	bastat/basta't	Hindi ako matatakot **bastat** kasama kita. *I will never be afraid **as long as** you are with me.* **Basta't** magtiwala ka sa Diyos, tutulungan ka Niya. ***As long as*** *you have faith in God, He will come to your aid.*
furthermore	gayundin	Nagpadala na ng tulong ang pambansang pamahalaan sa mga biktima ng bagyo. **Gayundin**, dumating kahapon ang grupo ng mga boluntaryong doktor at nars na magbibigay ng libreng serbisyo sa mga maysakit. *The national government sent aid to the typhoon victim. Furthermore, a team of volunteer doctors and nurses arrived yesterday to provide free medical services to those in need.*
just like or *just as*	gaya ng/tulad ng	**Gaya ng** napagkasunduan natin, ako ang maghahanda ng pagkain at ikaw naman ang mag-aayos ng entablado at sayawan para sa pagdiriwang. ***Just as*** *we have agreed upon, I will prepare the food and you will put together the stage and dance hall for the celebration.* **Tulad ng** sinabi ng prinsipal, suspendido ang mga klase habang inaayos pa ang mga gusali na nasira ng nagdaang bagyo. ***Just like*** *the principal stated, classes are suspended while repair work is ongoing on the buildings destroyed by the recent typhoon.*

10.3 **Relativizer and complementizer conjunctions** connect a relative clause or a complement clause to a main clause.

Na is used when the clause being connected is in the declarative or non-question form. Like the linker /na/, it has three possible forms: (1) a suffix /-ng/, which attaches to the word immediately preceding the relative or complement clause that ends in a vowel; (2) a suffix /-g/, which attaches to the word immediately preceding the relative or complement clause that ends in a consonant; and (3) a separate word /na/ following a word that ends in a consonant other than /n/ immediately preceding the relative or complement clause. Many speakers of Filipino use only the form /na/ consistently as a complementizer.

Kung is used when the complement clause being connected is in the interrogative or question form. The use of /kung/ as a relativizer is limited to clauses indicating location or direction. (See chapters on relative clause and complement clause for more details.) Here are some examples.

Relative clauses	**na**	Hinuli ng pulis ang lalaki**ng** nagnakaw ng telepono ko. *The police arrested the man **who** stole my phone.*
who		Ibinigay niya sa akin ang relo**ng** binili niya kahapon. *He/she gave me the watch **that** he/she bought yesterday.*
where		Iyan ang simbahan**g** binigyan namin ng donasyon. *That is the church **to which** we gave a donation.*
whom		Siya ang pintor **na** ipinaghanda namin ng pagdiriwang. *He/she is the painter **for whom** we organized the party.*
which		Kanser sa baga ang sakit **na** ikinamatay ng lolo ko. *Lung cancer is the disease **that** caused my grandfather's death.*
that		Ito ang lupa**ng** pagtatayuan ko ng aking bagong bahay. *This is the land **where** I will build my new house.*
	kung saan	Ito ang lupa **kung saan** ko itatayo ang aking bagong bahay. *This is the land **where** I will build my new house.*

Complement clauses	**na**	Nakita ko**ng** kinuha ni Mike ang libro sa mesa. *I saw* ***(that)****Mike took the book from the table.*
that		Narinig ko **na** may pagdiriwang sa bahay mo sa Linggo. *I heard* ***that*** *there will be a celebration at your house on Sunday.*
whether		Sinabi ng reporter **na** babaguhin ang patakarang pangwika sa mga eskuwelahan sa susunod na taon. *The reporter said* ***that*** *the language policy in schools will be changed next year.*
		Binanggit ng taga-ulat **na** sasampahan ng kaso ang mga tiwaling opisyal ng pamahalaan. *The reporter mentioned* ***that*** *charges will be filed against corrupt government officials.*
		Gusto ko**ng** hanapin ang mga lumang talaarawan ng aking lola. *I want to search for my grandmother's old diaries.*
		Dapat sila**ng** magdala ng kompyuter sa laboratoryo. *They need to bring their computers to the laboratory.*
	kung **+ ano** **+ sino** **+ saan** **+ bakit** **+ kailan** **+ paano** **+ gaano ka-**	Sinabi ni Maria sa akin **kung saan** tayo magkikita bukas. *Maria told me where we will meet tomorrow.*
		Nalaman ko **kung bakit** hindi sasama si Kim sa atin. *I found out why Kim is not coming with us.*
		Tinanong niya ako **kung kailan** ang aking kaarawan. *He/she asked me when my birthday is.*
		Ikinuwento ng kapatid ko **kung** paano siya nakauwi noong bumaha sa aming lugar. *My brother recounted* ***how*** *he was able to get home back when there was a big flood in our area.*

Nagtatanong siya **kung** puwede kang bumili ng tanghalian.
*He/she is asking **whether** you can buy lunch (or not).*

Any noun phrase (NP) within a sentence, whether it is the focus or nominative NP or not, can be relativized or take a phrasal modifier. In the following section, illustrative sentences are provided to show relativization of the subject or focused NP of the main clause. In the following examples, the head noun or relativized noun is in bold, and the relative clause is underlined.

Relativizing the actor NP in an AF sentence:

Dumating nang maaga **ang babaeng** nagtitinda ng prutas sa harap ng aming gusali.
***The woman** who sells fruits in front of our building came early.*

Nagbigay ng donasyon sa simbahan **ang matandang lalaking** nakatira sa lumang bahay sa dulo ng kalyeng iyan.
***The old man** who lives at the old house at the end of that street gave a donation to the church.*

Nakakatugtog ng iba't-ibang instrumentong pangmusika **ang estudyanteng** kalilipat lang sa aming eskuwelahan.
***The student** who just moved to our school can play several musical instruments.*

Relativizing the object NP in an object-focus sentence:

Nakita ko **ang mga artistang** magtatanghal sa palabas mamayang gabi.
*I saw **the actors** who are performing at the show tonight.*

Binili niya **ang parol** na ginawa ng kanyang kapitbahay.
*He/she bought **the Christmas lantern** that his/her neighbor made.*

Hinuhugasan ni Juan **ang mga gulay** na ibinigay ng kaibigan ko.
*Juan is washing **the vegetables** that were given by my friend.*

Relativizing the locative/directional NP in a location/direction-focus sentence:

Pinuntahan nina Jun at Rudy **ang parkeng** nasa ibabaw ng bundok.
*Jun and Rudy went **to the park**, which is located on top of the mountain.*

Tatawagan namin **ang ahensyang** nagbibigay ng tulong sa mga batang-lansangan.
*We will make a call **to the agency** that provides assistance to street children.*

Tinulungan nila **ang mga komunidad** na nasalanta ng bagyo.
They gave assistance/help ***to communities*** *that were battered by the storm.*

Relativizing the benefactive NP in a benefactive-focus sentence:

Ipinaghahanda nila ng tanghalian **ang mga bisitang** dumating kaninang umaga.
They are preparing lunch ***for the guests*** *who arrived this morning.*

Inihanap niya ng pansamantalang tirahan **ang mga taong** nawalan ng bahay dahil sa sunog.
He/she looked for temporary housing ***for people*** *who lost their homes in the fire.*

Ipaglalaba ni Aling Marina ng damit **ang mga turistang** nagbabakasyon sa aming baryo.
Mrs. Marina will do laundry ***for the tourists*** *who are vacationing in our village.*

Relativizing the instrumental NP in an instrumental-focus sentence:

Ipinambili niya ng meryenda **ang perang** ibinigay mo.
He/she bought snacks ***with the money*** *that you gave (him/her).*

Ipantakip mo ng iyong ulo **ang sumbrerong** ginawa ni Pedro.
Cover/protect your head ***with the hat*** *that Pedro made.*

Ipanghugas mo ng iyong sugat **ang sabong** inirekomenda ng doktor.
Wash/clean your wound ***with the soap****, which the doctor recommended.*

Relativizing the experiencer NP in an experiencer-focus sentence:

Natuwa **ang mga bisitang** nanood ng palabas sa plasa.
The guests *who watched the show at the plaza enjoyed themselves.*

Nagugutom na **ang mga boluntaryong** gumagawa ng palamuti para sa pagdiriwang.
The volunteers *who are making decorations for the celebration are feeling hungry.*

Dahil sa sobrang init, nahilo **ang batang** nagtitinda ng bulaklak sa labas ng simbahan.
Due to extreme heat, ***the young person*** *who is selling flowers outside the church felt faint.*

Relativizing the reason NP in a reason-focus sentence:

Ikinalungkot niya **ang balitang** narinig niya sa radyo kanina.
The news *that he/she heard on the radio saddened him/her.*

Ikinababahala nila **ang bagong patakarang** inaprubahan ng lokal na pamahalaan.
The new policy *that was approved by the local government worries them.*

Ikinagalak ng aking lola **ang pagdiriwang** na inihanda ng kanyang mga apo.
The celebration*, which was organized by her grandchildren, made my grandmother happy.*

Relative clauses may also be associated with unfocused NPs in the main clause. The following examples illustrate how unfocused NPs may also be relativized.

Relativizing the actor NP in an object-focus sentence:

Kinuha **ng paring** nangangalap ng abuloy ang perang nasa mesa.
The priest *who is collecting donations took the money on the table.*

Dadalhin **ng mga batang** sasama sa biyahe ang kanilang mga baong tanghalian.
The children *who are joining the trip will bring their own packed lunch.*

Isinusuot **ng mga mananayaw** na nagtatanghal sa parada ang katutubong mga kasuotan.
The dancers *who perform in the parade wear traditional costumes.*

Relativizing the object NP in an actor-focus sentence:

Para sa salusalo, magdadala si Anna **ng mga kakaning** niluto ng kanyang lola.
For the dinner celebration, Anna will bring ***rice cakes*** *that were prepared by her grandmother.*

Sumulat siya **ng tulang** babasahin ng klase namin sa aming pagtatanghal.
She wrote ***a poem*** *that will be read by our class for our presentation.*

Bumasa kami **ng artikulong** tumatalakay sa usaping panseguridad sa aming rehiyon.
We read ***an article*** *that discusses security issues in our region.*

Relativizing the locative/directional NP in an actor-focus sentence:

Tumulong sila **sa mga taong** nawalan ng bahay dahil sa lindol.
They gave assistance/help ***to the people*** *who lost their homes because of the earthquake.*

Maglalagay siya ng bulaklak **sa mesang** inilagay ko sa harap ng altar.
He/she is going to put some flowers ***on the table*** *that I placed in front of the altar.*

Tumingin kami **sa larawang** nakasabit sa dingding.
*We looked **at the picture** that is hanging on the wall.*

Relativizing the benefactive NP in an actor-focus sentence:

Kumuha ako ng bulaklak sa hardin **para sa aking kapitbahay** na nagdiriwang ng kanyang kaarawan ngayon.
*I got some flowers from the garden **for my neighbor** who is celebrating his/her birthday today.*

Nagluluto si Mario ng pansit **para sa mga batang** naglilinis ng kanyang bakuran.
*Mario is cooking noodles **for the kids** who are cleaning his yard.*

Bibili ako ng mga inumin **para sa aking mga kaibigang** manonood ng laro sa bahay bukas.
*I am buying drinks **for my friends** who are watching the game at my place tomorrow.*

Relativizing the instrumental NP in an object-focus sentence:

Niluto niya ang manok **sa pamamagitan ng hurnong** inayos ko kahapon.
*He/she cooked the chicken **using the oven** that I fixed yesterday.*

Pinutol niya ang punong mangga **sa pamamagitan ng lagaring** hiniram niya kay Lina.
*He/she cut down the mango tree **using the saw** that he/she borrowed from Lina.*

Nagbungkal siya ng lupa sa bukid **sa pamamagitan ng traktorang** binili niya sa kanyang tiyo.
*He/she tilled the land on the farm **using the tractor** that he/she bought from his uncle.*

Relativizing the experiencer NP in a reason-focus sentence:

Ikinatuwa **ng mga bisitang** nanood ng palabas sa plasa ang mahusay na pagtatanghal ng mga mananayaw at mang-aawit.
*The wonderful performance by the dancers and singers made **the guests** who watched the show at the plaza very happy.*

Ikinagalit nang husto **ng mga taong** sumakay sa bus ang pagsisiksikan ng sobrang daming pasahero.
*The overcrowding of passengers in the overloaded vehicle made **the people** who took the bus very angry.*

Ikinagulat **ng mga empleyadong** binigyan ng parangal sa pagdiriwang ang hindi-inaasahang regalong natanggap nila.
The unexpected gift that they received surprised ***the employees*** *who were honored at the party.*

Relativizing the reason NP in an experiencer-focus sentence:

Nalilito ang mga empleyado **dahil sa magkasalungat na mga impormasyong** natanggap nila mula sa pamunuan ng kumpanya.
Employees are confused ***because of conflicting information*** *that they received from the company's management.*

Nababahala ang mga residente ng dormitoryo **dahil sa ingay** na nagmumula sa mga tubo ng tubig sa kanilang gusali.
Dormitory residents are worried ***because of the noise*** *coming from the water pipes in their building.*

Natakot ang aking kapatid **dahil sa balitang** nabasa niya sa diyaryo.
My brother/sister got scared ***because of the news*** *that he/she read in the newspaper.*

Chapter 11

Sentence structures

This chapter presents the structure of basic sentences or single-clause structures in Filipino. It is divided into four sections: (1) simple predicative sentence, (2) non-*ang* sentence, (3) interrogative sentence or question formation, and (4) negation.

11.1 Simple predicative sentences

11.1.1 Predicate + subject

The most basic sentence in Filipino is what is commonly referred to as the predicate + subject pattern. In this book, the term **predicate** refers to that part of the sentence or clause that asserts or states something about the subject. In Filipino, it need not contain a verb. The term **subject** refers to the thing (person, place, object, event, or idea) discussed or described by the predicate. In a basic sentence, it is a noun preceded by the marker ***ang***, ***si***, or ***sina*** or an *ang* pronoun. In Filipino, the subject or *ang* phrase need not be the actor or doer of the action expressed by the verb, if there is one. Here are some examples.

Predicate subject additional information

1. Tumakbo si Pedro sa parke.
   (*Ran subjmarker–Peter–in the park.*)
   Peter ran in the park.

2. Dinalaw sina Maria at Ana ng nanay nila.
   (*Visited subjmarker–Maria and Ana genmarker–mother.*)
   Their mother visited Maria and Ana.

DOI: 10.4324/9781315739427-12

3. Masaya ang mga bata sa klase kahapon.
   (*Happy subjmarker–kids in the class yesterday.*)
   The kids in the class were happy yesterday.
4. Doktor ang tatay ko.
   (*Doctor subjmarker–father–my.*)
   My father is a doctor.

In the preceding examples, sentences 1 and 2 contain a verb in the predicate, but sentences 3 and 4 do not. In sentence 1, the subject (Pedro) is the actor/doer, but in sentence 2 the subject (Maria and Ana) is not the actor/doer. In all of the examples, the subject is always preceded by a subject marker.

Filipino sentences can be classified into three basic patterns based on the predicate that they have: nominal sentences contain a noun predicate, adjectival sentences contain an adjective predicate, and verbal sentences contain a verb predicate. Two other patterns are added here because these also generally follow the predicate + topic pattern, but these are not considered to be canonical basic sentences. Existential sentences contain an existential phrase (***may*** + noun) in the predicate; prepositional sentences contain a prepositional phrase. Here are some illustrative examples.

Sentence type	***Predicate***	***Subject***	***More information***
nominal	Guro (*is a*) *teacher*	si Pedro (*marker*) *Peter.*	sa Bato High School. *at Bato High School.*
	Pedro is a teacher at Bato High School.		
adjectival	Masipag (*is*) *hardworking*	ang kapatid ko. (*marker*) *my sibling.*	
	My brother/sister is hardworking.		
verbal	Nagtatrabaho *work*	sina Liz at Ann (*marker*) *Liz and Ann*	sa aklatan. *at the library.*
	Liz and Ann work at the library.		
existential	May salu-salo *have a party*	kami *We*	sa Linggo. *on Sunday.*
	We have a party on Sunday.		
prepositional	Nasa labas (*are*) *outside*	ang mga aso. *The dogs*	
	The dogs are outside.		

The constituent noun phrases following a predicate may generally be rearranged without changing the meaning of the sentence. In this sense, Tagalog does not have a strict word order rule. Generally, the subject comes last but not when it is a pronoun. Pronouns, unless they are used to express possession, must immediately follow the predicate.

11.1.2 Ay sentence

Ay **sentences** are often referred to as *inverted sentences*, and the word *ay* is called a sentence inversion marker. The word order of this sentence type (subject + ay + predicate) is the reverse of the *simple predicative sentence* (predicate + subject). This sentence pattern is often employed in more formal or less familiar or intimate speech event settings, such as when giving a formal presentation or a speech at a gathering, or speaking to a stranger or a person of authority. Here is a comparative chart of simple predicative sentences and ay sentences.

Sentence type	*Predicate + subject*	*Subject + ay + predicate*
nominal	**Abogado si Liza.** *(is a) Lawyer–Liza.*	**Si Liza ay abogado.** *Liza is a lawyer.*
	Empleyado siya sa bangko. *(is an) Employee–He/she–at the bank.*	**Siya ay empleyado sa bangko.** *He/she is an employee at the bank.*
adjectival	**Mabait si Jose.** *(is) Kind–(submarker) Jose.*	**Si Jose ay mabait.** *Jose is kind.*
	Madaldal ang bata. *(is) Talkative–the kid.*	**Ang bata ay madaldal.** *The kid is talkative.*
verbal	**Nag-aaral ang estudyante sa kapihan.** *(is) studying–the student–at the coffee shop.*	**Ang estudyante ay nag-aaral sa kapihan.** *The student is studying at the coffee shop.*
	Bumili ako ng bagong telepono. *Bought–I–a new phone.*	**Ako ay bumili ng bagong telepono.** *I bought a new phone.*
existential	**May konsyerto sila sa CCP sa Mayo.** *Have a concert–they–at the CCP–in May.*	**Sila ay may konsyerto sa CCP sa Mayo.** *They have a concert at the CCP in May.*
	May trabaho si Rosa tuwing Sabado. *Has work–Rosa–every Saturday.*	**Si Rosa ay may trabaho tuwing Sabado.** *Rosa has work every Saturday.*

prepositional	**Sa Biyernes ang kaarawan ko.** *(is)On Friday–my birthday.*	**Ang kaarawan ko ay sa Biyernes.** *My birthday is on Friday.*
	Nasa Maynila sina Kim at Doris. *(are)In Manila–Kim and Doris.*	**Sina Kim at Doris ay nasa Maynila.** *Kim and Doris are in Manila.*

11.1.3 *Equational sentence*

Equational sentences are sometimes referred to as *ang–ang sentences*, because both the predicate and subject are preceded by the noun marker *ang*. Like the *ay* sentence, the word order of this sentence type (*ang* subject + *ang* predicate) is the reverse of the *simple predicative sentence* (predicate + subject). This sentence pattern is often used to emphasize the subject or in response to the questions **alin** *which* and **sino** *who*. Here is a comparative chart of simple predicative sentences and *ay* sentences.

Sentence type	*Predicate + subject*	*Ang subject + ang predicate*
nominal	**Abogado si Liza.** *(is a)Lawyer–Liza.* *Liza is a lawyer.*	**Si Liza ang abogado.** *Liza is the lawyer.*
	Empleyado siya sa bangko. *(is an) Employee–He/she–at the bank.* *He/she is an employee at the bank.*	**Siya ang empleyado sa bangko.** *He/she is the employee at the bank.*
adjectival	**Mabait si Jose.** *(is) Kind–(submarker) Jose.* *Jose is kind.*	**Si Jose ang mabait.** *Jose is the one who is kind.*
	Madaldal ang tindero. *(is) Talkative–the salesclerk.* *The salesclerk is talkative.*	**Ang tindero ang madaldal.** *The salesclerk is the one who is talkative.*
verbal	**Nag-aaral ang bata sa klasrum.** *(is) studying–the student–in the classroom.* *The student is studying in the classroom.*	**Ang bata ang nag-aaral sa klasrum.** *The child is the one studying in the classroom.*
	Bumili ako ng bagong telepono. *Bought–I–a new telephone.* *I bought a new telephone.*	**Ako ang bumili ng bagong telepono.** *I am the one who bought a new telephone.*

existential	**May konsyerto sila sa CCP.** *Have a concert–they–at the CCP.* *They have a concert at the CCP.*	**Sila ang may konsyerto sa CCP sa Mayo.** *They are the ones with a concert at the CCP.*
	May trabaho si Rosa araw-araw. *Has work–Rosa–every day.* *Rosa has work every day.*	**Si Rosa ang may trabaho araw-araw.** *Rosa is the one who has work every day.*
prepositional	**Sa Biyernes ang kaarawan ko.** *(is)On Friday–my birthday.* *My birthday is on Friday.*	**Ang kaarawan ko ang sa Biyernes.** *My birthday is the one (happening) on Friday.*
	Nasa Maynila sina Kim at Doris. *(are)In Manila–Kim and Doris.* *Kim and Doris are in Manila.*	**Sina Kim at Doris ang nasa Maynila.** *Kim and Doris are the ones in Manila.*

11.2 Non-*ang* sentence

Some sentences in Filipino do not contain an *ang* phrase but are complete or full clauses nonetheless. Because of their structure, these sentences are sometimes referred to as 'subjectless' sentences or non-predicative sentences. This section outlines five commonly used sentence patterns of this type.

11.2.1 Existential or *may* sentences may or may not contain an *ang* phrase. They are used to indicate the existence of some noun modified by either /may/ or /mayroon/. Without an *ang* phrase, they are roughly equivalent to the English existential pattern containing the phrase *there is/there are*. Their negative counterpart /wala/, indicating absence of some noun, will be discussed in detail in the chapter on negation. There is a slight difference in the sentence structures of sentences that use /may/ and sentences that use the full form /mayroon/. The latter requires a linker immediately before the noun referent. Here are some examples.

May sentences

May mga tao sa labas.
There are people *outside.*

May mga batang naglalaro sa salas.
There are kids *(who are) playing in the living room.*

Mayroon sentences

Mayroong mga tao sa labas.
There are people *outside.*

Mayroong mga batang naglalaro sa salas.
There are kids *(who are) playing in the living room.*

11.2.2 Sentences with the pseudo-verbs /gusto, ayaw, kailangan/ always have the actor and object marked for genitive case regardless of the focus inflection of the main verb. When the main verb is an actor-focus (AF) verb, the sentence cannot contain an *ang* phrase. In the following examples, the genitive case marking on the actor is highlighted.

Gusto sentences

Gusto **ni Bob** na bumili ng bagong kotse.
*Want–**genmark.Bob** –AF.buy–genmark.car*
Bob wants to buy a new car.

Gusto **ng bata**ng kumain ng sorbetes.
*Want–**genmark.child** –AF.eat–genmark.ice cream*
The child wants to eat ice cream.

Ayaw sentences

Ayaw **ng estudyante**ng magdala ng mabigat na kompyuter.
The student *does not like bringing a heavy computer.*

Ayaw **ng nanay ko**ng sumakay sa eroplano.
My mother *does not like traveling by plane.*

Kailangan sentences

Kailangan **mo**ng kumuha ng bagong pasaporte.
You*need to get a new passport.*

Kailangan **ng kapatid ko**ng magpaluto ng pagkain para sa salusalo.
My sister *needs to have a caterer cook for her party.*

11.2.3 Sentences with verbs indicating recently completed action, such as the *pagka-* upon completion of the action verbs and *ka-* recent perfective verbs always have the actor marked for genitive case. In the following examples, the verb and the actor in these clauses are highlighted.

Pagka- upon completion of action verbs in a clause

Pagkakain natin, maglalakad tayo sa parke.
After we eat*, we will walk in the park.*

Pagkagradweyt ni Lina, nagturo na siya sa aming hayskul.
(Soon) After Lina graduated*, she started teaching at our high school.*

Ka + CV recent perfective verbs in a clause

Kaaalis lang ni Grace nang tumawag ang nanay niya.
Grace just left *when her mother called.*

Kagagaling lang niya sa trabaho kaya pagod pa si Lito.
He just came from *work so Lito is still tired.*

11.2.4 **Sentences with certain superlative adjectival forms,** such as those that take the prefix /napaka-/, and constructions of the form /ang + adj. root/ always have genitive case marking on the noun being described (see chapter on adjectives for a more detailed discussion of adjective forms). The adjective and noun referents are highlighted in the following examples.

Napaka- superlative adjective forms in a sentence

Napakahusay ng mang-aawit sa palabas na pinanood namin kagabi.
The singer *in the show that we watched last night* ***was very good.***

Napakamahal ng gasolina ngayon.
Fuel is very expensive *these days.*

Ang + adjective root superlative forms in a sentence

Ang galing ng direktor ng pelikula.
The director *of the movie* ***is very good*** .

Ang mura ng tiket na nabili ko.
The ticket *that I bought* ***is very cheap.***

11.2.5 **Impersonal sentences containing weather-related verbs** do not contain *ang* phrases, and often the verb by itself forms a complete sentence. Generally, these are either verbal or adjectival sentences.

Verbal sentences

Umuulan.
It is ***raining.***

Lumindol kahapon.
It ***quaked*** *yesterday. (There was an earthquake yesterday.)*

Adjectival sentences

Mainit ngayon.
It is ***hot*** *today.*

Napakahangin.
It is ***very windy.***

11.3 Questions

Questions in Filipino are either information questions or yes/no questions. Yes/no questions are formed either simply by using a rising intonation on a simple declarative phrase or with the insertion of the enclitic adverb /ba/. Information questions, on the other hand, consist of an interrogative pronoun in initial position.

11.3.1 **Polar or yes/no questions** are interrogative sentences answerable by *yes* or *no*. The question is formed by simply inserting the enclitic adverb /ba/ immediately after the predicate in a sentence. In the following examples, the declarative sentence counterparts are provided for comparison.

Declarative sentences	***Yes/no interrogative sentences***
Guro ang nanay ni Jose. *Jose's mother is a teacher.*	Guro **ba** ang nanay ni Jose? *Is Jose's mother a teacher?*
Masipag ang estudyante. *The student is hardworking.*	Masipag **ba** ang estudyante? *Is the student hardworking?*
Bibili siya ng bagong sapatos. *He/she will buy new shoes.*	Bibili **ba** siya ng bagong sapatos? *Will he/she buy new shoes?*
Mayroong tao sa kusina. *There is someone in the kitchen.*	Mayroon **ba**ng tao sa kusina? *Is there anybody in the kitchen?*
Nasa Laguna sina Lucy at Jim. *Lucy and Jim are in Laguna.*	Nasa Laguna **ba** sina Lucy at Jim? *Are Lucy and Jim in Laguna?*

11.3.2 **Information questions** ask for specific information by using an interrogative pronoun as a substitute for the missing information in the sentence initial position and marking the rest of the sentences with /ang/. Here some examples using some of the most commonly used interrogative pronouns. To provide some context, sample responses are also included. In conversational Filipino, the part of the response that does not directly address the question is often elided.

English	***Filipino***	***Sentences***
who	sino	**Sino** ang propesor mo sa Kasaysayan? *Who is your History professor?* – **Si Dr. Santos** ang propesor ko. – ***Dr. Santos*** *is my professor.* **Sino** ang nagluto ng hapunan? *Who cooked dinner?*

		– **Si Linda** ang nagluto ng hapunan. – ***It was Linda*** *who cooked dinner.*
what	ano	**Ano** ang iyong kurso? ***What*** *is your course?* – **Antropolohiya** ang kurso ko. – *My course is* ***Anthropology****.* **Ano** ang gagawin mo mamaya? ***What*** *are you doing later?* – **Magsisine** ako mamaya. – *I am* ***watching a movie*** *later.* **Anong oras** magsisimula ang sine? ***What time*** *will the movie start?* – **Alas dos** magsisimula ang sine. *The movie will start* ***at 2:00****.*
where *where – location* *where – from*	saan nasaan tagasaan	**Saan** ka pupunta pagkatapos ng klase? ***Where*** *are you going after class?* – Pupunta ako **sa kapeterya** pagkatapos ng klase. – *I am going* ***to the cafeteria*** *after class.* **Nasaan** ang mga inumin? ***Where*** *are the drinks?* – **Nasa pridyider** ang mga inumin. – *The drinks are* ***in the refrigerator****.* **Tagasaan** ang kaibigan mo? ***Where*** *is your friend* ***from****?* – **Taga-Bacolod** ang kaibigan ko. – *My friend is* ***from Bacolod****.*
when	kailan	**Kailan** ang piyesta sa bayan ninyo? ***When*** *is your town's festival?* – **Sa Oktubre** ang piyesta sa bayan namin. – *The festival in our town is* ***in October*** *.* **Kailan** ka maglalakbay sa Mindanao? ***When*** *are you traveling to Mindanao?* – Maglalakbay ako sa Mindanao **sa susunod na buwan**. – *I am traveling to Mindanao* ***next month****.*

why	bakit	**Bakit** nagbitiw sa kanyang trabaho sa bangko si Carla? ***Why*** *did Carla resign from her job at the bank?* – Nagbitiw siya sa kanyang trabaho sa bangko **dahil nakahanap siya ng trabahong may mas mataas na sweldo**. – *She left her job at the bank* ***because she found a better-paying job****.*
how	paano	**Paano** magluto ng kare-kare? *How do you cook kare-kare?* – Para magluto ng kare-kare, **kailangan mong . . .** – *To cook kare-kare,* ***you need to . . .***
how many	ilan	**Ilan** ang mga kapatid mo? ***How many*** *siblings do you have?* – ***Tatlo*** *ang mga kapatid ko.* – *I have* ***three*** *siblings.* **Ilang araw** ang bakasyon mo? ***How many days*** *is your vacation?* – **Limang araw** ang bakasyon ko. – *My vacation will last for* ***five days****.*
what position in a sequence	pang-ilan	**Pang-ilan** ka sa apat na magkakapatid? ***In order of birth, what is your position*** *among four siblings?* – **Pangatlo** ako sa apat na magkakapatid. – *I am the* ***third*** *of four siblings.* **Pang-ilang klase** mo ito ngayong araw? ***In the sequence of classes attended today, what is the position*** *of this class?* – **Pang-apat na klase** ko ito ngayong araw. – *This is my* ***fourth class*** *today.*
how much – asking about cost	magkano	**Magkano** ang isang kilong mangga? ***How much*** *is a kilogram of mangoes?* – **Dalawandaang piso** ang isang kilong mangga. – ***Two hundred pesos*** *is the price of a kilogram of mangoes.* **Magkano** ito? ***How much*** *is this?*

		– **Limandaang piso** iyan. – *That is **five hundred pesos**.*
how much – asking about degree of quality	gaano / ka-/ + adjective root word	**Gaano katagal** ang biyahe mula Maynila hanggang Naga? ***How long** is the trip from Manila to Naga?* – **Pitong oras** ang biyahe mula Maynila hanggang Naga. – *The trip from Manila to Naga lasts **seven hours**.* **Gaano kaanghang** ang sabaw? ***How spicy** is the soup?* – **Maanghang na maanghang** ang sabaw. – *The soup is **very spicy**.*

11.4 Negation

The use of the negators *huwag*, *wala*, and *hindi* is presented in this section. The negative of **gusto** *want* or *like*, which is **ayaw** *not want* or *not like* is discussed in the section on pseudo-verbs. In Filipino, negative sentences are formed by simply placing a negator before the predicate. In this position, it becomes the highest predicate, and thus attracts or pulls to the position immediately following it words that have clitic properties, such as enclitic adverbs and pronouns.

11.4.1 Huwag is used to express a negative command or exhortation. In a negative sentence, there is a linker between the verb and the word immediately preceding it. For comparison, the following examples include positive counterparts. The negator and linker are highlighted.

Affirmative command	***Negative command***
Lumabas ka. (*You*) *go outside.*	**Huwag** ka**ng** lumabas. (*You*) ***do not** go outside.*
Manood kayo ng telebisyon. *You all watch television.*	**Huwag** kayo**ng** manood ng telebisyon. ***Don't** you all watch television.*
Itapon nga ninyo ang mga papel. *You all throw away the papers.*	**Huwag** nga ninyo**ng** itapon ang mga papel. ***Don't** you all throw away the papers.*
Ipagluto mo sila ng almusal. (*You*) *cook breakfast for them.*	**Huwag** mo sila**ng** ipagluto ng almusal. ***Don't*** (*you*) *cook breakfast for them.*
Lumakad na tayo sa parke. *Let us walk in the park now.*	**Huwag** na tayo**ng** lumakad sa parke. *Let us **not** walk in the park anymore.*

11.4.2 Wala is used to negate existential or *may* sentences. It indicates absence of something or someone. In a negative sentence, there is a linker between the noun referent and the word immediately preceding it. For comparison, the following examples include positive counterparts. The negator and linker are highlighted.

Affirmative existential sentence	***Negative existential sentence***
May pera ako. *I have money.*	**Wala** ako**ng** pera. *I **do not have** money.*
Mayroon akong klase mamaya. *I have a class later.*	**Wala** ako**ng** klase mamaya. *I **do not have** a class later.*
May bisita pala sa salas. *I was surprised to see that there are guests in the living room.*	**Wala** pala**ng** bisita sa salas. *I was surprised to see that **there are no** guests in the living room.*
Mayroon nang parke sa sentro ng bayan. *There is a park in the downtown area now.*	**Wala** na**ng** parke sa gitna ng bayan. ***There is no** more park in the downtown area.*
Mayroong mga alagang hayop ang lolo ko. *My grandfather has pet animals.*	**Walang** mga alagang hayop ang lolo ko. *My grandfather **does not have** pets.*

11.4.3 Hindi is used to negate all other sentences, and no linker is needed to link the negator to other parts of the sentence. For a more thorough overview of its use, negation in all basic sentence types is illustrated by the following examples here, excluding existential sentence and prepositional sentences with the marker /nasa/. Their *ay* sentence counterparts are also provided to show the difference in structures.

Sentence type	*Affirmative predicate + subject* ***and ay sentence***	***Negative sentence***
nominal	Abogado si Liza. *(is a)Lawyer–Liza.* *Liza is a lawyer.*	**Hindi** abogado si Liza. *(is) not a Lawyer–Liza.* *Liza is **not** a lawyer.*
	Si Liza ay abogado. *Liza is a lawyer.*	Si Liza ay **hindi** abogado. *Liza is **not** a lawyer.*
adjectival	Mabait si Jose. *(is) Kind–Jose.* *Jose is kind.*	**Hindi** mabait si Jose. *(is) Not kind–Jose.* *Jose is **not** kind.*
	Si Jose ay mabait. *Jose is kind.*	Si Jose ay **hindi** mabait. *Jose is **not** kind.*

verbal	Nag-aaral siya sa kapihan. (is) *studying–he/she–at the coffee shop.* *He/she is studying at the coffee shop.*	**Hindi** siya nag-aaral sa kapihan. (is) *not–he/she–studying–at the coffee shop.* *He/she is **not** studying at the coffee shop.*
	Siya ay nag-aaral sa kapihan. *He/she is studying at the coffee shop.*	Siya ay **hindi** nag-aaral sa kapihan. *He/she is **not** studying at the coffee shop.*
prepositional	Sa Biyernes ang kaarawan ko. (is)*On Friday–my birthday.* *My birthday is on Friday.*	**Hindi** sa Biyernes ang kaarawan ko. (is)*Not on Friday–my birthday.* *My birthday is **not** on Friday.*
	Ang kaarawan ko ay sa Biyernes. *My birthday is on Friday.*	Ang kaarawan ko ay **hindi** sa Biyernes. *My birthday is **not** on Friday.*

Chapter 12

Clauses and conjunctions

Clauses in Filipino can comprise a word or group of words that express a complete thought. In contrast to English, clauses in Filipino do not need a verb to express a complete idea. Like many other languages of the world, Filipino distinguishes between independent or main clause and dependent or subordinate clauses. The following are examples of sentences containing a single independent clause. Only the first and last examples contain a verb (in bold).

Filipino	English
Umuulan.	*(It is)* ***raining**.*
Maaraw ngayon.	*(It is) sunny today.*
May tao sa labas.	*There (is) somebody outside.*
Maganda ang pelikula.	*The move (is) good.*
Guro ang aking nanay.	*My mother (is) a teacher.*
Nakapagluto na ako ng hapunan.	*I **have cooked** dinner already.*

12.1 Independent clause and coordinating conjunctions

An independent clause, also called main clause, expresses a complete thought and can stand alone as a sentence. The following examples are sentences containing two independent clauses connected by a coordinating conjunction.

Magluluto ka ba **o** kakain tayo sa labas?
*Are you cooking, **or** are we eating out?*

Naglinis kami ng garahe **at** itinapon namin ang lahat ng basura.
*We cleaned the garage, **and** we tossed all the rubbish.*

Masaya ang piyesta **pero** nakakapagod ang paghahanda nito.
*Festivals are fun, **but** preparing for it is very tiring.*

DOI: 10.4324/9781315739427-13

Huwag kang matakot **dahil** kasama mo ako.
*Do not be afraid, **for** I am with you.*

Natapos ko na ang aking proyekto **kaya** puwede na akong magpahinga.
*I finished my project already, **so** I can take a break now.*

Nanalo ang mga kandidato ng aming partido sa huling halalan. **Samakatuwid**, malaki ang posibilidad na masisimulan na ang mga programang pangkomunidad na matagal nang hinihintay ng aming bayan.
*Our party's candidates won in the last elections. **Therefore**, there is a good chance that the community programs that our town has long been waiting for will finally be initiated.*

Nagpahayag ng kanilang pagtutol sa pagtaas ng presyo ng langis ang mga tsuper ng dyip sa pamamagitan ng malawakang welga. **Gayunpaman**, mas malaki ang papel at impluwensya ng pandaigdigang merkado sa pagtatakda ng lokal na presyo nito.
*Jeepney drivers expressed their objections to the oil price increase through a general strike. **However**, world market conditions play a significant role and influence in determining local oil prices.*

12.2 Dependent clause and subordinating conjunctions

A dependent or subordinate clause does not express a complete thought but depends on the main clause to express a complete idea and cannot stand as a sentence by itself. Subordinate clauses can be further classified into three types: nominal clause, adjectival clause, and adverbial clause.

12.2.1 A **nominal clause** is a subordinate clause that functions as a noun. In Filipino, nominal clauses generally function as complements of classes of verbs that can take sentential subjects, such as reporting verbs and perception–cognition verbs. Like other languages, Filipino has verbs that can take an embedded clause or sentence as a verbal complement. Some embedded clauses may function as sentential subjects, while others may function as non-subject complements. When the embedded clause is in the declarative form, the complementizer immediately preceding it is the conjunction /na/. When the embedded clause is in the interrogative form, the complementizer immediately preceding it is the conjunction /kung/. With the exception of complements of pseudo-verbs, embedded clauses with the complementizer /na/ may be used consistently instead of having the phonologically conditioned forms /-ng/ after a vowel and /n/, and /na/ following a consonant. Here are some examples of complement clauses. The complementizer, /na/ or /kung/, is in bold, and the embedded clause is underlined.

Complement clause of a pseudo-verb

Gusto ko**ng** manood ng sine sa susunod na Linggo.
I want to watch a movie next week.

Dapat kayo**ng** magdala ng kompyuter bukas.
You (all) must bring a computer tomorrow.

Complement clause of actor-focus (AF) verbs

Naniniwala ako **na** magiging mabuting pangulo siya.
*I believe **that** he/she will be a good president.*

Nagtatanong ang kapatid ko **kung** bakit hindi kayo nakarating sa kanyang kasal.
*My brother/sister is asking **why** you did not make it to his/her wedding.*

Complement clause of object-focus (OF) verbs

Narinig ko **na** binigyan ng parangal ng lokal na pamahalaan ang iyong tatay.
*I heard **that** the local government gave your father an award of recognition.*

Ibinalita nila sa amin **kung** saan gagawin ang programa.
*They told us **where** the program will be held.*

Complement clause of location/direction-focus (LDF) verbs

Pinayuhan niya kami **na** makinig sa aming mga magulang.
He/she advised us to listen to our parents.

Sinabihan ni Juan si Maria **kung** kailan mangingibang-bayan ang pamilya niya.
*Juan told Maria **when** his family is moving overseas.*

A small set of nouns may also take nominal subordinate clause complements. The following examples show nouns in bold and the subordinate clauses underlined.

Trabaho ni Juan na linisin ang bakuran tuwing hapon.
*It is Juan's **job** to clean the yard every afternoon.*

Tungkulin niyang bantayan ang mga bata.
*It is his/her **responsibility** to watch over the children.*

Malaking **pagkakamali** kung ibibenta mo ang inyong lupa.
*It would be a big **mistake** if you were to sell your land.*

Mahirap na **responsibilidad** kung mag-aampon kayo ng bata.
*It would be a huge **responsibility** if you were to adopt (a child).*

Indefinite pronouns may also serve as or introduce nominal clauses. Some commonly used indefinite pronouns are

anuman	*whatever*	kahit ano	*anything*
sinuman	*whoever*	kahit sino	*anyone*
saanman	*wherever*	kahit saan	*anywhere*
kailanman	*whenever*	kahit kailan	*anytime*

12.2.2 An **adverbial clause** is a subordinate clause that functions as an adverb. This type of dependent clause is introduced by an adverbial conjunction modifying the situation expressed in the main clause in terms of time (when), frequency (how often), intensity (to what extent), condition, contrast, and cause and effect. Adverbial subordinate clauses may come before or after the main clause. In the next few paragraphs, the most commonly used conjunctions are listed, followed by some examples of their use. (Also, see chapter on connectors.)

Some of the most frequently used conjunctions indicating time and frequency are the following:

noong	*back when*
kapag	*when* or *whenever*
tuwing	*everytime*
mula nang	*since* or *ever since*
hanggang	*until* or *up to*
bago	*before*
pagkatapos	*afterward*
habang	*While*

Makakaalis na kayo **kapag** tumunog na ang kampana.
You can leave ***when*** *the bell rings.*

Nagluluto si Lisa sa kusina **habang** naglilinis si Ben sa salas.
Lisa is cooking in the kitchen, ***while*** *Ben is cleaning in the living room.*

Mula nang nawalan siya ng trabaho, naging masungit na si Lito.
Ever since *he lost his job, Lito has become short-tempered.*

Bago kayo pumasok sa eskuwela, mag-almusal muna kayo.
Before *you go to school, eat your breakfast first.*

Some frequently used conjunctions indicating cause and effect are the following:

dahil/sapagkat	*because*
kaya/kung kaya	*and so*
upang/para	*in order to*
at nang	*so that*

Nagawa ko lamang iyon **sapagkat** mahal ko kayo.
I only did that ***because*** *I love you all.*

Wala siyang mahanap na trabaho sa bansa **kaya** nagpasiya si Jun na mag-OFW.
He could not find a job in-country, ***so*** *Jun decided to work abroad.*

Upang makatulong sa kanyang pamilya, nagtrabaho si Luis sa Dubai.
In order to *help his family, Luis worked in Dubai.*

To express contrast, the following conjunctions are frequently employed:

kahit na	*even if*
subalit/subali't	*Although*
datapwat/datapwa't	*even though*
gayunman	*nevertheless*
samantala	*in spite of*

Kahit na mahirap ang trabaho bilang katulong, tiniis ito ni Emily.
Even if *the job as a maid was hard, Emily endured it.*

Lumalakas ang ekonomiya **datapwat** hindi natin ito direktang nakikita.
The economy is growing ***even though*** *we cannot directly see it.*

Mataas ang kanyang grado samantalang puro lakwatsa lang ang ginagawa ni Jim.
He got good grades ***in spite of*** *Jim constantly doing nothing but going out.*

Frequently used conjunctions to specify conditional situation are the following:

kung	*If*
kundi	*if not*
sakali man	*in case*
basta/basta't	*as long as*
baka/kung sakali	*just in case*

Pupunta ako sa salu-salo **kung** papunta rin kayo.
I am going to the party ***if*** *you all are going too.*

Magbotas kayo para nakahanda kayo **sakali mang** umulan at bumaha.
Wear boots so you can be ready ***in case*** *it rains and there is flooding.*

Kung sakaling mapadaan ka sa opisina, pakibigay mo ito kay Mr. Santos.
Just in case *you happen to stop by the office, please give this to Mr. Santos.*

In addition to those already mentioned, there are other conjunctive adverbials in Filipino that are commonly used in extended discourse and more detailed narrations, presentations, and conversations. Here are some frequently used ones:

gayundin	*furthermore*
at saka	*and also*
sa kabilang dako	*on the other hand*
bilang halimbawa	*for instance*
bilang karagdagan	*in addition*
kahit anupaman	*regardless*
ganoon man	*despite the fact*
kung anu't-ano man	*be that as it may*
gayunpaman	*Nevertheless*
samakatuwid	*Therefore*
sa katunayan	*in fact*
kung hindi man	*if not that*

12.2.3 Adjective clause. A dependent clause that functions as an adjective in Filipino has the structure of a relative clause or phrasal modifier. Generally, it follows or comes after the noun that it modifies and is marked or introduced by the linker *na*.

Filipino does not use (interrogative) relative pronouns, but instead it uses the linker *na* to express relativization or phrasal modification. It must be noted that contemporary use of Filipino in some media outlets considers the relative pronoun 'kung saan' as standard usage in free variation with the form *na* + locative-focus verb (LF).

Like single-word modifiers, such as adjectives, numerals, and colors, a relative clause is connected to the noun it modifies by a linker. Technically, modifiers in Filipino can precede or follow the noun they modify. However, in practice, there is a preference for single-word modifiers to come before the noun and relative clauses to follow the noun. In fact, both single-word and phrasal modifiers can occur together modifying the same noun. The verbal inflection for focus is most relevant in relativization because the head noun of a relative clause must always be the syntactic focus (or subject) of the clause. It must be noted, however, that a fairly recent linguistic innovation is to use the complementizer /kung/ when relativizing a head noun, which functions as the location (and sometimes direction) of an action or event instead of using an LDF verb. The examples provided here show the relativization of head nouns that have different syntactic functions. The head noun is underlined, while the linker and the relative clause are in bold.

Syntactic function of head noun	***Examples of relative clauses***
Subject of an AF verb	Nakita ko <u>ang lalaki</u>**ng pumatay ng aso ninyo**. *I saw <u>the man</u>* ***who killed your dog****.*

Object of an OF verb	Dinala niya sa salusalo ang pagkaing **niluto ng kanyang nanay**. *He/she brought to the party the dish* ***that was cooked by his/her mother****.*
Location of an LDF verb	Binisita namin ang lugar **na pinaglibingan ng aming lolo**. *We visited the place* ***where our grandfather was buried****.* or Binisita namin ang lugar **kung saan inilibing ang aming lolo**. *We visited the place* ***where our grandfather was buried****.*
Direction of an LDF verb	Kinausap ako ng estudyanteng **binigyan ninyo ng parangal**. *The student* ***to whom you gave an award*** *talked to me.*
beneficiary of a benefactive-focus (BF) verb	Siya ang bisitang **ipinagluto ng aking kaibigan ng hapunan**. *He/she is the guest* ***for whom my friend cooked dinner****.*
instrument of an instrumental-focus (IF) verb	Ito ang gunting **na ipinanggupit ko ng buhok ni Pedro**. *This is the pair of scissors* ***with which I cut Pedro's hair****.*
reason of a reason-focus (RF) verb	Isusulat ko ang balitang **ikasasaya ng mga tao sa aming bayan**. *I will write the news that which will be the cause of happiness of the people in our town.*

12.2.4 Relativizing the subject or focused noun phrase of the main clause

In the following examples, the head noun or relativized noun is in bold, and the relative clause is underlined.
Relativizing the actor noun phrase (NP) in an AF sentence:

Dumating nang maaga **ang babaeng** nagtitinda ng prutas sa harap ng aming gusali.
The woman *who sells fruits in front of our building came early.*
Nagbigay ng donasyon sa simbahan **ang matandang lalaking** nakatira sa lumang bahay sa dulo ng kalyeng iyan.

The old man *who lives at the old house at the end of that street gave a donation to the church.*
Nakakatugtog ng iba't-ibang instrumentong pangmusika **ang estudyanteng** kalilipat lang sa aming eskuwelahan.
The student *who just moved to our school can play several musical instruments.*

Relativizing the object NP in an OF sentence:

Nakita ko **ang mga artistang** magtatanghal sa palabas mamayang gabi.
*I saw **the actors** who are performing at the show tonight.*

Binili niya **ang parol** na ginawa ng kanyang kapitbahay.
*He/she bought **the Christmas lantern** that his/her neighbor made.*

Hinuhugasan ni Juan **ang mga gulay** na ibinigay ng kaibigan ko.
*Juan is washing **the vegetables** that were given by my friend.*

Relativizing the locative/directional NP in an LDF sentence:

Pinuntahan nina Jun at Rudy **ang parkeng** nasa ibabaw ng bundok.
*Jun and Rudy went **to the park**, which is located on top of the mountain.*

Tatawagan namin **ang ahensyang** nagbibigay ng tulong sa mga batang-lansangan.
*We will place a call **to the agency** that provides assistance to street children.*

Tinulungan nila **ang mga komunidad** na nasalanta ng bagyo.
*They gave assistance/help **to communities** that were battered by the storm.*

Relativizing the benefactive NP in a BF sentence:

Ipinaghahanda nila ng tanghalian **ang mga bisitang** dumating kaninang umaga.
*They are preparing lunch **for the guests** who arrived this morning.*

Inihanap niya ng pansamantalang tirahan **ang mga taong** nawalan ng bahay dahil sa sunog.
*He/she looked for temporary housing **for people** who lost their homes in the fire.*

Ipaglalaba ni Aling Marina ng damit **ang mga turistang** nagbabakasyon sa aming baryo.
*Mrs. Marina will do laundry **for the tourists** who are vacationing in our village.*

Relativizing the instrumental NP in an IF sentence:

Ipinambili niya ng meryenda **ang perang** ibinigay mo.
*He/she bought snacks **with the money** that you gave (him/her).*

Ipantakip mo ng iyong ulo **ang sumbrerong** ginawa ni Pedro.
*Cover/protect your head **with the hat** that Pedro made.*

Ipanghugas mo ng iyong sugat **ang sabong** inirekomenda ng doktor.
*Wash/clean your wound **with the soap**, which the doctor recommended.*

Relativizing the experiencer NP in an EF sentence:

Natuwa **ang mga bisitang** nanood ng palabas sa plasa.
The guests *who watched the show at the plaza enjoyed themselves.*

Nagugutom na **ang mga boluntaryong** gumagawa ng palamuti para sa pagdiriwang.
The volunteers *who are making decorations for the celebration are feeling hungry.*

Dahil sa sobrang init, nahilo **ang batang** nagtitinda ng bulaklak sa labas ng simbahan.
*Due to extreme heat, **the young person** who is selling flowers outside the church felt faint.*

Relativizing the reason NP in an RF sentence:

Ikinalungkot niya **ang balitang** narinig niya sa radyo kanina.
The news *that he/she heard on the radio saddened him/her.*

Ikinababahala nila **ang bagong patakarang** inaprubahan ng lokal na pamahalaan.
The new policy *that was approved by the local government worries them.*

Ikinagalak ng aking lola **ang pagdiriwang** na inihanda ng kanyang mga apo.
The celebration*, which was organized by her grandchildren, made my grandmother happy.*

12.2.5 **Relative clauses may also be associated with unfocused NPs in the main clause.** The following examples illustrate how unfocused or non-subject NPs may also be relativized.

Relativizing the actor NP in an OF sentence:

Kinuha **ng paring** nangangalap ng abuloy ang perang nasa mesa.
The priest *who is collecting donations took the money on the table.*

Dadalhin **ng mga batang** sasama sa biyahe ang kanilang mga baong tanghalian.
The children *who are joining the trip will bring their own packed lunch.*

Isinusuot **ng mga mananayaw** na nagtatanghal sa parada ang katutubong mga kasuotan.
The dancers*who perform in the parade wear traditional costumes.*

Relativizing the object NP in an AF sentence:

Para sa salusalo, magdadala si Anna **ng mga kakaning** niluto ng kanyang lola.

*For the dinner celebration, Anna will bring **rice cakes** that were prepared by her grandmother.*

Sumulat siya **ng tulang** babasahin ng klase sa aming pagtatanghal.
*He/she wrote **a poem** that will be read by our class for our presentation.*

Bumasa kami **ng artikulong** tumatalakay sa usaping panseguridad sa aming rehiyon.
*We read **an article** that discusses security issues in our region.*

Relativizing the locative/directional NP in an AF sentence:

Tumulong sila **sa mga taong** nawalan ng bahay dahil sa lindol.
*They gave assistance/help **to the people** who lost their homes because of the earthquake.*

Maglalagay siya ng bulaklak **sa mesang** inilagay ko sa harap ng altar.
*He/she is going to put some flowers **on the table** that I placed in front of the altar.*

Tumingin kami **sa larawang** nakasabit sa dingding.
*We looked **at the picture** that is hanging on the wall.*

Relativizing the benefactive NP in an AF sentence:

Kumuha ako ng bulaklak sa hardin **para sa aking kapitbahay** na nagdiriwang ng kanyang kaarawan ngayon.
*I got some flowers from the garden **for my neighbor** who is celebrating his/her birthday today.*

Nagluluto si Mario ng pansit **para sa mga batang** naglilinis ng kanyang bakuran.
*Mario is cooking noodles **for the kids** who are cleaning his yard.*

Bibili ako ng mga inumin **para sa aking mga kaibigang** manonood ng laro sa bahay bukas.
*I am buying drinks **for my friends** who are watching the game at my place tomorrow.*

Relativizing the instrumental NP in an OF sentence:

Niluto niya ang manok **sa pamamagitan ng hurnong** inayos ko kahapon.
*He/she cooked the chicken **using the oven** that I fixed yesterday.*

Pinutol niya ang punong mangga **sa pamamagitan ng lagaring** hiniram niya kay Lina.
*He/she cut down the mango tree **using the saw** that he/she borrowed from Lina.*

Nagbungkal siya ng lupa sa bukid **sa pamamagitan ng traktorang** binili niya sa kanyang tiyo.
*He/she tilled the land on the farm **using the tractor** that he/she bought from his/her uncle.*

Relativizing the experiencer NP in an RF sentence:

Ikinatuwa **ng mga bisitang** nanood ng palabas sa plasa ang mahusay na pagtatanghal ng mga mananayaw at mang-aawit.
*The wonderful performance by the dancers and singers made **the guests** who watched the show at the plaza very happy.*

Ikinagalit nang husto **ng mga taong** sumakay sa bus ang pagsisiksikan ng sobrang daming pasahero.
*The overcrowding of passengers in the overloaded vehicle made **the people** who took the bus very angry.*

Ikinagulat **ng mga empleyadong** binigyan ng parangal sa pagdiriwang ang hindi inaasahang regalong natanggap nila.
*The unexpected gift that they received surprised **the employees** who were honored at the party.*

Relativizing the reason NP in an EF sentence:

Nalilito ang mga empleyado **dahil sa magkasalungat na mga impormasyong** natanggap nila mula sa pamunuan ng kumpanya.
*Employees are confused **because of conflicting information** that they received from the company's management.*

Nababahala ang mga residente ng dormitoryo **dahil sa ingay** na nagmumula sa mga tubo ng tubig sa kanilang gusali.
*Dormitory residents are worried **because of the noise** coming from the water pipes in their building.*

Natakot ang aking kapatid **dahil sa balitang** nabasa niya sa diyaryo.
*My brother/sister got scared **because of the news** that he/she read in the newspaper.*

Chapter 13

Interjections, courtesies, and other lexical classes

Interjections, courtesies, and other lexical classes that are necessary for talking about familiar everyday topics are provided in this chapter.

13.1 Interjections are words or group of words that capture the sudden burst of emotion or energy on the part of the speaker as a reaction to the information being received or provided, or the situation that induced such a reaction. The following chart lists some commonly used interjections, everyday expressions, and conversation fillers.

Interjection and common expressions	***Equivalent English expressions***
Naku!	*Wow!/Oh my!*
Hay naku!	*Oh, gosh!*
(Ang) galing!	*Great!*
Talaga?	*Really?*
Talaga!	*Indeed!*
Aba!	*Oh, what a surprise!*
Hoy!	*Hey!/Hey there!*
Sus!/Diyos ko!	*Oh, my God!*
Susmaryosep!	*Jesus Christ!*
Sayang!	*Too bad!/What a pity!*
Kawawa naman!	*How pitiful!*
Aray!	*Ouch!*
Tumigil ka!	*Stop it!*
Grabe!	*Too much!*
Awat na!	*That's enough!*
Dali!	*Quick!*
Hala!	*Oh, no!*
Walanghiya!	*How rude!*
Sige!	*Okay!*

DOI: 10.4324/9781315739427-14

Sige na!	*Come on!*
Sige pa!	*More! More!*
Sige nga!	*Let's see what you can do.*
Hindi nga!	*You're kidding!*
Siyempre!	*Of course!*
Siguro.	*Maybe.*
Maaari.	*It's possible.*
Sigurado.	*For sure!/Certainly.*
Tumpak!	*Exactly!*
Bahala na!	*Come what may.*
Bahala ka!	*It's up to you.*
Sayang!	*Too bad.*
Ewan ko!	*I don't know.*
Siyanga!	*That's right!*
Oo nga.	*Indeed!*
Tara na!	*Let's go!*
Halikayo!/Halina kayo.	*Come on, let's go.*
Para!	*Please pull over.*
Bilisan mo!	*Hurry up!*
Saglit lang!	*Wait a second.*
Teka!	*Wait!*
Teka muna!	*Just wait!*
Hindi ba?/'Di ba?	*Isn't that right?*
Hindi bale.	*It's not important.*
Di bale na lang!	*Never mind.*
Sige na nga.	*Oh, alright.*
Ganoon ba?	*Is that right?*
Wala kang pakialam.	*It's none of your business!*
Huwag kang makialam!	*Don't meddle!*
Wala akong pakialam!	*I don't care!*
E ano ngayon?	*So what?*
Tama ka./Tama po kayo.	*You're right!*

13.2 Some useful expressions for **greetings and leave-taking courtesies** are provided here. For most expressions, simply adding the enclitic /po/ at the end of the sentence turns the expression into a formal or more polite courtesy appropriate when addressing someone older, of authority, or a stranger.

*Commonly used greetings and **leave-taking courtesies***	***Equivalent English expressions***
Kumusta (po)?	*Hello./How are you?*
Magandang umaga (po).	*Good morning.*
Magandang tanghali (po).	*Good noontime.*

Magandang hapon (po).	*Good afternoon.*
Magandang gabi (po).	*Good evening.*
Paalam (po).	*Goodbye.*
Sige (po).	*Bye.*
Hanggang sa muli (po).	*Until next time.*
Sandali lang (po).	*Please wait./Just a second.*
Maraming salamat (po).	*Thank you very much.*
Walang anuman (po).	*You're welcome (po).*
Mawalang-galang na po.	*Please excuse me.* (always formal)
Pasensiya ka na. (informal) Pasensiya na po kayo. (formal)	*I'm sorry./Excuse me.* (minor infractions)
Patawarin mo ako. (familiar) Patawarin po ninyo ako. (formal)	*Please forgive me.* (major infractions)
Tuloy ka. (familiar) Tuloy po kayo. (formal)	*(Please) come in.*
Ingat ka. (familiar) Mag-ingat po kayo. (formal)	*Take care.*

13.3 **Numerals** from three source languages are used in Filipino. Tagalog-derived numbers are used for counting, indicating order, and expressing monetary value, especially for numbers smaller than 10,000. Spanish-derived numbers are generally used for telling time and, interchangeably with Tagalog-derived numbers, in expressing monetary value. In spoken Filipino, especially among young people, English numbers are used interchangeably with Tagalog- and Spanish-derived numbers for almost all contexts where numerals are necessary. The prefixes /pang-/ and /ika-/ are used to form ordinal numbers.

13.3.1 Tagalog-derived numbers and their logic

	1–10	*10 x X*	*100 × X*	*1,000 × X*
1	isa	10 sampu	100 sandaan	1,000 sanlibo
2	dalawa	20 dalawampu	200 dalawang daan	2,000 dalawang libo
3	tatlo	30 tatlumpu	300 tatlong daan	3,000 tatlong libo
4	apat	40 apatnapu	400 apat na raan	4,000 apat na libo
5	lima	50 limampu	500 limang daan	5,000 limang libo
6	anim	60 animnapu	600 anim na raan	6,000 anim na libo
7	pito	70 pitumpu	700 pitong daan	7,000 pitong libo
8	walo	80 walumpu	800 walong daan	8,000 walong libo
9	siyam	90 siyamnapu	900 siyam na raan	9,000 siyam na libo

	10 + X	Units of 10 + X	Units of 100 + X
1	11 labing-isa	21 dalawampu't-isa	111 sandaan at labing-isa
2	12 labindalawa	32 tatlumpu't-dalawa	212 dalawang daan at labindalawa
3	13 labintatlo	43 apatnapu't-tatlo	313 tatlong daan at labintatlo
4	14 labing-apat	54 limampu't-apat	414 apat na raan at labing-apat
5	15 labinlima	65 animnapu't-lima	565 limang daan at animnapu't-lima
6	16 labing-anim	76 pitumpu't-anim	676 anim na raan at pitumpu't-anim
7	17 labimpito	87 walumpu't-pito	787 pitong daan at walumpu't-pito
8	18 labingwalo	98 siyamnapu't-walo	898 walong daan at siyamnapu't-walo
9	19 labinsiyam	29 dalawampu't-siyam	929 siyam na raan at dalawampu't-siyam

	Units of 1000 + X
1	1,001 sanlibo't-isa
2	2,012 dalawanlibo't-labindalawa
3	3,134 tatlong libo, isang daan, tatlumpu't-apat
4	40,564 apatnapung libo, limandaan, animnapu't-apat
5	50,235 limampung libo, dalawandaan, tatlumpu't-lima
6	615,786 anim na raan, labinlimang libo, pitong daan, walumpu't-anim
7	734,729 pitong daan, tatlumpu't-apat na libo, pitong daan, dalawampu't-siyam
8	835,607 walong daan, tatlumpu't-limang libo, anim na raan, at pito
9	910,750 siyam na raan at sampung libo, pitong daan, at limampu
milyon	1,987,654 isang milyon, siyam na raan walumpu't pitong libo, anim na raan, at limampu't-apat

13.3.2 Spanish-derived numbers for telling time

A complete answer to the question, 'Anong oras na?' (*What time is it?*), includes one of the following expressions to specify the time of day:

@ 5:00 am – 11:30 am	______ ng umaga	______ *in the morning*
@ 11:30 am – 12:30 pm	______ ng tanghali	______ *at noon*
@ 12:30 pm – 5:45 pm	______ ng hapon	______ *in the afternoon*
@ 5:45 pm – 11:45 pm	______ ng gabi	______ *in the evening*

@ 11:45 pm – 1:00 am ______ ng hatinggabi ______ *at midnight*
@ 1:00 am – 5:00 am ______ ng madaling araw ______ *at dawn*

Time	***Spanish derived***	***Tagalog/Filipino***
1:00	ala-una	ikaisa
2:00	alas-dos	ikalawa/ika-dalawa
3:00	alas-tres	ikatlo/ika-tatlo
4:00	alas-kuwatro	ikaapat
5:00	alas-singko	ikalima
6:00	alas-sais	ikaanim
7:00	alas-siyete	ikapito
8:00	alas-otso	ikawalo
9:00	alas-nuwebe	ikasiyam
10:00	alas-diyes	ikasampu
11:00	alas-onse	ikalabing-isa
12:00	alas-dose	ikalabindalawa

Time	***Spanish derived***	***Tagalog/Filipino***
12:05	alas-dose singko ng . . .	limang minuto makalipas ang ikalabindalawa ng . . .
12:10	alas-dose diyes ng . . .	sampung minuto makalipas ang ikalabindal-awa ng . . .
12:15	alas-dose kinse ng . . .	labinlimang minuto makalipas ang ikalabi-ndalawa ng . . .
12:20	alas-dose beynte ng . . .	dalawampung minuto makalipas ang ika-labindalawa ng . . .
12:25	alas-dose beynte singko ng . . .	dalawampu't-limang minuto makalipas ang ikalabindalawa ng . . .
12:30	alas-dose y medya ng . . .	ikalabindalawa at kalahati ng . . . tatlumpung minuto makalipas ang ikalabi-ndalawa ng . . .
12:35	alas-dose treynta y singko ng . . .	dalawampu't-limang minuto bago mag-ikaisa ng . . .
12:40	alas dose kuwarenta ng . . .	dalawampung minuto bago mag-ikaisa ng . . .
12:45	alas dose kuwarenta y singko ng . . .	labinlimang minuto bago mag-ikaisa ng . . .

12:50	alas dose singku-wenta ng . . .	sampung minuto bago mag-ikaisa ng . . .
12:55	alas dose singku-wenta y singko ng . . .	limang minuto bago mag-ikaisa ng . . .

13.4 The words for **days of the week and months of the year** are Spanish derived, except for the word for Sunday.

Months of the year				***Days of the week***	
Enero	*January*	Hulyo	*July*	Lunes	*Monday*
Pebrero	*February*	Agosto	*August*	Martes	*Tuesday*
Marso	*March*	Setyembre	*September*	Miyerkoles	*Wednesday*
Abril	*April*	Oktubre	*October*	Huwebes	*Thursday*
Mayo	*May*	Nobyembre	*November*	Biyernes	*Friday*
Hunyo	*June*	Disyembre	*December*	Sabado	*Saturday*
Example: Lunes, ika-16 ng Enero 2019				Linggo	*Sunday*

Chapter 14

Summary

The most salient Filipino grammatical markings, morphological forms, and syntactic structures are summarized in this section to serve as a quick reference guide for the reader or language learner.

14.1 Verbal inflection

Aspect

Form	*Affix*
Completed	*n-*
Incompleted	*n-* + C_1V_1 reduplication
contemplated	*m-* + C_1V_1 reduplication
infinitive/neutral	
recently completed	*ka-* + C_1V_1 reduplication *kaka-*
immediate post-completed	*pagka-*
Intermittent	*pa-* + C_1V_1 reduplication
immediate pre-contemplated	*pa-/papa-*

Focus (default focus forms: indicative)

actor (agent; doer)	*mag-*; *-um-*; some *ma-* (optional: *magsi-*)
object (patient)	*-in*; *i-*; *-an*; perception–cognition/stative *ma-*
location/direction	*-an*; *pag – an*; *ka – an*
Beneficiary	*ipag-*; *i-*
Instrumental	*ipang-*
experiencer (theme)	*ma-* (some *-in*; *-um-*)
Reason	*ika-*

DOI: 10.4324/9781315739427-15

Mood (mostly derivational)

Indicative	default verbal focus forms
distributive	actor focus: *mang-*
Reciprocal	actor focus: *mag – an*; some *mag-*
abilitative/potential	actor focus: *maka-*; *makapag-* object/locative/beneficiary/instrumental focus: *ma-*
Accidental	actor focus: *maka:-* object/locative/beneficiary/instrumental focus: *ma:-*
social – participative	actor focus: *maki-*
social – reciprocal	actor focus: *makipag-*; *makipag – an*
Causative	actor-focus 1: *magpa-* actor-focus 2: *pa – in*; *pag – in* object focus: *ipa-*; *pa – an* locative/directional focus: *papag – an*; *pa-* beneficiary focus: *ipapag-* instrumental focus: *ipapang-*

Pseudo-verbs (attracts/pulls enclitics, and GEN and NOM pronouns)

gusto/nais ayaw kailangan	*ng*-marked actor, regardless of the focus form of the main verb
dapat puwede/maaari bawal	actor case marker is dependent on the focus form of the main verb

14.2 Adjective derivational forms

Simple or bare roots	***No affixes***
ma- adjectives	*ma-*
optional noun plurality agreement	*ma-* + C_1V_1 reduplication
de-verbal forms: emotion/sensation inducing	*nakaka-* *ka-* + C_1V_1
denominal forms: has some quality similar to	*mala-*
denominal and de-adjectival forms: has affinity for/with	*maka-*
de-verbal forms: has the tendency/prone to do the verb	*mapag-* *mapang-*
de-verbal forms: habitual doer of the verb	*pala-*
de-verbal and denominal forms: for use in/by	*pang-*
de-verbal and denominal forms: in a postion . . ./ wearing . . .	*naka-*

Adjective inflection for degree of quality

unequal comparison	*mas ... kaysa*
equal comparison	*magkasing-*; *kasing-*
superlative	*pinaka-*
intensified	*napaka-*
	full stem reduplication
moderate quality	*ma-* + root reduplication

14.3 Adverbs

time	
past	noong+; kahapon; kanina; kamakalawa
present and recurring	ngayon+; tuwing; sa kasalukuyan
future	sa+; bukas; sa hinaharap
manner	
following a verb	*nang* + adjective
preceding a verb	adjective *na*
de-verbal/de-adjectival form	*pa-*

14.4 Conjunctions

coordinating	at; o; pero/ngunit; kasi/dahil; kaya; samakatuwid; gayunman; at saka; gayundin
subordinating	
adjective clause (relative clause)	Na
subordinating	na
noun clause (verbal complement)	kung
subordinating	
adverb clause: time	noong/nang; tuwing; mula; hanggang; bago; pagkatapos; habang; samantala
adverb clause: cause and effect	dahil/sapagkat; para/upang; nang sa gayon; kung kaya
adverb clause: contrast	kahit na; sa halip na; gayong; samantalang
adverb clause: condition	kung; kundi; kung sakali; sa oras na; basta't

14.5 Case markers

	Singular	***Plural***
subject – actor (AF) subject – patient (OF) subject – theme (EF)	Ang	ang mga

genitive – actor (OF)		
genitive – patient (AF)	Ng	ng mga
locative/directional	Sa	sa mga
beneficiary	para sa	para sa mga
instrumental	sa pamamagitan ng	sa pamamagitan ng mga
reason	dahil sa	dahil sa mga

14.6 Pronouns

(In a basic sentence, *GEN before SUB, except ka*; *ko + ka => kita*)

Personal	***Subject***	***Genitive***	***Oblique***
singular			
first person	ako	ko	sa akin
second person	ikaw/ka	mo	sa iyo
third person	siya	niya	sa kanya
plural			
first-person exclusive	kami	natin	sa amin
first-person inclusive	tayo	namin	sa atin
second person	kayo	ninyo	sa inyo
third person	sila	nila	sa kanila
Deictic/ demonstrative	***Subject***	***Genitive***	***Oblique***
near speaker			
singular	ito	nito	dito
plural	ang mga ito	ng mga ito	sa mga ito
near addressee			
singular	iyan	niyan	diyan
plural	ang mga iyan	ng mga iyan	sa mga iyan
far from both			
singular	iyon	niyon/noon	doon
plural	ang mga iyon	ng mga iyon	sa mga iyon

Interrogative pronouns

sino	*Who*	bakit	*why*
ano	*What*	paano	*how*
kailan	*when*	magkano	*how much*
saan	*where*	gaano ka-	*how (re. quality)*
nasaan	*where at*	ilan	*how many*
taga-saan	*where from*	tig-iilan	*how many each*

14.7 Enclitics or adverbial particles

(In a sentence, ***enclitics come before GEN and NOM pronouns, except ko, mo, and ka***)

na	pa	nga	lang	din	daw	po	ba	muna	naman	yata	kaya	sana	pala

The following are commonly used expressions with enclitic adverbs:

Na		***Pa***	
Wala na.	*no more*	Wala pa.	*none yet*
Hindi na.	*not anymore*	Hindi pa.	*not yet*
Sige na.	*Come on.*	Sige pa.	*Keep going.*
Puno na.	*already full*	Puno pa.	*still full*
Bukas na.	*already open*	Bukas pa.	*still open*
Sarado na.	*already closed*	Bu:kas pa.	*not until tomorrow*
Tara na.	*Let's go.*	Mamaya pa.	*not until later*
Tayo na.	*Let's go.*	Kanina pa.	*already done earlier*
Halika na.	*Let's go.*		
Tapos na.	*already done*		
Mamaya na.	*not now, later*		
Nga		***Lang/lamang***	
Oo nga.	*Indeed!*	Isa lang.	*Just one.*
Sige nga.	*Give it a try.*	Ako lang.	*Just me.*
Hindi nga.	*Emphatic no*	Ikaw lang.	*Only you.*
Wala nga.	*Emphatic none*	Wala lang.	*Nothing really.*
Sige na nga.	*Okay, I'll do it.*	Sige lang.	*Just keep going.*
Wala na nga.	*Indeed, it's gone.*	Kanina lang.	*Earlier today.*
Sige pa nga.	*Let me try it again.*	Mamaya na lang.	*Just do it later.*
Tara na nga.	*Okay, let's go.*		
Din/rin		***Daw/raw***	
Wala rin.	*None also.*	Wala raw.	*None, people say.*
Hindi rin.	*Not either.*	Hindi raw.	*Not, others say.*
Ako rin.	*Me too.*	Siya raw.	*He/she is doing it.*
Naman		***Sana***	
Wala naman.	*None really.*	Wala sana.	*I hope there's none.*
Hindi naman.	*Not really.*		
Heto na naman.	*Here we go again.*	Hindi sana.	*I hope it's not true.*
		Ito na sana.	*I hope this is it.*
Ikaw na naman.	*You again?*	Sana nga.	*I hope so.*
Oo naman.	*Yes, of course!*		
Oo nga naman.	*Yes, they have a point.*		

Pala		*Muna*	
Wala pala.	*Surprisingly, none.*	Wala muna.	*none yet*
Hindi pala.	*Surprisingly, no.*	Hindi muna.	*not yet*
Ikaw pala.	*Oh, it's you!*	Ikaw muna.	*You first.*
Kanina pa pala.	*Surprisingly, it happened earlier today.*	Ikaw na muna.	*You go ahead.*
Mamaya pa pala.	*Surprisingly, it's not happening until later today.*		
Mamaya na pala.	*Surprisingly, it's happening later today.*		

Po		*Ba*	
Wala po.	*No, ma'am/sir.*	Wala ba.	*Is there none?*
Hindi po.	*Not, ma'am/sir.*	Hindi ba.	*Isn't it?*
Kayo po.	*You, ma'am/sir.*	Talaga ba.	*Really?*

Sana		*Kaya*	
Sana nga.	*I hope so.*	Wala kaya?	*I wonder if there's none.*
Sana naman.	*I'm really hoping so.*	Hindi kaya?	*I wonder if it isn't.*
Wala sana.	*I hope none.*	Ano kaya?	*I wonder what . . .*
Hindi sana.	*I hope not.*		

14.8 Noun-forming affixes

Affixes	*Examples*
p- (de-verbal nouns)	
pag-	paglaya; pagsagot; pagsamba *liberation; answering; worshipping*
pag- + reduplication	pag-uusap; pagluluto; paghahanap *conversation; cooking; search*
pakiki-/pakikipag-	pakikisama; pakikipag-usap *getting along; discussion*
pang-	pang-aapi; pandurukot; pangangaso *oppression; pickpocketing; hunting*
ka – an (de-adjectival abstract quality)	kalayaan; kagandahan; kabutihan *freedom; beauty; goodness* or *kindness*
ka – an (denominal collective noun)	kababaihan; kabataan; kapulisan *womenhood; young people; policemen*
-an/-han (de-verbal place/location)	languyan; paaralan; pasyalan *swimming area; school; amusement park*

taga- (de-verbal noun referring to worker doing the verb)	tagalinis; tagalaba; tagahugas *janitor; laundry person; dishwasher*
mang- (de-verbal noun referring to worker doing the verb)	manggagawa; manggagamot; mang-aawit *worker; healer; singer*
mag- (de-verbal noun referring to worker doing the verb)	maglalako; magsasaka; magtataho *seller; farmer; sweet-tofu seller*

14.9 Sentence structures

Basic sentence

Predicate	***+ Subject***	***+ Additional information***
Noun	+ang noun	
Adjective		
Verb		
PP		
AdvP		

Ay sentence (formal situation; stylistic variation)

Subject	***+Ay***	***+ Predicate***	***+ Additional information***
ang noun		noun	
		adjective	
		verb	
		PP/AdvP	

Identificational (ang – ang sentence in response to sino and alin questions; emphasis on the subject)

Subject	***+ Ang***	***+ Predicate***	***+ Additional information***
ang noun		noun	
		adjective	
		verb	
		PP/AdvP	

14.10 Negation (attracts/pulls enclitics and GEN and NOM pronouns)

hindi	+ verb, adjective, sentence/clause
wala	+ linker + noun (opposite of *may/mayroon*)
huwag	+ infinitive verb (imperative/command)

References

Aganan, Fernanda P., et al. 1999. *Sangguniang Gramatika ng Wikang Filipino.* Quezon City: UP Sentro ng Wikang Filipino.

Almario, Virgilio S. 1997. *Tradisyon at Wikang Filipino.* Quezon City: UP Sentro ng Wikang Filipino.

Ceña, Resty Mendoza. 2012. *Sintaks ng Filipino.* Manila: The National Commission for Culture and the Arts.

Constantino, Ernesto. 1964. "The Sentence Patterns of Twenty-Six Philippine Languages." In Lingua 15: 71–154. Manila: Linguistic Society of the Philippines.

Constantino, Ernesto. 1969. "Sentence Patterns of Ten Philippine Languages." In *Readings in Philippine Linguistics.* Manila: Linguistic Society of the Philippines.

Cruz, Emily. 1975. *Subcategorization of Tagalog Verbs.* UP Quezon City: Archives of Philippine Languages and Dialects.

Cubar, Nelly I. and Ernesto H. Cubar. 1994. *Writing Filipino Grammar: Traditions and Trends.* Quezon City: New Day Publishers.

De Guzman, Videa P. 1978. *Syntactic Derivation of Tagalog Verbs.* Honolulu: University of Hawaii Press.

Himmelmann, Nikolaus. 2008. "Lexical Categories and Voice in Tagalog." In P. Austin and S. Musgrave (eds.), *Voice and Grammatical Relations in Austronesian Languages*, 247–293. Stanford: CSLI.

Kaufman, Daniel. 2005. "Aspects of Pragmatic Focus in Tagalog." In I. Wayan Arka and Malcolm Ross (eds.), *The Many Faces of Austronesian Voice Systems.* Canberra: ANU Press.

Kroeger, Paul. 1993. *Phrase Structure and Grammatical Relations in Tagalog.* Stanford: CSLI.

Malicsi, Jonathan C. 2013. *Gramar ng Filipino.* Quezon City: UP Sentro ng Wikang Filipino.

Mithun, Marianne. 1994. "The Implications of Ergativity for a Philippine Voice System." In Barbara Fox and Paul J. Hopper (eds.), *Voice: Form and Function*, 247–277. Amsterdam/Philadelphia: John Benjamins.

Nolasco, Ricardo Ma. 2003. *Ang pagkaergatibo at pagkatransitibo ng mga wikang Pilipino: Isang Pagsusuri sa Sistemang Bose.* Ph.D Dissertation. Unibersidad ng Pilipinas Diliman Quezon City.

Ramos, Teresita V. 1974. *The Case System of Tagalog Verbs*. Canberra: The Australian National University.

Ramos, Teresita V. 1985. *Conversational Tagalog, A Functional-Situational Approach*. Honolulu: University of Hawaii Press.

Ramos, Teresita V. and Maria Lourdes S. Bautista. 1986. *Handbook of Tagalog Verbs*. Honolulu: University of Hawaii Press.

Ramos, Teresita V. and Resty M. Ceña. 1990. *Modern Tagalog*. Honolulu: University of Hawaii Press.

Reid, Lawrence A. and Hsiu-chuan Liao. 2004. "A Brief Syntactic Typology of Philippine Languages." *Language and Linguistics* 5.2: 433–490.

Rubino, Carl. 2002. *Tagalog-English/English-Tagalog Dictionary*. New York, NY: Hippocrene Books.

Schachter, Paul and Fe T. Otanes. 1972. *Tagalog Reference Grammar*. Los Angeles: University of California Press.

Index

Made in the USA
Las Vegas, NV
31 October 2024

9b8b1f96-c902-406e-9232-b4e2d0ffdef9R01